S0-AIX-005

THE UNITED STATES OF
APPALACHIA

The United States of

APPALACHIA

✢

How Southern Mountaineers Brought

Independence, Culture, and

Enlightenment to

America

✢

JEFF BIGGERS

Shoemaker & Hoard

Copyright © 2006 by Jeff Biggers

All rights reserved. No part of this book may be used or reproduced in any manner whatsoever without written permission from the Publisher, except in the case of brief quotations embodied in critical articles and reviews.

Rosa Parks is quoted on p. 169 from "Giving Aunt Donnie Her Due," by Cynthia Stokes Brown, *Social Policy*, Volume 21, No. 3, Winter 1991. Used courtesy of *Social Policy*.

"Shadows from the Big Woods" excerpts on pp. 195 and 208 from *The Journey Home* by Edward Abbey, copyright © 1977 by Edward Abbey. Used by permission of Dutton, a division of Penguin Group (USA) Inc.

Every attempt has been made to secure permissions. We regret any inadvertent omission.

Library of Congress Cataloging-in-Publication Data

Biggers, Jeff.

The United States of Appalachia : how Southern mountaineers brought independence, culture, and enlightenment to America / Jeff Biggers.

p. cm.

Includes bibliographical references.

ISBN (10): 1-59376-031-0

ISBN (13): 978-1-59376-031-1

1. Appalachian Region, Southern—History.

2. Appalachian Region, Southern—Intellectual life.

3. Appalachian Region, Southern—Politics and government.

4. Appalachians (People)—History. 5. Appalachians (People)—Intellectual life.

6. Appalachians (People)—Politics and government. I. Title.

F217.A65B54 2005

975—dc22

2005023931

Book design and composition by Mark McGarry

Set in Dante

Map by Kat Kalamaras and Mike Morgenfeld

Printed in the United States of America by Malloy

Shoemaker ⎡S&⎤ Hoard

An Imprint of Avalon Publishing Group, Inc.

Distributed by Publishers Group West

10 9 8 7 6 5 4 3 2 1

Per Carla, per sempre

For my folks, makers of my first mountain

Montani semper liberi.

꘎

These things, or such as these, will come again; so too, the high heart and
the proud and flaming vision of a child—to do the best that may be in
him, shaped from this earth, as we, and patterned by this scheme, to wreak
with all his might, with humbleness and pride, to strike here from his
native rock, I pray, the waters of our thirst, to get here from his native
earth, his vision of this earth and this America, to hear again, as we, the
wheel, the whistle, and the trolley bell; so too, as we, to go out from these
hills and find and shape the great America of our discovery.

—THOMAS WOLFE, "Return," 1937

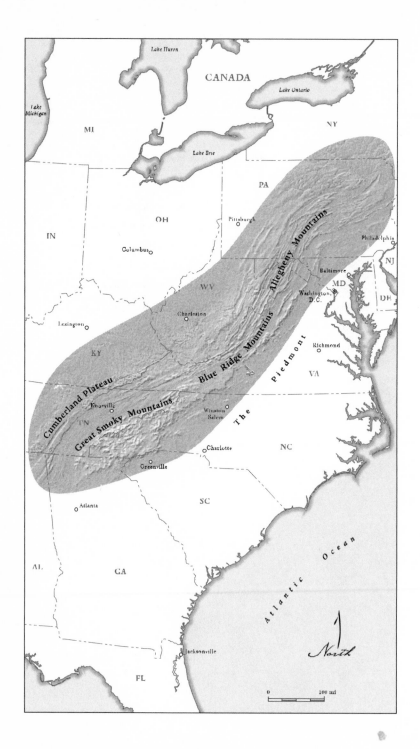

Contents

꙳

APPALACHIA NEEDS NO DEFENSE—IT NEEDS MORE DEFENDERS

～

BEYOND its mythology as a quaint backwater in the American imagination, Appalachia also needs to be embraced for its historic role as a vanguard region in the United States.

Vanguard Appalachia? The very word—*vanguard*—conjures up a plethora of images, though none in Appalachia. It's Thomas Jefferson at the Continental Congress in Philadelphia; it's George Washington plotting his campaign at Yorktown. William Lloyd Garrison, the great New England abolitionist, was in the vanguard of the antislavery movement; his transcendentalist Boston neighbors stood in the forefront of nineteenth-century American literature. The *New York Times,* in an era of yellow journalism, typified the vanguard press; the Village Vanguard jazz club in New York City provided the nation's music innovators with its hallowed stage. Martin Luther King, Jr., at the front of the civil rights movement, would be its modern political symbol. Expatriate Gertrude Stein might be its literary icon.

These are all reasonable examples, of course. And yet, would you believe me if I said an Appalachian preceded, led or influenced every one of these historic events or gatherings? That years before Jefferson completed the first draft of the Declaration of Independence, a back-woods settlement had already stunned the British Crown with its independence as a "dangerous example for the people of America." That an alliance of Southern Appalachian insurgents orchestrated their own attacks on British-led troops and turned the tide of the American Revolution. That a humble band of mountain preachers and writers published the first abolitionist newspaper in the nation and trained the radical Garrison. That a Cherokee mountaineer invented the first syllabary in modern times. That a back-hills young woman astounded the Boston literary circles in 1861, with the first American short story of working-class realism to be published in the *Atlantic Monthly*. That a young publisher from Chattanooga actually took over the *New York Times* and set its course for world acclaim. That the "high priestess of soul" put a spell on an audience at the Village Vanguard in 1959, with her blend of folk, jazz, gospel, country, and Bach-motif riffs she had learned in her Southern Appalachian hamlet. That a self-proclaimed "radical hillbilly" galvanized the shock troops of the civil rights movement and returned an African spiritual and labor song as its anthem. That the first American woman ever awarded the Nobel Prize for Literature was recognized for her family memoirs of West Virginia as much as for her literary contributions to the Far East.

FEW REGIONS in the United States confound and fascinate Americans like Appalachia. No other region has been so misrepresented by the mass media. Four paradoxical images have enjoyed incredible staying power: *pristine Appalachia,* the unspoiled mountains and hills along the Appalachian Trail, notwithstanding centuries of warfare, the wholesale destruction of the virgin forests by the timber industry, and the continual bane of strip mining; *backwater Appalachia,* home of the "strange land and peculiar people" in thousands of stories, novels, radio and TV programs and films, even though the region has produced some of the most important writers, artists, scientists, and politicians in the country; *Anglo-Saxon Appalachia,* once defined by *Merriam-Webster's Collegiate Dictionary* as a mountain region of "white natives," despite its role as a crossroads of indigenous cultures and vast immigrant and African American migrations for centuries; and *pitiful Appalachia,* the poster region of welfare and privation, the haggard faces greeting Charles Kuralt on *CBS News* on Christmas 1964, regardless of the tremendous wealth generated by the mountain range's mineral resources, timber, and labor force in the mines, mills, and factories, and today's tourist industry.

Untouched wilderness, poor white backward hillbillies.

In his best-selling analysis of the Buffalo Creek mining dam disaster in the 1970s, *Everything in Its Path,* eminent Yale sociologist Kai Erikson captured these stereotypes in an enduring judgment of Appalachian mountain culture: "It helps breed a social order without philosophy or art or even the rudest form of letters. It brings out whatever capacity for superstition and credulity a people come endowed with, and it encourages an almost reckless individualism."

FOR MOST READERS, the blood-curdling acts of Appalachian man's inhumanity to civilized man in the mountains, replete with inbred banjo pickers, violent feuds, moonshine, sexual deviltry, and miasmic gorges, have been put to rest. We are savvy enough to refrain from uttering "hillbilly" in mixed company. *Li'l Abner, Barney Google and Snuffy Smith, Hee Haw,* and *The Andy Griffith Show* are out; best-selling authors Barbara Kingsolver, Charles Frazier, Homer Hickam, and Robert Morgan are in. Sure, bizarre and offensive portrayals of Appalachians occasionally take place—during the research and writing of this book, CBS talent scouts combed the Southern mountains for corncob-piped rubes to participate in a proposed reality-TV show based on *The Beverly Hillbillies;* Abercrombie & Fitch dressed their manikins with a "West Virginia, It's All Relative" T-shirt; and a horror film, *Wrong Turn,* featured a promo about "six young people who find themselves being hunted by inbred cannibals in the woods of West Virginia"—but we've come a long way from the time of literary critic H. L. Mencken, who openly discussed reducing the birthrate of "inferior orders, for example, the hillbillies of Appalachia."

Still, the region's fame or infamy has forced writers and critics to dwell on what has been done to Appalachia, rather than what Appalachia has contributed to the world. For every *Deliverance* and its sodomites, we are quick to recall *The Waltons* in our collective memory, or more recently, the best-selling novel and Oscar-nominated *Cold Mountain* film. Or, in more tragic terms, for every Private Lynndie England, the defamed cigarette-lipped scapegoat of the Abu Ghraib prison scandal in Iraq, who hails from Fort Ashby, West Virginia, there is a heroic Private Jessica Lynch, from Palestine, West Virginia, molded into the image of Sergeant Alvin York, the Tennessee mountaineer and America's most famous soldier.

APPALACHIA, as author Wallace Stegner once remarked about the American Southwest, has been more a process than a place. Some critics would even say it has become an invention of its own. Sociologist Allen Batteau once voiced a common feeling that "Appalachia is a creature of the urban imagination." Since the first Spanish conquistador was informed of its existence in 1528 by distant tribes in Florida, Appalachia has certainly bewildered its explorers and inhabitants with its boundaries, its mystical forests, and its meaning.

But Appalachia does exist, both as a range and as a region. Beyond any singular culture, however, any "real Appalachia," the region has also endowed the nation with an enduring and conflicting treasury of innovations and innovators. That treasury, though, is rarely viewed beyond the surface or a few honorable exemplars—high lonesome singers and banjo players, black-faced coal miners, wizened front-porch storytellers—trotted out every so often to represent the entire region. Appalachian author Jim Wayne Miller once recounted an old tale about flat-boaters who traversed the Tennessee River at night, passing house after house with a "great fire burning, people dancing, always to the same fiddle tune." The boatmen didn't realize they were caught in the "Boiling Pot" eddy, going in circles around the same house and its unchanging scene, unaware of the region's greater wonders hidden in the forests like ginseng.

This is Appalachia's best-kept secret: Far from being a "strange land with peculiar people," the mountains and hills have been a stage for some of the most quintessential and daring American experiences of innovation, rebellion, and social change.

This book is an attempt to get off that flatboat and enter another part of Appalachia, or, in fact, we should say *Southern Appalachia,* that mountain spine and its valley tributaries that trundle along the eastern and Southern states from northern Alabama to southwestern Pennsylvania. (The Appalachian Regional Commission actually defines Appalachia from southern New York to northern Mississippi.) It is not a definitive history of the region; instead, it is a portrait of a hidden Appalachia on the cutting edge, full of revolutionaries and pioneering stalwarts, abolitionists, laborers, journalists, writers, activists, and artists overlooked among the lineup of conventional Appalachian suspects.

Putting aside the banjos and pot-lickers, casting aside both the wearisome slurs and sentimental postcards, and taking a break from recounting the evil deeds done unto mountaineers, this book seeks to show how a remarkable procession of Appalachian-born innovators have gone from these hills, as Thomas Wolfe wrote, to find and shape the great America of our discovery.

THE UNITED STATES OF
APPALACHIA

～

RANK STRANGERS

~

*I guess if it hadn't been for the radio it's no telling how long it
would have taken us to find out that we were hillbillies, or what kind of
songs we were supposed to sing.*

—JEAN RITCHIE, "The Mother of Folk Music"

ON THE EVENING before Halloween in 1944, with the United States
upended by wartime displacement, Martha Graham led her avant-garde
ballet troupe across a Washington, D.C., stage with the romantic yearn-
ings of pioneer homesteaders. Set in the western Pennsylvania hills,
Appalachian Spring reminded its war-weary audience of the courage,
faith, and simple joys of the first American frontier.

Graham, who entitled the ballet from a Hart Crane poem, envisioned
Appalachian Spring as a celebration of roots; in fact, like her contemporary literary icon Gertrude Stein, the modern dance luminary was born
in the Allegheny hill country, just outside Pittsburgh, in the late nineteenth century. Yet, despite its Appalachian title, the ballet's score and
reoccurring theme song, "The Gift to Be Simple," borrowed nothing from
mountain gospel or music traditions. The song was a Shaker melody.

Not that this mattered, of course. For the ballet's legendary composer, Brooklyn-born Aaron Copland, the Appalachian setting was not a
historical place, but an idealized homeland of rural American values. He

drew his inspiration from romantic Tin Pan Alley tunes and his world-renowned piano concertos, not dirgelike mountain ballads. More importantly for the audience in Washington, D.C., Copland's adaptation of folk music *sounded* Appalachian, the naive characters at the wedding party *seemed* Appalachian, and the beautiful score and dance provided a transient country with a much-needed reminder of the great American pastoral still embodied in the Appalachian region.

Copland won a Pulitzer Prize for his composition. Graham's choreography added to its seminal fame. *Appalachian Spring* remains America's most popular ballet today and is performed on school stages and in the most prestigious concert halls across the country.

FOR MANY of us, Appalachia first entered our lives in the form of music. Whether it is a local performance of *Appalachian Spring* or a country ballad on the radio, the region's ordained role as the Eden of American music has been well chronicled for years. In recent times, the phenomenal sales of the *O Brother, Where Art Thou?* film soundtrack, winner of the Grammy Award Album of the Year in 2002, launched a revival among mountain music enthusiasts across the country. A successful "Down from the Mountain" tour, composed of country and bluegrass musicians, extended the soundtrack's amazing run for two more years.

While it would seem easy to dismiss Copland's elegant phrasings of Shaker tunes as non-Appalachian music, the same case could be made for much of the "Down from the Mountain" bill; very few of the actual performers, or songs, originated from the mountains. The Southern Appalachians simply provided the setting, and the moniker, with a stamp of rustic authenticity.

This fact should not detract from the wonderful tour, or even *Appalachian Spring,* or set some narrow litmus test for "real" mountain music. To the contrary, it reminds us that far from being an idyllic Eden of music, sequestered by mountains and preserved in a time warp, the Southern Appalachians have been a burning ground in innovating and mixing modern musical trends.

Appalachia's infallible bond to country music, the so-called music of America, serves as a great example. We are told often enough that many of the top stars and trendsetters who have determined our music vernacular and memories originate from the Southern Appalachians. There would be no *Grand Ole Opry* without Roy Acuff; the modern-day Nashville scene and its monolithic sway over commercial country music could not have emerged without Chet Atkins's guitar licks and record-producing genius or the household recognition of Appalachian singers like Loretta Lynn, Dolly Parton, Dwight Yoakam, and the Judd family. It would be difficult to imagine bluegrass, gospel, and traditional folk music without Ralph Stanley's haunting voice and banjo licks, Doc Watson's flat-picking guitar, and Ricky Skaggs's mandolin.

These are only a few contemporary examples. Even more, it is not an exaggeration to suggest that the taproot of American country music comes from the Southern mountains, dating back to a makeshift studio in Atlanta in 1923, when an Appalachian fiddler gave birth to the country music recording industry. Playing a fiddle that had been carted across the Atlantic from Ireland with his ancestors in 1714, Fiddlin' John Carson, a former mill worker from the north Georgia mountains, represented the Scotch-Irish fiddle tradition that had first sounded in the Appalachian valleys in the earliest American experience. Soon joined by his guitar-strumming daughter, Moonshine Kate Carson, Fiddlin' John emerged as the iconic figure of "hillbilly records" and the poster image of the modern country music scene: poor white characters, toting their instruments and songs down from the hills.

Carson's Appalachian legacy is far more compelling and groundbreaking in modern American music. The first song he recorded for the OKeh Record company, "Little Old Log Cabin in the Lane," was not a Scotch-Irish air, rewritten in some lonesome Appalachian valley. It had been a popular 1870s minstrel tune written in a black dialect by a professional Louisville composer, W. S. Hays—a nineteenth-century counterpart to Aaron Copland. For a close listener, Carson's rendition on the fiddle would dispel any stereotype of an isolated rube. As a veteran performer and musical circuit rider, his performance captured the overlapping black-white musical experiences, from commercial and traditional sources, that had been imported and then reshaped in the Southern Appalachians.

THIS RECOGNITION of a more complex Appalachia, and its entangled history with African American music culture, was left out of Carson's marketing plan and was forever lost in our modern perceptions of Appalachian or country music. Realizing that they had tapped into a potentially lucrative hillbilly market, the New York–based OKeh Record company and its ambitious director, Ralph Peer, started mining the mountains for more musicians. Within a year, Ernest "Pop" Stoneman and several other acts released recordings with great success. Coaxed away by Victor Records, home of the inimitable Enrico Caruso, Peer wasted no time in returning to Southern Appalachia. Using Stoneman's financial success as a ruse to draw musicians, Peer set up a studio at the historic Appalachian crossroads of Bristol, Tennessee / Virginia, in 1927 and issued an open invitation for mountain acts to try their chance at winning a recording contract.

In what has been widely accepted as the big bang of country music, Peer attracted the history of Southern Appalachian music traditions in one setting: white and black musicians, church choirs and gospel quartets, Scotch-Irish fiddlers, banjo and harp guitar players, country string bands and medicine show performers, balladeers, and even a jazz combo. He also encountered a family trio of musicians from the Clinch Mountains in Virginia—A. P. Carter and his wife, Sara, and sister-in-law Maybelle—and a yodeler from Mississippi, Jimmie Rodgers, who had been based in the mountains around Asheville, North Carolina.

These two acts alone, which would go on to alter the course of country music, reached back into the region's multiracial and intersecting traditions. The Carters played a couple of gospel songs that had long circulated in the tiny mountain churches. They added some Scottish and Scotch-Irish ballads, and a popular nineteenth-century parlor piano song that had made its way "up the mountains" from the North. Rodgers sang a World War I ballad, and then yodeled to a minstrel tune from the 1860s.

The success of Peer's first acts will never be underestimated. It also led to a lot of the misperceptions grafted onto country music that still linger today. As part of a marketing ploy, Peer started the fashion of dressing down musicians with outdated work clothes and oversized hats, and promulgated the harebrained stereotypes of hillbillies. (Far from Peer's often quoted depiction of his first meeting with the Carter family, whom he likened to clodhoppers, the trio had arrived at the Bristol recording studio in their Sunday best.) But for all of his marketing bluster and racial repugnance, including his claim that he had "invented the hillbilly and nigger stuff," Peer's tenacity in attracting, producing, and urging songwriters to create new material guaranteed him a legendary role in modern music. And a tremendous fortune. With the advent of the radio sounding across the country by the mid-1920s, and the rise of the legendary *Grand Ole Opry,* the commercial engine of the day had found its musical jackpot in the hollows of Southern Appalachia.

Despite a life cut short by illness, Rodgers, "The Father of Country Music," emerged as one of the first recording stars in the nation. The Carter Family, "The First Family of Country Music," whose intergenerational bands and recordings attracted millions of listeners, reached a mythic status in the annals of American music, influencing the styles of innovators like Elvis Presley, Johnny Cash, and Bob Dylan. Some music critics even frame the family and its branches as a genre all to themselves: the originators of "traditional" Appalachian mountain music. In the process, countless old blues, folk ballads, and black minstrel and parlor songs, like the immortal "Wildwood Flower"—written by professional New Hampshire songwriter J. P. Webster in 1860—are erroneously credited to the Carters and relocated to Appalachia simply because of the magnitude of their recordings.

THESE FEATS didn't impress all the mountain music makers. Jean Ritchie, the Kentucky Cumberland "Mother of Folk Music," who became a beloved figure in the 1960s folk revival and whose musical family had been performing songs for over a century, wrote in her memoirs that "these hillbilly songs," as the radio claimed, "were sung all through the mountains, but we never had heard anything like them before."

The ballad "Rank Strangers to Me" is a fine example. Often described as one of the most famous "traditional" Appalachian mountain tunes—attributed to the Stanley Brothers for their haunting version—"Rank Strangers" was churned out in the Depression-era back offices of songwriter Albert E. Brumley, whose Arkansas and Missouri company served as the lyricist for the country and gospel industry for decades.

Like the score of *Appalachian Spring* or the stage presence of the "Down from the Mountain" tour, the commercial invention of "Rank Strangers" *became* Appalachian in our musical vernacular. In the meantime, a genuine Appalachian musical heritage and some of its most innovative and critical performers, far more reaching in their ambitions and influence, got left behind in the mountains, in the lyrics of the ballad's chorus, as rank strangers to you and me.

ON A WARM September evening in 1959, a young African American pianist and contralto dazzled a packed crowd at the Town Hall in New York City with her improvised versions of jazz ballads, folk songs, spirituals, pop tunes, Broadway musicals, and piano riffs with a Bach motif. Her recordings earlier that summer had taken the industry's breath away with her riveting performance of "I Loves You, Porgy" from the Broadway musical *Porgy and Bess*. The record had sold over a million copies in the jazz and blues section of record stores across the country.

In truth, the twenty-six-year-old woman's repertoire defied categories. It signaled the arrival of a modern diva and an innovator on the piano, not simply a jazz crooner. Some patrons, like those at the small Midtown Bar and Grill on Pacific Avenue in Atlantic City, understood this; over the past few years, the young woman had played at the Atlantic City dive and other bars in Philadelphia, pounding out tunes for six hours an evening in an attempt to earn enough money to return to her classical piano studies at the prestigious Julliard School in New York City.

As always, she introduced herself with a conjured show-name: Nina Simone. When she launched into a haunting version of the traditional ballad "Black Is the Colour of My True Love's Hair," no one in the performance hall in New York City knew that she had first learned this appropriated "mountain ballad" in her native Southern Appalachian town of Tryon, North Carolina.

In that same year, across town in the NBC-TV recording studios, an American icon was preparing his top-rated weekly TV program, *The Perry Como Show.* Wearing his trademark cardigan sweater, perfecting the ultimate cool and sway of a ballad crooner, Perry Como was celebrating the first gold record ever registered by the Recording Industry Association of America. The master of the romantic ballad, Como and his silky baritone had sold millions of records over the last two decades as the voice of the wholesome heartthrob of America. When he casually peppered his show with folk songs, such as the country music anthem "Wildwood Flower," hardly anyone realized that the son of Italian immigrants had first learned this "Carter mountain ballad"—one of his first in English—in his native Appalachian mill town of Canonsburg, in southwestern Pennsylvania.

Throughout the heady years of gold records and Christmas specials, the TV icon never lost touch with his folk roots. He spent his summers in the mountain village of Saluda, North Carolina, down the dirt road from Simone's childhood haunts, because it reminded him of his home.

DESPITE their origins and influences, Simone and Como were not considered Appalachian musicians, of course. And they never would be. Not that the Big Apple was unaware of the region and its musical traditions. The late 1950s had heralded the beginnings of another "Appalachian revival." The accepted boundaries of this revived Appalachian music had been relegated to a narrow hollow in a music industry fashioned more by the outside world of marketing than by the abilities of the inhabitants in the mountains. In the process, non-Appalachian performers also head-lined this revival.

One of the most frequently championed performers of "traditional Appalachian mountain music" was the wondrous Bill Monroe, the mandolin-playing "father of bluegrass," who was not Appalachian. Nor were his groundbreaking bluegrass compositions and stylistic innova-tions traditional. By the time the western Kentucky native stole the show at the Newport folk festivals in the 1960s with his "folk music in overdrive," he had set the stage for a generation of mountain music enthusiasts. Others in the Appalachian revival had never even visited the region. For example, by 1959, as Monroe and his Blue Grass Boys churned out an acoustic alternative to commercial country, rockabilly, and rock and roll—headlined by a "hillbilly cat" named Elvis Presley—something else was brewing in California. The Kingston Trio, a clean-shaven trio of Palo Alto students, had transformed a Southern Appalachian dirge into a catchy number-one hit that had suburban housewives whistling across the nation. Sweetly harmonizing the "Tom Dula" ballad about a real-life wife murderer in the North Carolina mountains, the Kingston Trio chimed in standard English, "Hang down your head, Tom Dooley." Meanwhile, John Cohen, a New York City–based performer with the New Lost City Ramblers, toured that same year through the Kentucky Cumberlands and "discovered" coal-mining banjo player Roscoe Holcomb. Riveted by the emotional intensity of Hol-comb's singing, Cohen returned to New York and coined the "high lone-some sound" that suddenly defined the entire Southern Appalachian experience in a single phrase.

Despite his portrayal as an untamed mountain genius unaware of the outside world, Holcomb's repertoire, like that of Simone and Como, was anything but insular. He played a bewildering array of old ballads and fid-dle tunes from the British Isles, nineteenth-century minstrel and parlor room songs, Tin Pan Alley, commercial hillbilly and Western swing hits, gospel hymns, African American work songs, and his favorite blues by fel-low Southern Appalachian singer Bessie Smith, the legendary "Empress of the Blues."

Far from being a static or unmovable phenomenon, mountain music was on the move, and hardly lonesome.

SIMONE'S story begins, like the history of music in Southern Appalachia, long before the Civil War, when immigrants, African slaves, and American settlers a generation or two removed from the British Isles, Northern Ireland, Germany, and other European countries pressed into the Carolinian mountains for tracts of land or jobs in the nascent iron and timber industries. Some found a place on the increasing stretches of the railroad. Many of these immigrants and slaves toted instruments, such as the fiddle, banjo, piano, drums, mandolin, and zither, and brought to the region their centuries-old styles of singing.

From this cultural encroachment, an inevitable convergence in ways of life took root in the mountains. As an amalgam of this mountain history, Simone celebrated a Cherokee great-great-grandmother, a Scotch-Irish relation torn into her maternal past—her mother had been named Kate—and her African heritage, which had been replanted in the Carolinas.

Born Eunice Waymon in 1933, she found herself at a piano keyboard at the age of three, thumping out tunes by ear. Her house had always been a musical one, though not necessarily for pleasure. Her mother had been a piano player in her youth, often accompanying her husband, who had been a singing and dancing entertainer. When her mother became a Methodist minister, gospel hymns replaced all forms of heathen diversion; Simone's father pined for "The Darktown Strutters' Ball," which his young daughter knocked off when her mother was not around.

At the age of six, the child prodigy found herself as a regular church pianist. While other kids played tag, Simone developed a discipline that required her to perform for hours on the weekends and several nights a week. Many churches, including the evangelical Holiness Church, sought out her remarkable playing. In turn, their revivals generated a level of emotion and complex rhythm patterns that, Simone declared, "came straight out of Africa."

The gospel experience was not wasted on the young girl. Beyond the critical discipline and staying power demanded by the revivals, Simone acknowledged the "vital part of rhythm" she had learned in the shifting scenes in the church. "Gospel taught me about improvisation," Simone wrote in her autobiography, *I Put a Spell on You*. "How to shape music in response to an audience and then how to shape the mood of the audience in response to my music."

Gospel may have shaped her music, but Bach provided the child prodigy with a passion to become a world-class classical pianist. Her abilities stunned the mountain town. When she accomplished all that was possible with an English piano teacher at the teacher's backwoods mansion, the racial divide of the village was temporarily bridged by a campaign to raise special funds to send the young girl to a better school. Nonetheless, Simone's parents were forced to stand in the back during her concerts in town. The mere fact that these concerts occurred shattered the monolithic facade of Southern Appalachia as a remote cultural wasteland: an African American child prodigy, under the guidance of an immigrant English patrician (married to a Russian), performing Bach for an extremely rural and forest-bound community in the 1940s.

With the town's support, Simone attended Julliard in New York City, only to be turned down by the classical piano bastion of the Curtis Institute of Music, in Philadelphia, in the early 1950s, despite the high recommendations of her well-known Julliard professors. For Simone, the rejection remained a wound of racism that she would never forget. Out of desperation, she began her secret performances in the Atlantic City and Philadelphia bars. Within a few years, she became a star on the jazz and pop music circuits.

Her conflicts with the racial barriers and social problems of the day, however, had just begun. In 1963, outraged by the murder of civil rights activist Medgar Evers and the terrorist bombing of a black church in Birmingham, Alabama, which resulted in the deaths of four little girls, Simone sat down and wrote one of the most blistering denouncements in pop music history. With "Mississippi Goddam," she thrust herself into the role of figurehead in the civil rights and black liberation movements.

One song, "Old Jim Crow," reminded the South of its minstrel past. Another ballad, "To Be Young, Gifted and Black," became an anthem for a wide audience in the 1960s, as well as civil rights groups, such as the Congress on Racial Equality. "To Be Young, Gifted and Black" recalled being "haunted" by her Southern Appalachian youth and her striving to become the first black classical pianist, "but my joy of today, is that we can be proud to say, to be young, gifted and black."

Author of scores of jazz, blues, pop, and folk songs and hailed as the high priestess of soul, Simone had the ability to cross musical borders. This ability, fashioned so early in her Appalachian childhood, reinforced her iconoclastic rapport with the music industry. By the end of the 1960s, however, fed up with the racism in the country and the underhanded dealings in the entertainment industry and forever outraged by her narrow classification as a jazz singer, Simone set off on a series of migrations to Barbados, Liberia, Switzerland, and then France. She continued to record abroad and sell out huge crowds; her compositions were translated into several other languages, including Chinese. In the 1980s, she returned to the top of the American pop charts with a new recording of one of her first hits, "My Baby Just Cares for Me."

Despite her distance, Simone's influence on the region's traditional artists was overlooked by the media, but not lost on its performers. As mountain music enthusiasts, including Bob Dylan and legendary rock guitarist Eric Clapton, made their homage to the purity of Holcomb's high lonesome sound in the Cumberlands, the Appalachian banjoist would beguile his visitors with a mesmerizing rendition of the "House of the Rising Sun," a traditional blues (most likely based on an English ballad) that Simone had made famous at a live recording at the Village Gate club in New York City in 1961.

The high priestess of soul died in 2003 in southern France, an expatriated Southern Appalachian whose mountain origins had long been excised from her public persona, though not by her own doing. In her memoirs, Simone recalled a critical period in her life in the mid- to late 1930s, when she and her father lived in a rustic cabin in Lynn, North Carolina, an African American mountain hamlet defined more by the forest than any cluster of modern conveniences. Simone and her father cultivated a garden and roamed the mountain trails as he recuperated from an illness, in "one of the most beautiful forests you would see anywhere." For the internationally acclaimed diva whose life would be identified with so many conflicts, the mountain retreat remained the arcadian home of her entangled roots.

ONLY TWENTY YEARS before Simone tarried in the woods, English folklorist Cecil Sharp had combed those very same mountains in North Carolina, in search of Appalachian ballad singers and his own version of an arcadian lifestyle "just exactly what the English peasant was one hundred or more years ago." In fact, he recorded hundreds of old ballads from the British Isles, many preserved in the same dialects and phrasings from a century or two before.

When Sharp published some of his findings in his celebrated book, *English Folk Songs from the Southern Appalachians,* in 1917, he reinforced the fashionable trend of perceiving Southern Appalachia as a chain of "sequestered mountain valleys" trapped in a time warp. In essence, Appalachia was a region inhabited only by pure Anglo-Saxon or, at worst, Scotch-Irish descendants, where time and cultural ways had been frozen.

Yet, for every ballad, air, or fiddle tune that Sharp recorded, he dismissed numerous others that did not fit with this neat theory that Appalachian mountaineers were the last pure Anglo-Saxons. His findings in Appalachia were less about mountaineers than a crusade to bring England back to its folk traditions and musical idiom. African Americans, of course, were not part of this history; Sharp reviled their settlements in the Southern Appalachians as a "lower race," and lamented the presence of "tobacco, molasses and niggers."

Sharp's work, like that of many other "song catchers" in the Southern Appalachians, has dominated the musical depiction of the region ever since. Although he never entered them in his chronicles, Sharp also encountered an overwhelming number of gospel hymns, African spirituals, Tin Pan Alley tunes, minstrel songs, and labor and field blues that

Appalachians considered part of their heritage, as well. These songs, played by both his "English peasants" and those from the communities of black Appalachians and southern European immigrants, didn't square with Sharp's vision, and therefore they remained outside the purview of music enthusiasts. A few other details about the mountaineers also failed to fit Sharp's definitions: He lamented in one letter that even the most remote cabins were tidy, clean, and befitting "respectable suburban families," when he preferred "dirt and good music" as bedfellows.

Sharp wasn't alone in his selective view of Appalachian singers and musicians. In 1905, Emma Bell Miles, an Appalachian writer based in Chattanooga and the surrounding mountain hamlets, wrote an endearing portrait of mountaineers that still remains an important text: *Spirit of the Mountains.* For Miles, though, the thousands of blacks living in her area—more than a third of the inhabitants of her Chattanooga—didn't exist on a single page. Instead, she highlighted the romantic joys in her stories of "dulcimore" players, plucking "faint monotonous chords" on the strings, "into the weird and plaintive harmony of which they were capable." The dulcimer's origins, as well, remained mired in lore as an ancient English import, overlooking its zither origins in the nimble hands of German immigrants.

Sharp's rejection of gospel music, however, is a curious detail for Southern Appalachia. In his quest for "traditional ballads," a puzzled Sharp declared that the mountaineers "misunderstood our requirements and would give us hymns instead." The hymns, in fact, after a century of singing, had long been grafted onto Appalachian traditions. Since the summer of 1801, massive camp revivals had swept through the mountain region with religious fervor, introducing spirituals and shape-note singing styles that had their origins in Sharp's beloved England. Transplanted to New England before the American Revolution and then into the South and Southern Appalachia after they had lost popularity among more classical hymns, the gospel songs emphasized community singing largely without instruments. Psalms and hymns repeated easy refrains and eventually spun off into harmonies that would serve as the basis for contemporary four-part gospel harmonies. Itinerant singers and preachers spread the songs, and songbooks, throughout Appalachia's country churches. For mountaineers in the most remote areas, many without instruments, these quickly became the "traditional" songs.

As Simone noted in her own experience in a small mountain village, the presence of black gospel singers and their spirituals would have been even harder for Sharp to dismiss. Galvanized by the famous Fisk Jubilee Singers, the Tennessee-based group that had performed concerts at some of the most famous venues—including the White House—since the 1870s, African American gospels and slave songs had been published, distributed, and performed throughout Southern Appalachia a half century before Sharp's visit.

W. C. HANDY recorded an African spiritual called "The Rocks and the Mountains" during the same year that Simone was living in the forests with her father. For the "Father of the Blues," nature was not some abstract invention of Sharp's English romantics, but an integral part of his own childhood in the forests. Handy was raised in an African American community on Handy's Hill in northern Alabama, on the outskirts of Southern Appalachian hill country. His proximity to the Appalachian cultural boundaries was as close as Bill Monroe's small-town roots in western Kentucky.

So, why do critics and historians consider Monroe's modern bluegrass, and not Handy's traditional blues, part of the "real" Appalachia? Or, for that matter, why do we exclude John Coltrane, the jazz innovator raised in High Point, North Carolina, on the piedmont edges of Southern Appalachia, while moving the mountains for bluegrass and folk heroes like Monroe, Earl Scruggs, Merle Travis, Johnny Cash, John Prine, and Iris DeMent and the hundreds of other country musicians who grew up in California or western, midwestern, or Southern low-country towns or urban settings?

The simple answer is one of marketing: Since its inception in the early twentieth century, the recording industry and its radio and TV counterparts have always appealed to their customers through a tidy division of the races. Hillbilly, country, folk, and then bluegrass records were placed in the white slots; "race" or "black" music, such as the blues or jazz, filled the other. Radio and TV shows booked their musicians accordingly. Whether these genres had transmuted or lifted parts or players from each other mattered little to a vendor, and a society, intent on keeping the races separate.

All stereo marketing and stereotypes aside, true Appalachian mountain music traditions came into being as an inexorable blend of black and white musical innovations. Most innovators, white or black, Appalachian or non-Appalachian, quickly acknowledged this aspect of the music. Monroe often went out of his way to recognize the amazing versatility and influence of African American fiddler and guitar player Arnold Shultz on his own legacy; Monroe had cut his teeth at local dances in Rosine, Kentucky, backing up Shultz on the guitar. A. P. Carter, who is lauded more than anyone else in launching modern country and hillbilly music in the 1920s, relied heavily on black guitar player Lesley Riddle, from the mountain town of Burnsville, North Carolina. For over a decade, Riddle helped Carter comb the mountains for new ballads and other songs. Unlike Carter, Riddle possessed an incredible ability to quickly memorize and transcribe songs. His unrecorded legacy, of course, vanished with his death.

Handy's blues serve as a telling reminder of this mix. In a pioneering recording in 1925, the legendary Uncle Dave Macon and his Hillbillies band sold a half million copies of their version of the "Hill Billie Blues," which was a reworking of Handy's "Hesitation Blues." Macon had learned his trade from black musicians at medicine and minstrel shows. In turn, his band's rendition of Handy's blues literally gave rise to the "hillbilly" moniker in country music.

In truth, Handy interpreted the "symphonies of unpremeditated art" in his woodlands in a manner deeply connected to a mountain way of life. Far from any urban reality, the wilderness provided his first sense of jazz, blues, and gospel techniques. The birds engaged in call and response; while some trilled cadenzas, others belonged to an outdoor choir. He envisioned the scales of robins carrying an alto theme to the melodies of the bobolinks. In his autobiography, he delighted in the idea of nature as his muse:

> There was a French horn concealed in the breast of the blue jay. The tappings of the woodpecker were to me the reverberations of a snare drum. The bullfrog supplied an effective bass. In the raucous call of the distant crow I would hear the jazz motif. The purple night would awaken a million crickets with their obligations of mournful sound, also the katydid, and down the lonely road the hooves of the galloping horses beat in syncopation. As I grew older I added the saxophonic wailing of the moocows and the clarinets of the moody whippoorwills. All built up within my consciousness a natural symphony. This was the primitive prelude to the mature melodies now recognized as the blues.

One other historic event in Southern Appalachian music occurred in the same year Simone lived in the woods. In the fall of 1937, Bessie Smith died in a car accident in Mississippi. She was forty-three. The Empress of the Blues received a funeral parade that brought out thousands of mourners in Philadelphia. Her death was soon mired in gruesome and untrue accounts of racial discrimination and charges of neglect. The achievements of her extraordinary life, though, especially for Handy, Simone, Holcomb, and a legion of other singers, did not simply disappear into her unmarked grave. As one of the pioneers in blues and jazz, Smith's emergence out of Southern Appalachia remains one of the overlooked stories in the history of American music.

From Handy's Lawrence County in northern Alabama, the Smith family had followed the migration of African Americans in the 1880s and arrived in the booming river town of Chattanooga in the Southern Appalachians. Bessie's father was a Baptist minister whose paltry salary forced him to work at times in the iron mills. Her mother joined the ranks of laundrywomen serving the white elite. Settling in the west Chattanooga neighborhood called Bluegoose Hollow, the Smiths managed somehow to buy a home, which Bessie referred to as a "ramshackle cabin," in the muddy lanes of the hollow. While a relative would later describe the neighborhood as "kind of wooded, like the country," Chattanooga's rising mills were always in sight.

By the age of nine, Smith had lost both parents, in an era when pellagra, tuberculosis, and other diseases roved at random through the poor mountain communities. It set the young girl on a peripatetic path. Raised by her older sister, who had also fallen into the washerwoman sector, a young Bessie found herself freed from the conservative mores of the Baptist Church and now on the move from one rental unit to the next. She roamed the back warrens of Chattanooga on roller skates. Within a short time, she joined her older guitar- and piano-playing brother—who was seventeen years her senior—on the lively West Ninth Street as street performers. Another brother had already joined a traveling vaudeville group.

African Americans made up at least a third of the citizens of Chattanooga in this period, and nowhere was the vibrancy of the river town's black culture more dynamic than on West Ninth. By the turn of the century, as Bessie took to the streets as a singer and dancer, over twenty taverns and inns lined the main boulevard, alongside shops, barbers, and the magical venues of theaters that hosted minstrel and vaudeville shows from around the country. Smith wasn't alone on the streets; Roland Hayes, who would go on to a celebrated opera career as a tenor, got his start on the same corners.

Like Holcomb, Smith's repertoire was a mixed bag of parlor room music, Tin Pan Alley songs, minstrel tunes, and vaudeville numbers popular in her time. The boom of ragtime, and the continual draw of vaudeville and medicine shows, provided an outlet for African American innovators and musicians in a period that otherwise would have kept them outside the performing halls. For all of their elements repugnant to our modern sensibilities, black minstrel shows introduced the genius of African American musicians to an outside audience; Handy, like many other blues and jazz musicians, started in a minstrel show. Smith was often headlined in her early period as a "favorite Tennessee coon shouter."

LARGELY IGNORED for their role in the twisted roots of "traditional" mountain music, the minstrel shows first emerged in Appalachia in the late 1820s. As a popular variety show, white entertainers took the stage in burned-cork-painted blackface, performing a "walkaround" comedy routine in a derisive version of a so-called black dialect. The show was wildly theatrical, introducing deficient black characters through song and dance routines based in rural settings. Quartets performed, often backed by a harmonizing chorus. Playing the instruments of slaves—banjos, bones, homemade tambourines, and drums—and appropriated fiddles from their British Isles and Irish counterparts—the minstrels sang contemptuous and debasing renditions of field and labor songs, and "burnt cork songs of comic love."

The minstrel shows packed crowds from the most remote corners of the Southern mountains to the largest stages in New York City. Their huge success generated an endless line of songwriters, who churned out thousands of ballads and songs, some borrowed from older British Isles and Irish traditions. Like any musical parody, many of the songs lambasted the elite cultural trends and players and most ethnic and immigrant groups as much as they cast blacks in the mold of brainless, slovenly, and exotic creatures. To be fair, a handful of minstrel shows eventually made forays into the temperance movement, touted patriotism, and even shared some antislavery sentiments. Nor were the minstrel songwriters all hacks; composers included historical figures such as marching band icon John Philip Sousa; popular song pioneer Stephen Foster, who had declared in 1852 that he would become "the best Ethiopian songwriter"; and Irving Berlin.

From the minstrels emerged the character of Jim Crow, who danced his way onto the American stage as early as 1828. Legendary Ohio songwriter Dan Emmett reinvented himself as the "Virginia minstrel," after learning the banjo from a black mountaineer circus performer in western Virginia, and soon provided the South with its "Dixie" anthem at his minstrel shows in 1859. His version of one song, "Turkey in the Straw," originally titled "Zip Coon" and adapted from an old ballad in the British Isles, still appears in various publications as an "Appalachian classic" for children.

Beyond their themes and songs, the minstrel shows popularized an instrument that has often been held up as the musical symbol of Appalachia: the banjo. Most historians agree that the ancient stringed instrument made its way across the Middle East, the Magreb of Africa, and into western African communities over centuries of interchange. Transported across the Middle Passage by African slaves to the Caribbean and then the Atlantic coast of the Americas, the four-string gourd "banjer" started to appear in American slave accounts and drawings in the early eighteenth century. It remained a slave instrument for decades, brought out for weddings, dances, and other rituals that soon seeped into the white communities in the South. Its appearance in the Southern Appalachians resulted from the influx of slaves in the mountains. Laborers in the swine drives from the mountains into the lower markets passed along banjo tunes. Others would have picked up the instrument and songs down the waterways that brought barges and black musicians onto the outer edges of the region. Traveling circuses and medicine shows soon made the banjo a key feature, as well.

By the mid-1800s, the banjo became a common fixture at mining and timber camps and on the construction sites of the railways through Appalachia. One of the most famous railroad or folk songs to come out of the mountains recounts the exploits of a black railroad worker in West Virginia in the 1870s: "John Henry." Reminding us that the American railroads were laid not only with whiskey and tea—Irish and Chinese laborers—but with large crews of African Americans in the Southern Appalachians and Ohio River valley, John Henry became a household American name as the larger-than-life figure taking on the steel-driving machines.

By 1880, minstrel shows dominated America's stages of entertainment. A banjo craze hit the country at the same time, especially among middle-class women in the North, prompting banjo factories to open in Philadelphia and other urban centers.

Southern Appalachian women did not miss out on the banjo boom. Fashioning their own or ordering them from their dog-eared Sears & Roebuck catalogs, mountain women took the lead in incorporating the instrument into the minstrel songs, blues, and British and Irish ballads and airs that had been rewritten into Appalachian settings and events. Virtually every banjo legend who emerged generations later in the bluegrass boom, such as Earl Scruggs and Ralph Stanley, would acknowledge the vital role of a banjo-playing sister (in Scruggs's case) or mother (for Stanley). In fact, the first commercial recording of an Appalachian banjoist was by Samantha Bumgarner, from a mountain village in North Carolina. Bumgarner cut a record for Columbia in New York City in 1924, right after Fiddlin' John Carson's historic recording. One of her songs, "Shout Lou," had been based on a minstrel tune.

IRVING BERLIN'S involvement in the minstrel parodies recalls a parallel turn-of-the-century musical phenomenon that would have an equally dramatic impact on Southern Appalachian music: Tin Pan Alley. Employing a kinder, gentler vision of a rural South, professional songwriters based on 28th Street in New York City tapped into the same American fascination with "Dixie" and its mountain neighbors—a fascination that also filled the magazines and fiction racks. Joined by scores of professional writers in New York, many of them Eastern European Jewish immigrants like Berlin, these urban composers produced reams of fashionable and romantic tunes about a rural America that was completely foreign to them. By 1909, when the Tin Pan Alley term became popular, millions of copies of sheet music had been printed, sold, and hoisted into the American parlor rooms, heralding a New York City version of the South as a bucolic, molasses-slow, and romantic land perfumed by magnolias and sweet potatoes and held in the bosom of loving mammies. The mystique of Bessie Smith's Chattanooga, for example, had inspired a young Berlin to write his first nostalgic hits, including "Down in Chattanooga" and "Tell All the Folks in Kentucky (I'm Coming Home)."

THERE WAS very little nostalgia in Bessie Smith's blues. And though she would record a devastating version of "Baby, Won't You Please Come

Home," she wasn't referring to the "ramshackle cabin" where she had been raised.

After a short stint in various vaudeville shows, and as a dancer on a chorus line, Smith met Gertrude "Ma" Rainey in Atlanta in 1910 and later joined her traveling troupe. The encounter, while it has dispersed into racy legends about kidnapping and sexual diversion, remains truly historic because it placed the young Chattanooga singer in the company of "The Mother of the Blues."

Along with the popular Tin Pan Alley and minstrel tunes of the times, Rainey weaved in country blues traditionally associated with Southern black guitar players and male singers. Drawn from labor and field songs, topical events, and elements of African gospels, Rainey's blues spun the stories in the voice and concerns of a black woman. As a breakthrough in the period, she not only sang but also wrote her own lyrics, opening the doors to a new era of modern blues compositions by women. The strength and defiance in many of the songs, girded by Rainey's emotional intensity and rich voice, made Smith "cry all over the place."

Rainey and Smith packed the black vaudeville houses and minstrel shows throughout the South. They followed a trail of venues that soon evolved into the Chattanooga-based Theater Owners' Booking Association, a black-run network that sought to raise the standards of performances and promote black performers. By 1915, Smith was drawing sold-out crowds for her powerful performances, including a special homecoming appearance at Chattanooga's largest theater. Like Rainey, Smith started singing her own versions of the blues. According to one critic, Smith's genius was in her ability to take the classic twelve-bar blues and its three verses beyond an expected rhythm and repetition, and rephrase them with vocal effects, improvised lyrics, and dramatic pauses and timings. Along with the classic songs of love and love lost, drinking and carousing, Smith wrote and sang about the working lives and struggles of black women, flood victims, domestic violence, and jailhouse dramas.

When Mamie Smith (no relation) made the first recording of a woman blues singer in 1921, selling over a hundred thousand copies in a month, Bessie Smith's ascent to the vinyl records was inevitable. She had become one of the most popular blues performers in the country. Nonetheless, it took a couple of tries to break into the recording industry. One company refused to record her in 1921 because they found her style too rugged. The OKeh Record company, which would soon be combing the Southern mountains for white performers, even overlooked one of her test recordings. In 1923, on the brink of bankruptcy, Columbia Records in New York City launched its "race" music series with Smith's "Downhearted Blues." She earned $150, and signed away the royalties. The record sold 780,000 copies, confirmed the Empress of the Blues as one of the top music acts in the country, and propelled Columbia Records into the recording limelight.

Rejecting the racial and sexual protocols of the day, Smith's legendary acts of defiance have been highlighted in numerous books and essays. Chroniclers tend to get bogged down in her bisexual affairs, bottomless drinking, stage antics, jealous rages, vicious fights—including a knife-stabbing she received on the back streets of Chattanooga—and flamboyant flights of indulgence as a star. She made scores of records and became one of the highest-paid acts in the business. Her powerful recording of "Nobody Knows You When You're Down and Out" turned an unknown blues into a famous jazz standard. Moving herself and various family members to Philadelphia and perennially fleeced by her no-good first husband, Smith managed to burn through her fortune in the prosperous Jazz Age of the 1920s like any other fur-coat-wearing and diamond-jewelry-loving flapper. Openly contemptuous of the white public, her rendition of "'Tain't Nobody's Bizness If I Do" revealed a fascinating glimpse into her own life perspective:

> *There ain't nothing I can do,*
> *Or nothing I can say, that folks don't criticize me.*
>
> *But I'm going to do just as I want to anyway*
> *And don't care if they all despise me.*

More importantly for the legacy of the blues, she shaped her icono-clastic role as a successful, irreverent, and brilliant entertainer in a time when white women had just earned the right to vote and blacks contin-ued to languish under brutal racial discrimination. Physically imposing as well, Smith became legendary for her boldness in confronting the Ku Klux Klan or other detractors at any of her performances in the South. In her recording of "Young Woman's Blues" in 1927, she rejected the "respectable" role of submissive blacks in a white-dominated society and mocked any regard for sexual restrictions. Her biting lyrics reminded lis-teners of her incredible self-made success and an unquenchable desire to "drink good moonshine and rub these browns down."

With the country seeping into economic ruin in 1930 and all record sales plummeting, she recorded "Black Mountain Blues," a tongue-in-cheek song that conjured up a nightmare scenario of her Appalachian mountain past of feuds, violence, and wild-eyed jealousy, seasoned by her unabashed love for the "unsealed jar" of moonshine:

> Black Mountain people are bad as they can be,
> Black Mountain people are bad as they can be,
> They uses gun powder just to sweeten their tea.

"Black Mountain Blues" was ultimately a marketing disaster, eerily sym-bolizing that African blues and Appalachian settings didn't mix in the public perception. Like many other black entertainers in the hard-pressed music industry during the Depression, Smith floundered to maintain a foothold of survival, playing smaller venues and shared billings. Her tragic death occurred just as she had begun to cross over to the jazz scene.

Only months before her car accident in 1937, a Chicago newspaper asked Smith about her musical influences. Eschewing the obvious blues divas like Ma Rainey, she singled out fellow Southern Appalachian blues-man W. C. Handy as one of her main inspirations. In turn, gospel diva Mahalia Jackson, jazz legend Billie Holiday, and rock-and-roll star Janis

Joplin would all pay homage to Smith's impact on their own iconoclastic styles and careers. Joplin even recorded "Black Mountain Blues" in 1963. Outraged that Smith had been buried in Philadelphia in an unmarked grave, Joplin donated most of the money for a proper gravestone three decades later.

For novelist Ralph Ellison, who would see his literary star rise a generation later during the era of Simone, Smith was more than a blues singer. Echoing the mystic tributes that had accompanied Graham's feat of *Appalachian Spring* or the Carter Family's mountain gospel rendition of "Will the Circle Be Unbroken" or Simone's own "To Be Young, Gifted and Black," again elevating the Southern Appalachians to a mythical role outside the bounds of geography, Ellison declared that Smith had been "a priestess, a celebrant who affirmed the values of the group and man's ability to deal with chaos."

Dealing with chaos, indeed, would be a fair assessment of the forces behind a lot of Appalachian music and culture over the past three centuries. It might even best define the region's inception. Beginning her music memoir with an account of her Appalachian town's founding after a bloody conflict in the mid-1800s, Simone reminded outsiders that the earliest episodes of chaos in the Southern mountains took place between her Cherokee, European, and African ancestors. As we will see in the first chapter, out of this chaos emerged an extraordinary innovation that would rival any of the music contributions from the region.

Chapter One

THE TRAIL OF WORDS

꘠

The earth is a great island floating in a sea of water,
and suspended at each of the four cardinal points by a cord hanging down
from the sky vault, which is of solid rock. When the world grows old and
worn out, the people will die and cords will break and let the earth sink
down into the ocean, and all will be water again.

—JAMES MOONEY,
"How the World Was Created," *Myths of the Cherokees*

WHEN JAMES MOONEY collected this rendition of the Cherokee genesis from a storyteller in the 1880s, the eminent ethnologist, whose published work would become a bedrock of Cherokee history and mythology, knew that several other versions existed. Nor were they only in oral form, as we are quick to assume from indigenous American cultures. For over a half century at that point, the Cherokee had written down their thoughts, gossip, stories, medical formulas, political acts, and tribal secrets in their own script. Thousands of pages had been published in the form of newspapers and books. What has remained unpublished might even be more precious.

What Mooney couldn't know, like any other observer in the harsh post-Reconstruction days, was how prophetic this creation story would be for the founder of the Cherokee syllabary. *And all will be water again.*

THE INFAMY behind the horrific betrayal and removal of the Cherokee and other indigenous eastern tribes, culminating with the Trail of Tears in 1838, is well known and generally taught in the schools. History, we are often told with a certain air of resignation, is written by the victors. The invention of the Cherokee syllabary by Sequoyah, an indigenous scientist and linguist from Southern Appalachia, turns that tragic history on its head, allowing us to return to an extraordinary time of resurgence in American history and an era of slaughter, ruin, and rebirth.

We refer to him today as Sequoyah, a name immortalized by those marvelous trees in northern California, yet the definitive origins of his name and parentage are unclear. In fact, virtually everything about this linguistic mastermind, from his birth to his death to the personal trials behind his invention, remains mysterious and open to interpretation. Few other figures in American history could lend themselves so well to legend. Nonetheless, when we collect all the shreds of historical evidence left in his wake, like his wondrous *talking leaves*, and examine them within the perspective of his region's historical shift, we find that Sequoyah's personal story is larger than one life or one language. It is inseparable from the birth of Southern Appalachia, the breach of its great mountain ranges, and the conflicting interests of its inhabitants.

When Sequoyah entered the Cherokee world in a small village in the Little Tennessee Valley in the late 1760s or early 1770s, his indigenous nation's dominion over the region had already reached a point of irreversible decline. His mother's clan played a prominent role in tribal affairs; one of his uncles, called Corn Tassel by the English-speaking world, was an important elder and spokesman at the time.

Sequoyah's paternity, however, belied the complex interactions taking place in the Appalachian Mountains. He was most likely the son of Nathaniel Gist (also known as Guess or Guest), a Maryland-born trailblazer who had roved among Cherokee settlements for over a decade, making Sequoyah's birth an umbilical cord between the colluding realities of the Cherokee and American colonists in the region's evolving history. It would be an overstatement to call Sequoyah, as a product of this union, the first-born modern Appalachian. But his experience reminds us that the early historians' insistence on reserving that right for Americans of European ancestry doesn't quite tell the full story.

Following a common practice among indigenous people in his period, Sequoyah used two names: one in Cherokee and one in English. The actual Cherokee name, like many indigenous terms, was transliterated into *Sequoyah*. Linguists and Cherokee speakers fail to agree today on the meaning of the name in its original language.

In many respects, the English name is more remarkable for its probable familial connection. As a silversmith, and on his documents, including treaties, Sequoyah signed or was referred to as George Gist or Guess, the name his mother had also given him at birth.

THE EARLIEST Gist scion in the American colonies, a prosperous English merchant in late seventeenth-century Baltimore, married into the family of Oliver Cromwell, England's legendary Lord Protector. By 1750, Christopher Gist, Sequoyah's apparent grandfather, had walked away from his family's prominence in the emerging coastal cities and reinvented himself as a trader and backwoodsman on the Yadkin River, in the northwestern hills of the Carolinas. Recognizing his intrepid skills in the forests, the Ohio Land Company, which included George Washington's older brother Lawrence among its investors, soon hired Gist to survey the mysterious lands on the other side of the "great mountains."

As members of one of the most powerful land companies in the colonies, the Ohio Land representatives couldn't wait any longer to discover what lay beyond the western shadows of the Appalachians. Those shadows, of course, were in the hands of the French and various allied and unaligned indigenous nations. The determined land speculators had already gobbled up huge swaths of the western Virginia valleys; in 1748, George Washington, barely old enough to shave, had helped found a thermal-bath settlement for British Lord Fairfax at Berkeley Springs in today's West Virginia.

Gist's mission was simple: He had to catalog the prime real-estate

stretches down the Ohio River, across the Blue Ridge, the side river valleys, and the Cumberlands, and up to present-day Louisville in the Bluegrass region. His instructions carried geographical and geological aims:
to take an "exact account of soil, quality and product of the land," especially all large bodies of "good level land."

Gist didn't travel alone. He set off from Old Town on the Potomac
River in Maryland with an unnamed teenage African slave. This footnote
of frontier partnership is a telling reminder of the African presence on
every exploration in Southern Appalachia, dating back to Cabeza de
Vaca, who was the first shipwrecked Spanish conquistador in the sixteenth century to hear about the fabled land of "Apalachen" and who followed the lead of a Moroccan scout and slave.

No ordinary foul-smelling "long hunter" (i.e., a hunter who disappeared into the wilderness for long spells equipped with a flintlock rifle),
the likes of whom would provide the literary imagination with an endless number of gritty Appalachian stories, Gist has remained a rank
stranger in frontier history. His groundbreaking journey, though, wonderfully observed in his correspondence, provided a balanced view of the
realities of the earliest American trailblazers. His notes were accurate
and well written; he had obtained a decent level of education. Deeply
spiritual, he had insisted on reading prayers from the Bible to irascible
traders he encountered on Christmas Eve. He mourned the death of an
exotic bird. While undeniably committed to the British Crown and its
private American land companies, Gist also recognized the territorial
realities and cultural ways of other nations and participated in their ceremonies. He took note, the story goes, of the admonition of a Delaware
leader who challenged Gist about European land claims: "If the French
claim all the land on one side of the river and the English claim all the
land on the other side of the river," the indigenous leader asked, "where
is the Indians' land?"

In fact, Gist's journals exhibit a deliberation that dispels the cutthroat
savagery of the woods. His letters remind us that diplomacy, more than
the buckskin knife, was the most effective instrument of the solitary
wanderer on the range. In the end, Appalachia transformed Gist into a

mountaineer, as reliant on peace offerings, buffalo tongue, herbs, and indigenous sweat lodges as on any colonial comforts.

GIST'S TRANSMONTANE exploration, more than a decade before Daniel Boone's celebrated entrance into Kentucky, was a watershed for the American colonists. Within seven months, having confronted a busy traffic of tribes, traders, and scurrilous French competitors and the heartbreak of losing a pet bird, Gist returned and regaled the Washingtons and their counterparts with descriptions of the vast pasturage and lush valleys west of the mountains. In eastern Kentucky, he had taken a mammoth tooth from the Pleistocene Epoch and samples of a black rock that would irrevocably alter that region's destiny: coal. Gist's narrative confirmed the Virginians' dreams and redoubled their British American resolve to expand their fortunes across the Appalachians. Within a year, he found himself back across the range on another fact-finding venture. By 1753, he would be escorting George Washington, twice saving his life from treacherous waters, according to legendary accounts, in the wunderkind soldier's first forays to treat with the French forces in the Ohio River valley.

CHRISTOPHER GIST'S second journey introduces Nathaniel Gist, his teenage son and Sequoyah's father, into the historical picture. After suffering frostbite in the winter of 1752 in the northwestern Virginia mountain explorations with his father, Nathaniel headed south along the Great Path (described in historical documents as both a trade and war route) that ribboned across the range like the original Appalachian Trail and ventured into the heart of the Cherokee upland country. The fractured world the younger Gist encountered, the same his Cherokee son Sequoyah would inherit, was far from any paradisiacal forest of undisturbed wilderness.

According to Mooney, the Cherokee had been *the* mountaineers in the South, "holding the entire Allegheny region from the interlocking head-streams of the Kanawha and the Tennessee southward almost to the site of Atlanta." He traced their historical land claims across the Virginias, Tennessee, Kentucky, the Carolinas, Alabama, and Georgia. But Mooney's observations, as the Gists discovered on their journeys, didn't necessarily reflect the complexity of overlapping indigenous land claims along the mountainous spine of the Southeast, or the full extent of Cherokee expansion.

The Appalachian Mountains, like any chain of peaks and valleys in the world, had served as a natural borderland between numerous indigenous peoples and outside invaders for centuries. Like any frontier outpost, these geographical boundaries were uncertain, hardly impassable, and constantly changing. If anything, the Appalachians functioned more as a corridor of conquest between east and west, interlocking the vast Ohio River valley and the Atlantic coast. The Great Path served all parties south to north, from the farthest stretches of the Iroquois nations to the lower valleys of the Creeks. Between periods of warfare and treaty, this well-worn transit zone functioned as the Cherokee people's prime hunting grounds and the territory of their own frontier settlements.

As early as 1753, a nineteen-year-old Nathaniel Gist had just returned from "his people at the Cherokees," according to the letters of his father, Christopher. This thoughtful recognition of "his people" was no small admission for the elder Gist: The family branches of their clan had multiplied across the Maryland frontier to Virginia, the Carolinas, and eventually the Ohio Valley.

The Cherokee Overhill villages that Nathaniel joined (in today's far eastern Tennessee Valley) represented only one part of the Cherokee people's broader network of tribal associations. When the first British traders began to establish relationships with the Cherokee in the 1620s, the Europeans encountered scores of villages, each independent yet affiliated by tribal accords, ranging from the Lower towns on the Savannah River to the Middle towns in today's Carolina piedmont, to the Overhill towns across the Southern Appalachians. The traders, including French and Spanish competitors, helped give birth to a new economy based first on indigenous slaves and goods and then on deerskin and fur. An equally vital component of this trade economy included military alliances and warfare.

This new economy and set of alliances created its own turmoil. From the north, the Cherokee had battled and entreated a plethora of small tribes, the displaced Shawnee and the powerful Iroquois confederacy; from the east, they had battled and entreated the Catawba, among others; from the south and west, they had battled and entreated the Creek, Choctaw, and Chickasaw. By the early 1700s, the imperial ambitions of the French, unfolding along the Ohio and Mississippi valleys, the Spanish in Florida and the Mississippi Valley, and the British along the Atlantic coast had turned the Southern Appalachians into an international theater of war. With the indigenous rivals on the front line, the Cherokee fell into "chronic warfare" for the next century.

WARFARE SYMBOLIZED one aspect of the holy trinity of modern conquest for the Cherokee: Disease and the upheaval of their socioeconomic exigencies were equally devastating. From their initial contact with Europeans in the sixteenth century, all indigenous groups had dealt with the wreckage of foreign diseases. In the eighteenth century alone, four smallpox epidemics swept through Cherokee communities, with merciless results. As a courier between these two worlds, Christopher Gist fell victim to the disease in 1759 in South Carolina.

Beyond the internal ruin of disease, the increasing involvement of the Cherokee in the deerskin and fur trade, mainly with the British, also led to a complete breakdown of their traditional ways. According to sociologist Wilma Dunaway, whose research on early American economies has completely revamped modern perceptions of frontier development in Southern Appalachia, the Cherokee people's full-scale plunge into the skin trade led to an abandonment of a self-sustaining culture, dislocated their native forms of governance, and made them virtually dependent on British trade and commodities for their daily survival in little over half a century. By 1730, capitulating to the British demands for a centralized system to regulate trade, the Cherokee reorganized their ancient traditions of alternating peacetime and wartime leaders in each village and appointed single leaders to preside over designated trade zones.

With trade, of course, came more conflicts over territory. The Cherokee found themselves in the paradoxical situation of requiring more hunting grounds to keep up their fur-skin trade and relenting to the land demands of the expanding colonists. The Cherokee had already made their first land concession in the Carolinas in 1721. Many more giveaways were to follow.

The Cherokee, however, did not simply allow themselves to be trampled by British boots with ease. Every step of European advancement came at a tremendous price. In truth, Cherokee dependency on the British should be described in modern terms as a codependency. The British, like the French, recognized from the onset of their conquest that the Cherokee were the key players in deciding the fate of any colonization in the south. For this reason, the British halted slave raids against indigenous communities and began to supply the Cherokee with guns and the invaluable Caribbean rum for their own purposes by the early seventeenth century.

When the French and Indian Wars (with the British) finally came to a head in the mid-1750s, the British nervously courted, implored, and then cajoled the Cherokee into an alliance. In 1754, in the throes of conflict with the French and their own indigenous allies, rising military leader George Washington cautioned the Virginia governor to place "all possible respect and the greatest care" on arriving Cherokee soldiers. "One false step," Washington wrote, "might lose us all that, and even turn them against us."

Two key players in maintaining this vital British-American alliance with the Cherokee were none other than Christopher and Nathaniel Gist. Both had served as scouts and soldiers in Washington's defeated regiments in other Ohio Valley campaigns. Their roles as negotiators and messengers between the British Crown and the Cherokee Nation, however, would far surpass any military prowess.

SUPPLIED BY HIS FATHER, Nathaniel began his trading among the mountain Cherokee in the northeastern corner of Tennessee in the early

1750s. Along with a competing trader by the name of Richard Pearis, Nathaniel settled on an island along the fork of the Holston River. This "Long Island," part of present-day Kingsport, had been a sacred treaty ground used by the Cherokee and other tribes. Personal conflicts between Nathaniel and Pearis, however, prevented any formal trading license from the Virginia governor and eventually festered into a domestic dispute that spilled over into Cherokee village politics. Pearis's connubial involvement with a Cherokee woman, like those of Nathaniel and most traders, added to the drama. The result over their quarrel was ruinous for the British. Entrusted by the Virginia governor to solicit Cherokee assistance in the brewing French and Indian Wars in the north, Nathaniel failed amid the confusion of the traders' controversies.

By 1756, preparing for another assault against the French alliances, Washington wrote again that he considered the Cherokee "the best if not only troops fit to cope with the Indians [with the French] in such grounds." Once more assigned with the diplomatic charge of appealing for Cherokee forces, Nathaniel succeeded this time and even led a Cherokee division.

Despite such alliances and even the construction of British forts on Cherokee territory, the relationship between the two sovereign nations remained tenuous at best. A long-brewing war between the Cherokee, the British, and their Carolinian colonists broke out in late 1759 and festered in sporadic and bloody battles over two years. The Cherokee sacked Fort Loudoun in the Little Tennessee Valley, among other outposts; the British and colonial militias razed numerous lowland Cherokee towns. British troops eventually occupied Nathaniel's Long Island.

While ostensibly in the service of the British forces, Nathaniel—more than his father—walked a difficult if not ambiguous path, as he would many times, in the conflicting role of messenger, negotiator, soldier, and Cherokee consort. Amid the ashes of Cherokee defeat in 1761, as indigenous families retreated further into the forests of the Southern Appalachians, he returned to the Overhill settlements on his own. This cohabitation among the rival nations was remarkable for someone in Nathaniel's position. He was no lone-wolf trader or hunter, like scores of fellow travelers in the backwoods, devoid of any allegiances. As a representative of the Crown, invested in the interests of the American colonists, Nathaniel also found he couldn't afford to neglect the exigencies of the mountain Cherokee in the process. His decisions, ultimately, reflected the evolving reality of life and trade in the Southern Appalachians and the incompatible demands of the region's inhabitants. This connection with various groups of people would have its price: Years later, Nathaniel was briefly imprisoned, then vindicated and pardoned, as a traitor to the American Patriots, accused of having served as a spy on behalf of the Cherokee.

While Gist attempted to reopen the Long Island dispute a number of times, applying for a title to the land directly from the Virginia governor, his claim failed to be realized in his lifetime. He went on to have an impressive array of experiences over the next twenty-five years of his life, serving as a colonel in the American Revolution and settling in the Bluegrass region of Kentucky as a wealthy land and slave owner.

An important postscript, though, about that troubled piece of real estate on Long Island brings us full circle to the probable birth of his son Sequoyah. After a punishing exchange of battles with the British and American colonists in 1776 and 1777, including a self-destructive Cherokee attempt to destroy illegal American settlements on treaty-recognized Cherokee mountain territory, several of the Overhill leaders finally agreed to a truce and major land concessions. The treaty was held on Long Island, where Corn Tassel—the highly respected elder for the Overhills, uncle of Sequoyah, and would-be brother-in-law of Nathaniel—made a stinging appeal for peace. He first lambasted the settlers' demands for more territory. Then, as recorded by an English immigrant, he examined the divergent destinies of the mountaineers, be they British, American, or Cherokee:

> Indeed, much has been advanced on the want of what you term civilization among the Indians, and many proposals have been made to adopt your laws, your religion, your manners and your customs. But, we confess that we do not yet see the propriety, or practicability of such a

reformation, and should be better pleased with beholding the good effect
of these doctrines in your own practices than with hearing you talk
about them, or reading your papers to us upon such subjects. . . . The
great God of Nature has placed us in different situations. It is true that
he has endowed you with many superior advantages; but he has not cre-
ated us to be your slaves. We are a separate people.

Corn Tassel then wrote into the treaty his objection to the transfer of
the title of Long Island to any person or entity with the exception of
Nathaniel Gist, "for whom and themselves it was reserved by the Cherokees . . . and desired that Col. Gist might sit down upon it when he
pleased, as it belonged to him and them to hold good talks on." Corn
Tassel referred to Sequoyah's father as his friend and brother and as "one
of my own people."

Corn Tassel's demands were overlooked. The island was finally ceded
to the federal government of the United States in 1806. But a strange, if
not extraordinary event occurred in 1976, nearly two centuries after Corn
Tassel had made his speech on Nathaniel's behalf. The City of Kingsport,
in conjunction with the Mead Corporation, handed back the title to a
section of the sacred island to the Eastern Band of the Cherokee, marking the first land transfer (or return) to the indigenous inhabitants since
1785. In deference to Sequoyah, the tribe accepted the land in the name of
Nathaniel Gist.

As his literate American father, Nathaniel appears to have played
little role in the life of Sequoyah. Raised in the traditional Cherokee settlement of Tuskegee (Taskigi) in the Little Tennessee Valley with his
mother, Sequoyah never learned to speak, read, or write in English.

He spent his youth like others in his native community, ranging
across the Southern Appalachians and foothills as a hunter, a soldier, and
then as a blacksmith. In this mesh as an artisan and occasional combat-
ant, serving as late as 1812–1813 in campaigns against the Creek Red
Sticks, Sequoyah witnessed the exchange of written communications by

merchants and military officers and pondered the creation of a written language for his Cherokee people.

Even today, it is hard to imagine the audacity and terminal curiosity of such an undertaking. Critical to Sequoyah's tenacity, of course, was a basic tenet that his uncle, Corn Tassel, had made clear to the warring parties on Long Island: The Cherokee were a separate people endowed with their own extraordinary abilities. In Sequoyah's mind and in response to naysayers, there was no reason that the Cherokee could not invent their own written language. According to one story, Sequoyah once turned to a doubting friend in the early days and showed him a rock. After making a few scratches on the rock, Sequoyah handed it to his friend and said, "See, anyone can write their own language."

At the same time that Sequoyah was undertaking his tedious work, an American missionary had also created an orthography of the Cherokee language, using the Roman alphabet. While this version had some success among an English-speaking elite, it failed miserably among the majority of Cherokee. It was not their language.

That Sequoyah drew from this Roman alphabet of the English-speaking communities is indubitable; he also explored other sources of literary invention. Ancient petroglyph markings covered stones throughout the region. As a silversmith, Sequoyah had used his own artistic symbols for years to indicate various products and transactions. In the early phase of his work, in fact, he attempted to make a series of marks for every word, until the sheer numbers exhausted that possibility.

As the years progressed and experiments with the logographic options proved unworkable, Sequoyah's breakthrough occurred phonetically when he realized he could identity eighty-six distinct Cherokee sounds or, specifically, a vowel or consonant plus a vowel. At this point, incorporating letters from an English-language Bible (some accounts include a McGuffey reader), a Greek text, and forms of his own invention, Sequoyah designed a symbol for each sound.

The development of his syllabary chart took more than a decade of full-time research. It didn't transpire without controversy, a tremendous amount of ridicule, and constant disappointment. The notion of creating an alphabet, or a syllabary in Sequoyah's case, of course, would be considered a mad and impossible enterprise by most people. After several years of failure, most of Sequoyah's friends and family assumed he had come under the influence of some sort of dementia. The English-speaking Christian elite was not only dubious but also terrified of Sequoyah's work, as if it indicated a possible regression to the old ways.

Most Cherokee remained indifferent, assuming that his "foolish undertaking," as defined by one spokesman, was a predetermined fool's errand. Some chastised Sequoyah for his lack of regular work. The most suspicious, including his wife, however, thought the inventor might be dragging them into tribal shame or, worse, embarking on a plan of witchcraft. Coaxing him outside a small laboratory he had constructed for his research, they set fire to his mounds of papers and notes, destroying years of deliberation. The incident only renewed Sequoyah's resolve and perhaps functioned to shift his work toward a more phonetic approach.

In 1821, when he was living along the Coosa River, in the northeastern part of Alabama, Sequoyah unveiled his hard-earned results in public. He had instructed his young daughter in the syllabary. A fluent Cherokee speaker only needed to memorize the eighty-six (then modified into eighty-five) symbols and sounds, to utilize the system. Once his daughter had convinced the community of the syllabary's effectiveness, trading messages with Sequoyah from a long distance, other children began to learn to read and write in the written language. The inventor and his daughter made a formal presentation in front of the nation's leaders in north Georgia later that year.

The Cherokee leaders reacted in a jumble of poorly feigned indifference and outright disbelief. For the English-speaking Christian elite Cherokee, who had embraced the paradoxical task of distancing themselves from indigenous mores to prove their nation's ability to assume modern American ways, the syllabary came as a shocking reminder of the still formidable power of the monolingual Cherokee-speaking and traditional majority in the Southern Appalachians and foothills. Here was Sequoyah, a non-Christian traditionalist, an eccentric but valued elder who had been involved in treaties and war, unschooled and unable to speak, read, or write in English, who had done the impossible: One of their own Cherokee had created a written alphabet for the nation.

Sequoyah's own English paternity, too, disturbed a common assumption that Cherokee of mixed-blood ancestry were easily assimilating into an English-speaking American culture. Christian missionaries, who had become increasingly influential in daily affairs, fretted that the syllabary would lead their converts away from the King James Bible.

The outside missionaries were not the only souls unnerved by the invention. For the proponents of the manifest-destiny policies of the early-American postcolonial establishment, his invention devastated their well-worn proclamations that the nonliterate indigenous nations were inherently deficient, and therefore disposable.

THE GREAT MAJORITY of the Cherokee, 85 percent of whom were monolingual Cherokee speakers, adopted the syllabary as their very own, while the indigenous nation's elite adjusted themselves to the reality of the invention. Within a short period, according to one missionary, Sequoyah's written language was "spreading through like fire among the leaves." Other observers marveled at the ease with which Cherokee learned the syllabary. Another missionary wrote with an unmasked enthusiasm: "They can generally learn it in one day and in a week become writing masters and transact their business and communicate their thoughts freely and fully on religious or political subjects by writing."

When Sequoyah made a journey to Arkansas in 1822 to demonstrate his invention, he brought with him letters and documents from Cherokee friends and family members. He returned to Alabama and Georgia with a trunk load of letters in response.

At this point, the Cherokee leaders had no choice but to celebrate Sequoyah's work and his role in the nation. The syllabary proliferated beyond their control. Without any schools, but by "teaching each other in the cabins and along the roadside," an estimated two-thirds to three-quarters of the Cherokee communities were literate and using the syllabary for their personal needs within three years. This statistic, of course, far surpassed the literacy levels among the Cherokee's English-speaking neighbors in the region. Amid the jubilant times, tribal officials announced plans to create a newspaper, publish books and other texts, and establish a Cherokee library and museum.

Though English remained the official language, as an appeasement to the elite's relationship with the American government, all legal documents and tribal affairs were translated and published in Cherokee. The missionaries, who had assumed the syllabary would draw away from their Christian texts, threw themselves forward into translations; a syllabary version of the Gospel of John was completed by 1824. Samuel Worcester, an unusually enlightened Congregationalist missionary who had been instrumental in securing a typeface and printing press from Boston, concluded that "if books are printed in Guess's [Sequoyah's] character, they will be read; if in any other, they will lie useless."

The passion for literacy among the Cherokee, and the possibilities it had unleashed, amazed outside observers. According to one visitor, the most precious items in demand in the villages were pens, ink, and paper. Political speeches, an important practice in Cherokee oral culture, were suddenly transcribed and recorded. One of Sequoyah's first literary acts, in fact, had been to write out a speech on land boundaries and disputes. Written messages now linked the Western and Eastern bands of the nation. Traditional Cherokee healers, herbalists, and spiritual conjurers began to record their ancient knowledge, formulas, and secrets.

On top of the officially published books, newspapers, and other documents, the foremost value of the syllabary might be found in its role of empowerment and self-representation for the majority of the Cherokee in their private lives. As a vision of autonomy, as much as a vehicle for writing, Sequoyah's syllabary allowed virtually every Cherokee, without the intrusion of English-speaking outsiders or the control of quarreling tribal factions, to record their own personal story in the Southern Appalachians.

In effect, a true renaissance was taking place in the American South, and the invention of the Cherokee linguist ensured an account of its history.

IN THE WINTER OF 1828, as if demarcating the shrinking Appalachian boundaries of the Cherokee communities, a courier departed from the village of New Echota in north Georgia and journeyed around the mountains in the southern tier of the Carolinas, Tennessee, and the foothills of Alabama. Other couriers had set off to the western territories in Arkansas. The historic nature of their trips might seem commonplace today, but in that moment it recognized the astonishing resiliency of the Cherokee. The couriers were delivering a newspaper, the *Cherokee Phoenix*. The name could not have been more poignant. After generations of hostilities and invasion, territorial relocation and social breakdown, intertribal strife, disagreement and growing disparity, and the complete reorientation of daily life, a new vehicle had emerged from the ruins of the Cherokee to unite their disparate communities.

As the first bilingual indigenous newspaper in the United States, printed in both English and Sequoyah's alphabet, the *Cherokee Phoenix* signaled an exciting cultural rebirth taking place in the Southern mountains and lower Alabama and Georgia communities. With their population expanding for the first time in a generation, the Cherokee now numbered over 13,500, with thousands of other Cherokee living in the Arkansas territories. Having shifted largely to an agricultural and small-industry economy, their communities operated without debt and developed export markets in cotton, tobacco, wheat, apples and peaches, and livestock. Houses, farms, and even large plantations had been raised. A network of roads wound throughout the area; mission schools and churches had been built in various Cherokee villages.

At a time when the young nation of the United States struggled to mold its own regional and national identities from a broad amalgam of languages, cultures, religions, histories, and economic interests, Sequoyah's syllabary and its impact on the Appalachian region emerged as a startling exemplar of the enduring force of indigenous groups in the country. When the Cherokee held their convention in 1827 and adopted a written constitution, a greater percentage of their sovereign nation would have been able to participate in and read the document than would their American counterparts at the historic unveiling of the U.S. Constitution in Philadelphia. We would be hard pressed to identify an American phenomenon that had brought such full-scale participatory democracy to any other region in so quick a time frame.

To the horror of Appalachian abolitionists, the Cherokee people's shifting economy also mirrored the social realities of the American South in a very tangible manner. A majority of the indigenous nation had embraced the Christian sects of the Moravians, Baptists, United Brethren, Congregationalists, Methodists, and Presbyterians, while a small elite had become owners of over 1,300 African and African American slaves, who numbered 10 percent of the population.

While all of these indicators would be evidence of the Cherokee people's acculturation of early-nineteenth-century American ways, one key element in their lives and nation remained distinctly Cherokee: their language. No one could have been more imbued with a sense of dogged optimism and determination for the future than Sequoyah. Three months after the first issue of the *Cherokee Phoenix* rolled off the printing press, leaders of the rising nation in Washington, D.C., courted him like an elder statesman. Sequoyah had ventured to the capital to take part in another treaty for the Cherokee, dealing with land exchange and resettlement in the western territories. In the process, politicians hailed him as a genius, the press celebrated his invention, and the federal government honored him with a $500 award for "the great benefits he has conferred upon the Cherokee people, in the beneficial results which they are now experiencing from the use of the alphabet discovered by him." He returned to his region as a modern-day legend, compared to Cadmus, Moses, and Gutenberg.

While courtship in Washington would have been flattering, and the award no small sum for the times, the sixty-year-old Sequoyah was probably most heartened by the reception his work had finally gained among his own nation, especially in the form of the newspaper. After decades of dissension, the elder relished the sense of unity he had triggered among his divided people.

FAR FROM BEING an isolated and unknown aberration of one indigenous group in the southern forests, the news of Sequoyah's work spread rapidly across the country. Instilled with a broader Pan-American vision for indigenous nations, the aging inventor even visited several other western indigenous groups in an effort to demonstrate his chart. He hauled a supply of papers and other materials in an old oxcart and carried out workshops to encourage other tribes to devise their own creations. He functioned as an ambassador of indigenous sovereignty, debunking the common assumptions in that period that associated the lack of literacy among indigenous groups with their lack of societal organization. More so, the Cherokee elder remained a dedicated traditionalist to his last days. He refused any assimilation into American culture or the English language. He openly rejected a growing belief that his invention "elevated" the Cherokee, as many missionaries and English-speaking Cherokee sought to claim, as if to distinguish them from other "uncivilized" tribes. According to one portrait of the inventor in this period, Sequoyah viewed his syllabary as a way of simply providing the literary record of the Cherokee people's beloved cultural ways and aspirations, not altering them.

Years later, an article in another bilingual newspaper, the *Cherokee Advocate*, placed Sequoyah's life and work within the framework of another Cherokee myth:

> When the Indian and the white man were created, the Indian, being the elder, was given a book, while the white man received a bow and arrows. Each was instructed to take good care of his gift and make the best use of it, but the Indian was so neglectful of his book that the white man soon stole it from him, leaving the bow in its place, so that books and reading now belong of right to the white man, while the Indian ought to be satisfied to hunt for a living.

The subtext of this legend, of course, would suggest that the Cherokee had never lacked the means or right to literacy, but had it stolen by the British and Americans. Sequoyah's remarkable invention updates the myth from a modern perspective and makes his syllabary a Cherokee act of struggle, even resistance, a reclaiming of what had been rightfully theirs. A book now joins the bows and arrows as a vital part of Cherokee culture.

Sequoyah's invention had become the weapon for a new writing of history.

SEQUOYAH'S DEATH, like his birth, remains a mystery. In 1843, a frail man who was most likely in his eighties, Sequoyah departed on horseback from Oklahoma with a few companions, in search of a renegade group of Cherokee who had fled to northern Mexico. Forever the ambassador, he played the role of an elder statesman of the Cherokee in the western territories, actively involved in uniting the various factions.

Within a decade of the incredible Cherokee renaissance in the Southern Appalachians, the sovereign nation of the Cherokee had been fraudulently bilked of its lands in north Georgia and the surrounding areas, largely due to the discovery of gold and relentless land speculation. The nation was then forcefully relocated from its treaty-guaranteed territories in the Southern states to the Indian Territories in Oklahoma. Over one-third of the nation almost certainly died during this wintertime Trail of Tears in 1838. This history remains one of our nation's most despicable betrayals and tragedies.

Falling quite ill on his journey into Mexico in 1843, Sequoyah decided to rest in a cave while his companions searched for help. According to follow-up reports, Sequoyah had brought along his writing materials and papers. His body was never found; he is assumed to have died in the cave, the location of which remains unknown today, though several later searches have suggested various areas. His widow continued to receive a special pension awarded to Sequoyah, the first literary annuity in the country.

When the Tennessee Valley Authority (TVA) decided in the late 1970s to flood the Tellico area of the Little Tennessee Valley as part of its development plans in the region, the authority met with an initial burst of resistance by the Eastern Band of the Cherokee, a federally recognized tribe based in the North Carolina mountains, among others. As the plans progressed the TVA courted tribal officials with promises of undertaking archaeological excavations and surveys, and the Tellico Dam project was finally signed into effect. (The TVA would also name one of its nuclear reactors after Sequoyah.) A small faction of the Cherokee, including a descendant of Sequoyah, made a final plea before the Federal Court of Appeals to halt the project. Invoking a clause of religious freedom, lawyers argued that the plaintiff, Ammoneta Sequoyah, had a historical right to collect sacred medicine in the area. The appeal failed.

An opinion of the court summed up the American experience of the Cherokee in devastatingly honest terms: "Though cultural history and tradition are vitally important to any group of people, these are not interests protected by the Free Exercise Clause of the First Amendment."

Sequoyah's birthplace, as well as the sacred Cherokee village of Chota, was destroyed and completely inundated by the artificial lakes within six weeks. *And all was water again.*

Chapter Two

THE FIRST WASHINGTON, D.C.

+~+

A set of people in the back part of this colony, bordering
on the Cherokee country . . . to all intents and purposes, have erected
themselves into, though an inconsiderable, yet a separate State.

—LORD JOHN MURRAY DUNMORE,
Royal Governor of Virginia, 1774

ON JULY 5, 1776, a messenger on horseback skirted the Great Path along
the Southern Appalachians, fording creeks until he emerged onto the
piedmont forests near the Yadkin River, not far from Salisbury, North
Carolina. The horseman's saddlebag was light. He possessed only a few
documents, all signed and sealed by wax. He punished his horse across
the Tory-controlled villages in North Carolina until he arrived at the
headquarters of the regional Patriots.

Despite the subversive nature of his act, the messenger on horseback
was not delivering a declaration of independence. On the contrary, he
carried a declaration of dependence: the petition by a chain of renegade
settlements in the Southern Appalachians to devolve their bona fide status of independence and join the "glorious cause of liberty" as an
annexed district of the revolutionary state of North Carolina. They proclaimed themselves the inhabitants of the "District of Washington."

If we consider the prologue of the American Revolution as the long, tedious task of unhinging British control over the daily lives, lots, and rights of American colonists, not simply as a series of random acts of outrage or uprising, what unfolded in that simple petition from the Appalachian backwoods was nothing less than a dramatic reckoning in American history. Without firing a single shot at the redcoats, long before any tea was thrust into any harbor or before any state or national congress had gathered to draw up a declaration of independence, these outlaws recounted how they had moved themselves beyond the boundaries of British control, negotiated with the Cherokee as their own sovereign entity, and established a self-governing community, replete with its own laws, courts, elected officials, diplomats, and militia.

Whether or not the North Carolina Patriots recognized the landmark role of the petitioners, the British Crown and its agents had; it had long considered these mountaineers a "dangerous example to the people of America," as the royal governor of Virginia had written the British secretary of state for colonial affairs in 1774. The governor accused the Appalachians "of forming governments distinct from and independent of His Majesty's authority."

On November 19, 1776, the Provincial Congress of North Carolina formally approved the annexation of the petitioning Appalachian communities. The inhabitants of the District of Washington traded in their free-style form of independence for the revolutionary cause. The extraordinary nature of their dangerous example, though, had not been an empty gesture. For four years, from 1772 until the horseman's arrival in 1776, native-born Americans, immigrants, and slaves in the mountains of Southern Appalachia had provided the thirteen colonies with their first raw version of improvised democracy.

HISTORY has always reminded us of the cycles of population in prime real-estate areas. This self-styled District of Washington, a wedge of mountains and river valleys in today's northeastern corner of Tennessee, would be no exception. The area lay in the middle of an ancient corridor of hunting, trade, and settlement. The district's center, the Sycamore

Shoals off the Watauga River, sat in an abandoned clearing of old Cherokee fields, bordered by burial grounds. Skulls and bones abounded.
When Daniel Boone, on the payroll of a private land company, passed
the Holston Valley in 1769, he even noted the absence of the Cherokee,
an eerie if somewhat comforting realization that the region had transformed in his own short tenure of exploration.

Boone's note, as was often the case with his observations, was pre-
scient. By the spring of 1769, with various waves of long hunters, traders,
homesteaders, and their slaves staking claims along the Appalachian
waterways, the Cherokee authority over the region had been shattered.
Within a short time, the ancient name of the Cherokee River itself
would reflect the region's change; it transformed into the Tennessee
River on surveyors' maps. The incoming settlers, therefore, arrived not at
the birth of a region, but in the wake of a passing regime, as they repop-
ulated the forest communities.

There was just one problem: The still unnamed District of Washington was technically on the wrong side of the king's proclamation line.
As an appeasement to the territorial concerns of indigenous nations like
the Cherokee, who had aided the British in their territorial wars with
the French in the Ohio Valley, the Royal Proclamation of 1763 strictly for-
bade any colonial settlement west of the Appalachians and prohibited
any private person from purchasing land directly from the indigenous
inhabitants.

In truth, the British Crown drew this imaginary iron curtain across
the mountains as a last-gasp attempt to control the mounting advances of
the American land companies and colonists. By 1763, the frontier pulsated
with colonial ambitions of conquest. Arable plots of land for common
settlers, poor immigrants, entitled soldiers, veterans of the French and
Indian Wars, and, most importantly, the insatiable land speculators were
increasingly hard to come by in the piedmont and Southern low country.
Even on the edges of Southern Appalachia, such as the valleys of the
Blue Ridge Mountains in Virginia, wealthy plantation owners, private
land companies, and British partisans had swept up colossal estates and
prime land holdings. While the proclamation line served as a temporary

reproach to official land schemes, the temptation of crossing those great mountains remained irresistible.

Nonetheless, incursion over the line had now become a contemptuous act of outlaws.

THE IMAGE of an outlaw clashes, in some respects, with the common portrayal of the Appalachian pioneers, those freedom-loving and slightly feral backwoods people, guided more by their muskets than their ability to read the letter of the law. Moreover, romantic historians, largely out of a disingenuous tendency to justify American encroachment on indigenous lands, place these coon-capped souls within the backdrop of a virgin paradise unclaimed by the human touch. The Appalachian frontier people, we are often told, were rugged, individualistic freedom fighters who cleared the trails and forests on behalf of civilization, spurred by an innate need for unfettered liberty, not a calculating desire to gain property titles or political power.

The experience of the Gists among the warring Native American–European alliances dispelled many of these misleading images of untouched wilderness. The Appalachian mountain range had just gone through more than a century of massive change and irreparable warfare. The self-proclaimed District of Washington, on the other hand, making its political stand in the back valleys and mountains of Southern Appalachia, added an even more complex, fascinating, and largely ignored aspect to the prerevolutionary frontier. Beyond the "glorious cause of liberty," as they declared, these mountain rebels were law-savvy slave-owning real-estate agents. But they were forthright. Their cause cut to the heart of the American Revolution: land rights.

In effect, these mountaineers did not only serve in the vanguard of the independence movement. They were, in fact, some of colonial America's shrewdest politicians, albeit tucked away in a mountain stronghold and eventually branded outlaws for their legal maneuvers, not their feats with a gun.

They didn't realize, of course, that the mountain range and its ancient conflicts would ultimately determine their fate and the direction of their own democracy.

FAR FROM the unlettered coon-capped frontiersmen in the bear-hunting yarns made famous by fellow Tennessean Davy Crockett, the first mountaineers in the District of Washington came from surprisingly diverse backgrounds. William Bean, one of the first long hunters to settle on the lower Watauga waterway, was an educated merchant, militia officer, and plantation and slave owner who had arrived from southern Virginia with a supportive entourage. He could trace his noble Highland Scottish origins back to the reign of King Malcolm II. Bean's ancestors would claim the foiled character of Duncan, in Shakespeare's *Macbeth,* as one of their own. The first family members from Inverness had arrived in Virginia in the 1650s and prospered.

Jacob Brown, who became Bean's neighbor in 1771 and was a Virginian by birth, married into a wealthy South Carolinian family. With his own cadre of associates, he settled an area south of Bean, along the Nolichucky River. Brown "purchased" the rights to a choice riverside spot on Cherokee lands from another squatter, who was illegally holding the land himself. Far from being the stereotypical lonesome frontiersman, Brown had courted the financial support of the prodigious McDowell family, one of the most powerful clans in the Carolinas, and then set up a mercantile business. He had much greater ambitions; in time, he would also become a prosperous slave owner and real-estate baron. In his personal matters, though, Brown was less fortunate; the District of Washington courts eventually tried him for adultery.

More affluent than Bean or Brown, John Carter soon settled another group of Virginians on the southwestern fork of the Holston River, affixing the third angle of the district's triangle. Carter was related to the notorious Robert "King" Carter of the Corotoman Plantation in Lancaster County, Virginia. One of the richest men in the colonies, King Carter had over one thousand slaves working his vast landholdings at the time of his death in 1732. The Carters' English ancestors had been prominent leaders in the Tidewater region since 1635. With one hand still on his business interests in southern Virginia, the slave-owning John Carter set up his own mercantile and land-speculating outpost in the mountain settlement.

Other ambitious gentry from Virginia joined Carter, Bean, and Brown, crossing into the mountain valleys with their china tea sets, silver candle holders and turkey platters, and other heirlooms from Europe. Many of these families brought African slaves, as well.

Not all Washingtonians were Tidewater aristocrats, of course. Arriving on the heels of Bean, a young James Robertson had left behind the brewing political turmoil of North Carolina in 1769 and followed the wanderlust of his lifelong friend Boone, who had declared in his memoir, "Curiosity is natural to the soul of men." After making a survey of the region and clearing his own fields near Sycamore Shoals, the Scotch-Irish Robertson retrieved his family and settled in the area with a cluster of friends. A literate, keenly aware farmer and backwoodsman, Robertson rose from his modest beginnings to become a celebrated figure in the history of Tennessee, one of the founders of Nashville, a prosperous slave-owning politician, a medical expert on treating scalped heads, and a diplomat among the Southern indigenous tribes.

By 1771, these notable pioneers—Bean, Brown, Carter, and Robertson among them—had been joined in the area by nearly one hundred households and their extended families, all of whom had cleared plots of land along the valleys and ridges. Unlike many of the earliest frontier communities launched by a singular church or personality, such as the Moravian's founding of Wachovia (today's Salem, North Carolina), the ranks of these newer settlements included an assortment of religious sects and social strata. Most of the settlers had trickled in as groups, related by kin or colony.

The Africans and African American slaves among them have remained largely unnamed, though they are accounted for in wills, deeds, and other legal documents. The first significant recognition of slaves emerged during a period of warfare. Nonetheless, their roles alongside the trailblazers, clearing the forests and fields, raising the barns and cabins, and protecting the interests of their owners, were indispensable.

The extremely delicate social relations that endured in the mountains should not be underestimated; the first mountaineers were a diverse lot. They ranged from myriad English, Welsh, Scottish Highlanders, Lowlanders and Scotch-Irish (Ulstermen), German, Swiss, French, and Spanish to African and indigenous inhabitants. Two settlers of French Huguenot ancestry, John Sevier (originally spelled Xavier) and David Crockett (de Crocketagne), the grandfather of the legendary coon-capped icon, played key roles in the District of Washington. The celebrated Boone was the product of English Quakers who had immigrated to the Pennsylvania backcountry.

Much has been made in recent historical chronicles of the Scotch-Irish role on the American frontier, especially in Appalachia and the Ohio Valley. The District of Washington was no exception. Emerging from centuries of borderland wars in the Scottish Lowlands and then a century of conflict in the northern plantations of Ulster in Ireland, the Scotch-Irish were greeted variably by chroniclers of the period as "white savages" or indefatigable frontier people who quickly served in their destined role as border fighters.

In truth, the Ulsterites flowing into the Appalachian mountain valleys were not all a "pack of beggars," as one of the royal governors labeled them, but included many prosperous peddlers. Andrew Greer, an Ulster immigrant from Londonderry, worked his way down the Virginia Blue Ridge, becoming one of the key traders along the Holston and Watauga waterways. He settled in the District of Washington a few years before the Beans. He engaged in the dangerous but extremely lucrative role of the mule-packed dealer. With the Cherokee deep in warring conflicts and in need of various European products, guns, and powder, the Ulsterman reaped huge profits and sowed the grounds, according to one historian, "of a considerable estate."

One other group of notable settlers found their way to the District of Washington: radical Patriots, fleeing the fallout of the Regulator movement in the Carolinas. Considered by some historians a Southern counterpart to New England's antistamp Patriots, the Regulators were a ragtag array of colonists who objected to the extortionist policies of British officers and the uneven handling of justice in the backcountry. Their protests eventually turned violent and uneven in their own hands; they disrupted the courts, sprang their comrades from jail, and attacked anyone they considered on the side of the Tories. The British forces finally crushed an armed uprising by thousands of Regulators in the late spring of 1771, at the Battle of the Alamance in North Carolina, triggering the flight of many Regulators into the Southern Appalachian forests. Their departure did not transpire without notice. For a Moravian clergyman traveling in the Appalachian region, the mountains swelled with "many strangers . . . who do not wish to be under the law."

WITH SO MANY settlers spilling across the proclamation line in this pivotal eastern Tennessee corridor, the Cherokee appealed to the British authorities for help, declaring that the foreign muskets of squatters echoed around their hunting grounds like hawks. Represented by agents for two private land companies in the region, the British Crown negotiated the Treaty at Lochaber, South Carolina, in 1770, reestablishing the Cherokee borderline across the Appalachians. The treaty was not without its own political machinations; the two land companies managed to extract considerable land concessions for their own interests in the process.

The home of the Washingtonians, however, that peculiar wedge in the Southern mountains, was left out of the transaction. The land sat in neither Virginia nor the Carolinas. It remained unquestionably a strip of Cherokee territory, intersected by three major waterways, a good thirty miles south of the Lochaber line and fifty miles west of the proclamation line.

While the Washingtonians would later plead ignorance of these new borders, it would take a generous suspension of skepticism to believe them. No one was more familiar with the landmarks and waterways than the mountaineers. They had surveyed each rock, valley, and creek in the region. Their ranks even included professional surveyors.

In truth, this bevy of frontier people recognized that they had squatted on one of the most strategic corridors in the Southern Appalachians. Their views had turned Boone poetic; he claimed he felt "like the man in the Bible who owned the cattle on a thousand hills." One Washingtonian leader hailed the mountain valleys as "the promised land." One step removed from the British laws and land holdings of Virginians and Carolinians, this area also represented a vulnerable breaking spot in the vast territories of the Cherokee, who were literally in the throes of warfare with other indigenous groups and southern colonists. The settlers knew, like everyone in the American colonies, that their conquest would come at the expense of the Cherokee, not at the mercy of the British Crown.

IN THE MEANTIME, flanked by the Cherokee leader Attacullaculla, who had been part of a Cherokee delegation that had visited the London Court of King George III, the British agent in charge of the southern tribes officially ordered the mountaineers in 1771 to relinquish their holdings and abandon the area. The British demand was unequivocal and nonnegotiable.

The response to the British agent became one of the first decisive acts of coordinated civil disobedience in the American rebellion. The mountaineers didn't budge. Nor did they fire any weapons or rush into a confrontation like stereotypical war-hungry Scotch-Irish or untamed hunters. Instead, they convened, joined forces, organized their plans, and then concocted one of the most ingenuous plots in the nation's history to circumvent treaty laws and resist British authority. Incorporating themselves as the Watauga Association, they simply leased the land from the Cherokee for ten years.

According to the Royal Proclamation of 1763, no colonist could permanently settle west of the Appalachians or purchase land directly from the indigenous nations. The mountaineers proposed to do neither; by leasing the land from the Cherokee on a supposed ten-year lease, they were neither permanent nor purchasers.

Convincing the Cherokee was another matter. For this purpose, backwoods veteran Robertson and a member of the Bean family journeyed to the Overhill towns and negotiated with the Cherokee leaders. Implicit in the two men's actions, of course, was the understanding that the mountaineers functioned as a sovereign entity that required no permission and granted no authority to the British officials. Robertson and Bean dealt with the indigenous nations without a British agent or command at their side, operating as a completely independent American entity.

The incorporation of the district added to the democratic marvel of this affair. The mountaineers proved they were not simply a rabble of individual squatters seeking out small parcels of land without any consideration of the rest of the community. With the express intent of governing themselves, they drew up articles of association and a code of laws that were signed by every individual (which meant, in the terms of the period, every free male of European ancestry who was a head of household) in the surroundings. Their articles were not homespun or limited in scope. The settlers replicated the Virginia laws, though with one historic exception: Their association excised any reference to royal authority. According to an early nineteenth-century historian affiliated with members of the association, if any settler refused to sign the code of the laws, "he was debarred from its benefits. But there were no recusants."

The actual documentation of the association's 1772 articles has long disappeared, though the historic petition delivered to the Provincial Congress of North Carolina in 1776 recounted the community's extraordinary dealings and decision to set up its own independent government. Responding to the "consent of the people," the community declared it had formed a court to handle civil and criminal matters, including deeds, wills, and other public business such as marriage licenses. A sheriff was appointed; a clerk was selected; and five magistrates were elected "under the denomination of trustees," to carry out the letter of the laws.

IN THEIR NEGOTIATIONS with various Cherokee leaders, Robertson and Bean made two important discoveries: The leadership structure of the Overhill Cherokee villages was in disarray, and the British grip over the region was becoming increasingly transparent. Identifying elder Cherokee leaders amenable to land concessions, Robertson finalized the ten-year lease of the land in exchange for trade goods, muskets, and cash. The terms of the lease had one clear stipulation: The settlers could not advance beyond the boundaries of the agreement. Not to be outdone, Brown negotiated his own lease for a large tract of land on the Nolichucky River. He financed the deal through his association with the prominent McDowell family in North Carolina.

Romantic historians have gone to great pains to depict a flowering of wilderness democracy that is devoid of factions or discrimination and inspired by the high mountain winds of freedom. In 1816, Moses Fisk, a northern missionary turned Tennessee historian, described the community as "little protected, controlled or recollected by any government whatsoever, as their co-tenants the bears."

In truth, the mountaineers couldn't have been more organized, stratified, and concerned about their renegade status. The Virginian elite, all slave owners and land speculators, dominated the first positions of magistrates and trustees. This doesn't necessarily detract from the Washingtonians' achievement of independence, but acknowledges their extremely volatile situation. Their greatest fear, they later wrote in their petition, was being considered "a lawless mob."

In fact, the mountaineers were dealing not only with the repercussions from the British and the Cherokee, but also with incursions from other settlers potentially opposed to their united front. The mountaineer communities swelled with colonists fleeing the upheavals of the Regulators in the Carolinas and fugitives absconding from the Virginia backcountry law. Murderers, horse thieves, robbers, and debtors appeared daily in the pioneers' clearings.

THE ASSOCIATION'S unfurling of its lease with the Cherokee stunned the British agents. Immobilized by a web of treaty language, the English couldn't do anything but stammer, fret, and silently admit the mountaineers' manipulation of the laws. The agreement, however, augmented the divisions among the Cherokee, especially among younger leaders who were not in favor of allowing further encroachment on their lands.

While the Washingtonian and Cherokee relations would eventually dissolve into unrestrained warfare on both sides, a few glimmers of relative peace and even collaboration took place in the early phase of the agreement. Beyond their day-to-day trading, the neighboring communities took part in joint celebrations and commingled without alarm. There were even attempts at atonement when individual settlers ambushed innocent Cherokee. On two separate occasions, the Washingtonians called Robertson into his diplomatic role with the Overhill towns, promising to capture and punish the murderers. Likewise, the Cherokee alerted the settlers along the Watauga in advance of rebellious war parties that did not have the support of the elder leaders.

These moments of coexistence did not last long. By 1774, the Cherokee were disgruntled with the settlers' intransigence and increasing expansion, in violation of their lease terms. Cherokee hunting parties, deeply invested in their own skin trade, had even been rebuked from entering Cherokee lands along the confluence of the Watauga and Nolichucky waterways. Once again, responding to the Cherokee entreaties for order, the British agents and the royal governor of North Carolina officially ordered the mountaineers to remove themselves from their illegal settlements immediately. Once again, the mountaineers defied the orders.

B Y 1774, signs of American resistance to the Intolerable Acts and other British measures had begun to shake the king's control of the colonies. Earlier in the winter of 1773, of course, feather-topped rebels had dumped a shipment of tea into the Boston Harbor. The tremors for change in the backcountry, however, rippled with intrigue, forever with an eye to crossing the mountains for new land holdings. No one was more aware of this pulsing demand to surmount the watershed of the Appalachians than the British authorities themselves. In the spring of 1774, Lord John Murray Dunmore, the royal governor of Virginia, wrote the British secretary of state for American affairs about the festering circumstances. Explaining the colonists' exasperation over increasingly stalled land allocations, he singled out the Washingtonians and their unique mutiny in the Southern Appalachians. His description remains one of the most illuminating documents about the settlements:

> In effect, we have an example of the very case, there being actually a set of people in the back part of this colony, bordering on the Cherokee country, who, finding they could not obtain titles to the land they fancied, under any of the neighboring governments, have settled upon it without, and contented themselves with becoming in a manner tributary to the Indians, and have appointed magistrates, and framed laws for their present occasions, and to all intents and purposes, have erected themselves into, though an inconsiderable, yet a separate State; the consequence of which may prove hereafter detrimental to the peace and security of the other colonies; it at least sets a dangerous example to the people of America, of forming governments distinct from and independent of his majesty's authority.

Dunmore's letter, while explicitly stating the British alarm about the settlement's example of independence, reminds us that the mountaineers were operating well within the public view. The news of their exploits had made them pariahs in the eyes of the royal government, but enviable scalawags in the eyes of the colonists on the Virginian frontier. Respected merchants and land speculators like Carter, Bean, and many others continued to maintain some of their assets in Virginia; their periodic visits would have been nothing less than public updates on the settlements' boldness. Brown also kept his financial backers, the McDowell family in North Carolina, abreast of his developments.

Elsewhere in the central Appalachians, land speculators and backwoods settlers confronted the increasing hostilities of the Shawnee-led resistance on the frontier. The displaced and unwavering Shawnee had unleashed a series of attacks on surveyors and settlers along the spine of the mountains, as far south as the Cherokee territories. The most infamous episode had been the fatal assaults on Daniel Boone's party into Kentucky. Just as the Washingtonians knew that Cherokee resistance, not British resolve, would ultimately determine western expansion, those on the Virginian frontier recognized that the Shawnee and their allies stood as the last barrier.

The colonists got their frontier war. At the time of Dunmore's letter, an all-out campaign was launched against the Shawnee-led insurgency in the Ohio River valley. The royal governor ordered the raising of militias from the borderland settlements, adding to the complexity of the British relationship with the increasingly rebellious mountaineers. Dunmore, a Scottish laird who held the last governorship in Virginia, must have known he was inciting a risky affair. Although historians have generally referred to the military campaign as Dunmore's War, perhaps even considering it a ruse to sidetrack the colonists' growing moves toward sedition, the campaign was sought, fought, and successfully carried out by American frontiersmen. Other historians, noting the role of the backcountry militias and the extraordinary number of revolutionary leaders that emerged from the campaign, consider Dunmore's War the first battle in the American Revolution.

The dispatch of a group of riflemen from the District of Washington positioned the Appalachian mountaineers in a critical military role. On October 10, 1774, as a disputed story goes, Washingtonians Valentine Sevier and Robertson detected the Shawnee-led soldiers gathering at Point Pleasant, on the banks of the Kanawha River, while Sevier and Robertson were on a hunting trip. The mountaineers quickly alerted the American forces. One of the most atrocious and costly battles ever described between the indigenous soldiers and militias ensued, leading to the surrender of the Shawnee leader Cornstalk and his troops within a day. Dunmore and his entourage, though, were nowhere near the fighting. Arriving to negotiate a peace settlement, the royal governor drew the wrath of the Americans for his resistance to unleashing the militias deeper into indigenous-held areas. Regardless, Dunmore and the frontiersmen returned home as heroes, and the gates to the cherished Kentucky lands effectively opened.

Refusing to align with the Shawnee, the Cherokee stayed out of Dunmore's War, but they understood its warning. The divided tribe clearly viewed the massive military response by the frontiersmen and their British authorities with trepidation. The vast lands west of the Cumberlands, which they also considered their hunting grounds, were now in the hands of a Dunmore peace treaty that took no consideration of the historical claims of the Cherokee. At the same time, the ever-present Boone, whose failed expedition to Kentucky in 1773 did little to dampen his ambitions, rekindled a business alliance in a scheme that would place the Cherokee and the Washingtonians at the center of the greatest real-estate venture in American history.

FAR FROM BEING the solitary wanderer of the frontier, as he is generally portrayed, Boone was frequently on the payroll of Richard Henderson, an infamous land speculator of colonial America. Raised in Virginia, Henderson had been appointed a judge in the North Carolina backcountry by the royal governor in the late 1760s. The assignment carried its own burdens; the Regulators sacked Henderson's court at one point. However judicial his concerns, though, Henderson's eyes remained fixed on the Appalachians and the great beyond. In the late-1760s, he had hired Boone to survey choice lands west of the mountains. A handful of other business ventures went awry, depleting Henderson's assets, but not his land speculation plans. When news of Dunmore's victory sounded across the colonies, Henderson retired from the bench, replenished his investment chests with a roster of leading land speculators, and set out for the Overhill towns of the Cherokee.

Henderson's scheme was simple: He proposed to purchase the entire tract of Cherokee-claimed territory, from the Kentucky to the Cumberland rivers, roughly 20 million acres (modern-day Kentucky and northern Tennessee) for ten thousand English pounds, most of which would be paid in goods. In the tradition of the Washingtonians, Henderson and his investors identified the most willing Cherokee leaders and hosted them in North Carolina to preview the wished-for goods, including desperately needed arms, gunpowder, and metal products. With the selected Cherokee leaders convinced, Henderson set a date for a final rendezvous at the District of Washington heartland on the Watauga River.

Meanwhile, the Washingtonian mountaineers prepared for the gathering with a tremendous amount of expectation and planning. Henderson's scheme, in effect, placed them in an even more precarious situation. It also forced them to reconsider their own status as phantom tenants on Cherokee land. Beyond their refusal, twice, to relocate from the illegal land holdings, they would now play host to the illegal purchase of Cherokee territory by non-British investors. The royal governor of North Carolina had pronounced the once venerable Henderson a "land pirate," and his act criminal and seditious.

At the same time, the elder Cherokee leaders justified their capitulation on several grounds. Their demands for the removal of the settlers had been futile; the British ability to carry out Cherokee jurisdiction in the mountain country had been exposed as powerless. For the weary and overextended tribe, the faraway Kentucky lands proved to be even more difficult to defend. In fact, as a historically contentious territory between indigenous nations, the western Cumberland hunting grounds had become a no-man's-land of conflicts.

Overwhelmed by their own divisions and battles with other indigenous groups like the Creek and Chickasaw, as well as by encroaching American colonists on other fronts, and deeply in need of weapons and supplies, the Cherokee believed that an agreement with Henderson provided a welcome windfall. Still, a young Cherokee leader, called Dragging Canoe by the English-speaking world, excoriated the elder leaders for their surrender of the lands. He considered their transaction fraudulent. Making a promise he would keep, he declared that "a dark and bloody cloud" hung over the Cumberland lands. Within a short time of the historic meeting, Dragging Canoe and a cadre of insurgents reorganized their Chickamauga settlements in the lower Tennessee River area and began a series of raids.

When Henderson and his brigade arrived at Sycamore Shoals in March 1775, carting along the caravans of promised goods, the Washingtonians had already devised their own plan. With the same aplomb that they applied to their historic petition, the mountaineers explained that "persons of distinction were actually making purchases forever; thus yielding a precedent, and supposing many of them, who were gentlemen of the law, to be better judges of the constitution than we were," they had rounded up a committee of investors to purchase their own previously leased land.

The days of legal maneuvers had come to an end. The mountaineers announced their outright secession from the British.

After days of festivities and oratory, in Cherokee fashion, Henderson signed his Transylvania Purchase at Sycamore Shoals, which would go down in American history as one of the largest private real-estate transactions. Hundreds of settlers and thousands of Cherokee from the around the region gathered to witness the occasion. Among them was Nathaniel Gist. With Henderson's ink still wet, the Washingtonians purchased their formerly "leased" settlements, covering nearly two thousand square miles. Brown, again financed by McDowell, obtained an equally large tract of land along the Nolichucky waterway. As recompense for the sacking of his trading post, Carter and his investors took a large strip of land along the South Holston River and parts of Henderson's corridor through the valley and then purchased additional plots in what would become Carter's Valley.

THE REAL-ESTATE rebellion generated by the purchases at Sycamore Shoals had an unintended effect: democracy. Parceling out the land plots through their own self-described land office, the mountaineers declared in their historic petition that they reserved "those in our possession in sufficient tracts for our own use," and resolved to "dispose of the remainder for the good of the community." At first, a handful in the community, such as Carter and emerging leaders like Robertson and John Sevier, a Virginia-based militia leader and land speculator who had joined the community by 1773, purchased multiple holdings far beyond any of those held by common farmers and woodsmen. With his vast holdings, Brown immediately began to hawk his plots to the highest bidders. The exigencies and confusion of the brewing American Revolution, however, worked against the real-estate ambitions of the speculators.

While the famous shots would sound at Lexington one month after the real-estate rebellion in the mountains, the District of Washington land speculators still had to recognize that their transaction with the Cherokee remained illegal in the eyes of the authorities, British or American. The issued titles and deeds remained illusory in the hands of the purchasers. In the end, unlike virtually every other corner of land development in Appalachia and surroundings, attempts by large landowners like Carter and Brown to lease their holdings through the speculative efforts of land jobbers failed to attract a legion of outside buyers for more lucrative fees. Only the brave and the convinced individuals committed to the speculators' real-estate scheme, effectively warding off absentee investors and transients. As a result, small yeoman farmers emerged as the principal purchasers of the plots in the District of Washington, with the majority holding between two hundred and four hundred acres each.

Appointing a trustee and land title office, the Washingtonians mapped out and sold plots, despite no official authorization or legal recognition of their actions or, technically, any long-term rights to their deeds. Such a movement on the behalf of a diverse group of settlers took a tremendous amount of organization and a real leap of faith among its participants. In essence, every Washingtonian was agreeing to buy into a treasonous enterprise of his own invention, as a covenant-bound community.

The high level of complicity in such an act of defiance led some settlers to leave. For the great majority, though, as the young Robertson proclaimed, this undertaking by the mountaineers made them "the advance guard of civilization."

The joint venture of the settlements also highlighted the cooperative nature of the backwoods people and their ability to sustain themselves. Along with their communally governed civil and criminal affairs, the settlers collaborated on planting, harvesting, corn shucking, flax pulling, and other activities; cabins and barns were raised together. Religious festivities, dancing and sports events, and even horseracing brought the clusters together. Along with hunting the obvious abundance of wild game, the settlers, many of whom had been prosperous farmers in Virginia and the Carolinas, tended cattle and pigs, while cultivating the indigenous staples of corn, potatoes, squash, pumpkins, and melons; others raised hemp, flax, vegetables, and some wheat. The plethora of traders supplied salt, sugar, gunpowder, fabric, and metal products. In the end, the district's self-reliance was as much an accomplishment as was self-governance in the mountains.

This level of democracy in land distribution and self-governance by an elected body, accidental or not, underscored the mountaineers' singular feat in prerevolutionary American history. The local citizenry not only governed the District of Washington, but also jointly owned its property. In their historic petition, the settlers also touted the "legality" and fair representations in their elections. Remarkably, out of the 115 signatures on the 1776 petition, only 2 marked an X by their name, which again underscores the high level of literacy among the mountaineers. In the process, no single faction or family maintained an iron grip on power. In fact, the signers of the land purchase in 1775—most likely the elected magistrates at the time—did not include any of the original leaders of the first association in 1772, indicating a turnover of elected trustees, not an entrenched regime of gentry.

Democracy, of course, was a confused and untidy process. Slavery abounded in the District of Washington. Only one woman has been identified in available documents as a landowner in the district prior to the Revolution; she was Catherine Choate, most probably the widow of an infamous horse thief who had been strung from a tree. Nonetheless, some nineteenth-century historians, like the venerable George Bancroft, went to great lengths to champion these mountaineers and their independent democracy; Bancroft hailed the Watauga Association as a republic. In Theodore Roosevelt's *Winning the West* chronicles, which avidly sought to glorify the nation's settlement of the frontiers and highlight its so-called Anglo-Saxon contributions, the mountaineers represented the "first free and independent community on the continent."

All these descriptions have their detractors and fans. The Washingtonians were not, of course, the first American settlement in the Appalachians. More accurately, they were the first community in our nation to collectively defy British land laws and treaties, associate themselves as an elected self-governing entity accountable to their own authority and codes, issue their own land titles and deeds, carry out their own trials of civil and criminal justice, engage in diplomatic and business transactions with separate indigenous nations, and raise their own militia.

THE MOUNTAINEERS' acts of independence and dependence converged in the petition delivered by horseback to the revolutionary council of North Carolina in 1776. Reuniting the settlements on the Watauga, Nolichucky, and South Holston river ways, the District of Washington formally came into being as an undisputed mountain stronghold in the self-described "glorious cause" of the Patriots. It hailed the "new united colonies" as its guide. By being the first community in the colonies to name itself after the Patriot commander, the district made the most unflinching commitment to the American Revolution.

Beseeching the North Carolina Patriots to annex them as a province or district in the revolutionary colony, the Washingtonians offered their militia to the common cause and submitted themselves to the judgment of the Provincial Congress. At that very moment, a group of mountaineer riflemen had been dispatched to the defense of the Patriot cause in Charleston, South Carolina.

The petition also made clear the mountaineers' tremendous concern for protection. This, in fact, had not been their first petition; a similar document appealing for annexation had been turned down by the revolutionary Virginia governing body, which feared any escalation of tension among the Cherokee on their southwestern borders. The Virginians, in effect, still considered the mountaineers outlaws.

But the District of Washington had arrived at a point of no return. As the last ultimatum concerning insubordination to the Crown, British agents had already ordered the Washingtonians to demonstrate their allegiance to the king, remove themselves to the southern province, or risk all-out warfare by the Cherokee. The mountaineers took the British threat seriously for the first time. British agents had reportedly distributed sixty horses loaded with weapons, gunpowder, and supplies among the Cherokee in the lower Tennessee Valley by the spring of 1776. Meanwhile, an alliance of northern Appalachian and Ohio River valley tribes had met with the Cherokee to discuss a joint military campaign against the settlers on the frontier. The defeated Shawnee leader of Dunmore's War, Cornstalk, had returned to battle in a strategic alliance with Dragging Canoe.

As the newly elected head of the District of Washington, Carter responded to the British orders with the community's long-perfected stall tactics; he declared the Washingtonians loyal to the Crown and requested a short delay in organizing any departure. Amazingly, the British authorities and the Cherokee accepted the appeal. In the meantime, while the mountaineers waited for a response to their petition, they alerted their longtime neighbors and militias in the Virginia Blue Ridge and feverishly constructed two forts.

Only two weeks after the American Patriots had clamored into the streets to celebrate their Declaration of Independence and the Appalachian mountaineers had sent their historic petition to the North Carolina revolutionary government, an armed force of hundreds of Cherokee soldiers descended on the District of Washington settlements in a three-pronged attack. The settlers had been warned in advance by a handful of traders. Abandoning their smaller fort, the overmatched Washington militia leaders armed their African slaves and every settler, male and female, in an effort to hold off the assault. While the Cherokee destroyed the settlements in Carter's Valley, the settlers behind the fort at Sycamore Shoals managed to withstand a two-week siege. Remarkably, Dragging Canoe's forces also failed to take a stockade from unyielding armed settlers at the historically sacred Long Island claimed by Nathaniel Gist. The Cherokee finally abandoned their assault when a Patriot militia arrived from the southern Virginia Blue Ridge.

The importance of the Washingtonian resistance in holding off the

Cherokee invasion should not be understated within the context of the American Revolution. As the British Crown's important military allies, the Cherokee and other indigenous insurgents played a potentially explosive role on the western frontier. The defeat of the District of Washington outpost could have easily resulted in a deluge of military incursions by the Cherokee into the valleys of Virginia. Instead, the costly victory at Sycamore Shoals by the mountaineers served as a buffer and effectively gave the militia forces in Virginia, Georgia, South Carolina, and North Carolina the needed time to organize a massive military campaign. Launching an all-out assault on four fronts, thousands of militiamen from the lower colonies razed Cherokee villages throughout the Southern Appalachians and piedmont, burning and pillaging, taking an estimated two thousand Cherokee lives. The campaign resulted in a devastating Cherokee surrender in 1777.

The war on the southern frontier was not over, of course. The battles between the Cherokee and the American colonists lingered for another generation.

The first District of Washington, in the meantime, was no longer an independent settlement of renegades. The mountaineers had thrown in their lot with the American Patriots. Little did they know that they would soon be launching one of the most crucial battles in the American Revolution.

Chapter Three

DOWN FROM THE MOUNTAIN

In short, if you wish or deserve to live, and bear the name of men, grasp your arms in a moment and run to camp. The Back Water Men have crossed the mountains.

—MAJOR PATRICK FERGUSON,
British Commander in western Carolina, 1780

IN THE FALL OF 1777, as the king's men occupied the Patriot hub of Philadelphia after their triumph at the Battle of Brandywine, a cocky British officer by the name of Patrick Ferguson scoffed that the Americans had "learnt to rely on their heels." Ferguson's boasting was not unfounded. The euphoria of the independence drive in 1776 had yielded to the British refusal to withdraw without a fight. Every American Patriot victory had been countered with a devastating British reply elsewhere in the colonies. With his heroic crossing of the Delaware a distant memory, Patriot Commander George Washington would lament the sorry state of his troops, holed up miserably in the Jersey province in the winter of 1779–1780, one of the coldest in the short American experience.

Unpaid and distraught over their wretched conditions, the Continental troops had been rife with desertion and mutiny. Washington even hanged a couple of mutineers who had called for an uprising in the military. At the same time, the commander in chief found himself defending roguish elements in his troops and backcountry militias that were plundering the scarce resources of defenseless American settlers, Loyalist or Patriot, especially in the hinterlands. Morale could not have been lower. And this was only in the north.

Despite this declining campaign, the American Patriots still held the British line, whether it was by sea or land. No significant territorial shift had been made in the war since 1778. Such a deadlock made the architects of the British (and American) campaigns look south with suspicion, as if a few stars and stripes could be plucked from the American flag. Diplomats on both sides of the Atlantic Ocean even considered a compromise truce that might have rendered the Carolinas and Georgia to British control, in lieu of the Crown's relinquishing the northern colonies. Whether this proposal was ever given a thorough consideration is less important than the perceived Tory allegiance of the southerners.

In need of a new strategy to reinvigorate his forces, Lord George Cornwallis and his British generals convinced themselves that the wealthy plantation elite and Loyalist sympathizers in the south would rally to their side. At first, this southern strategy proved successful. Savannah fell with little resistance in 1778. Landing British forces on the Carolina coast, Cornwallis envisioned a march that would lead to Washington's home in northern Virginia. The redcoats started with the most prosperous city in America: Charleston, South Carolina, the plantation capital that had defied the first British assault in the summer of 1776.

This southern campaign, in fact, was not without foundation. The south had become a refuge for huge numbers of Loyalists. Even worse, a formidable Patriot force was in disarray; *nonexistent* might be a better word. By the spring of 1780, Washington declared to the Continental Congress that the weak state of his forces in the south had "laid me under great embarrassments."

LITTLE did the Patriot commander know that his expression of concern was an understatement. After a protracted battle off the Sea Islands and Carolinian harbors, the British troops marched into Charleston on

May 12, 1780. Two weeks later, a British colonel ignored a white flag of surrender by Continental troops near Waxhaws, South Carolina, and butchered hundreds of disarmed Patriots. Within two months, the British forces and Loyalist militias occupied the southern coastline, storming to the North Carolina border with ease.

Matters only got worse for the Patriots. In one of the most poorly planned battles of the Revolution, Continental General Horatio Gates, an English commoner who had risen to become a British officer, only to immigrate to western Virginia and take up the cause of the Patriots, led a large American charge of soldiers and militiamen to a horrendous defeat at Camden, South Carolina, in July. Cornwallis boasted: "There never was a more complete victory." A day later, British troops unleashed "indiscriminate slaughter" against more Continental troops and militia members at nearby Fishing Creek.

With the American Patriot forces decimated and on the run, Cornwallis and his British forces marched on to North Carolina as planned. Confident of victory and the uprising of southern Loyalists, the British commander declared the American insurrection to be over in the south. He smugly instructed the Loyalists to confiscate the plantations of any Patriots, treat the enemy without mercy, and hang any traitor to the British Crown.

The British success in the south further discouraged Washington and his Continental Congress. After Benedict Arnold, as commander of West Point, was exposed as a spy and defected to the British side later that fall, Washington declared that his Patriot cause was on the "brink of the precipice."

To cover his western flank, Cornwallis had sent the swaggering British officer Ferguson to suppress whatever American rebellion continued to stir in the backcountry along the Southern Appalachian frontier. While his alterations to the breech-loading rifle ensured his military legacy, Ferguson's uncompromising and vicious reputation suited the task of taming the wilds in the western Carolina frontier. The British officer, who had risen through the ranks during conflicts in Europe and the Americas, earning a commission as a major and inspector of militia by 1779, held a particular contempt for the American colonists. He had been permanently injured during one battle, by British bayonets, no less, that disabled one arm. The mountaineers, in his mind, were nothing less than barbarians.

Ferguson felt so sure of his troops that he issued a notorious ultimatum to all American Patriots, or "backwater men," in the Southern Appalachians. He selected a captured mountaineer to serve as his courier. His message was simple: "If they did not desist from their opposition to the British arms, he would march over the mountains, hang their leaders, and lay their country waste with fire and sword." The Scotsman's demand was not offered casually. Ferguson directed his courier to personally deliver the message to Isaac Shelby, a Southern Appalachian guerilla leader who had brazenly descended from the mountains in August 1780 and raided the British forces at Musgrove's Mill in the Carolina hills.

SHELBY'S extraordinary life spanned an entire epoch of historical change in Appalachia. Born in 1750 at the foot of North Mountain near Frederick, Maryland, the son of a Welsh immigrant, he moved with his pioneering family to the North Holston River valley in the southern Virginia mountains as a young man. In 1774, he served under his father's command in Dunmore's War against the Shawnee in the Ohio River valley. Instead of returning to the Blue Ridge, the younger Shelby stayed behind and explored Kentucky and the surrounding Cumberland Mountains for another year, planting the seed for his eventual return.

The outbreak of the American Revolution brought Shelby back to his family's Southern Appalachian base, where he immediately rose to the rank of captain in the Virginia militia. In the shadow of his father, who became a general, Shelby was appointed a special commissioner, entrusted with coordinating the supplies for militia and Continental troops on the Appalachian frontier and as far as Detroit. By 1779, Thomas Jefferson had recognized his leadership abilities and commissioned him as a major in the Virginia militia. The vast Shelby landholdings on the Holston River valley, ironically, straddled both sides of the Virginia–North Carolina mountain border. As the American forces reorganized themselves in the uncertain period of 1780, Shelby took command of a militia division in the North Carolina mountains as a colonel.

Kentucky, though, would never leave Shelby's blood. After the Revolution, he returned to become the new state's first governor, in 1792. By the time of his death in 1826, Shelby was considered one of the most respected and powerful politicians in the country.

RESPONDING to the pleas from the McDowell family, which was an early investor in the District of Washington land schemes, Shelby didn't hesitate to raise a mounted division of riflemen to join the routed piedmont rebels in the summer of 1780. He did more than organize his own regiments. Devising a military strategy of his own, Shelby issued a call for all militia units along the Southern Appalachian range to unite in their attacks on the British.

Shelby's boldness preceded him in the region. He and his men had become legendary "yelling boys" guerillas, imitating the Cherokee war scream in their relentless sneak attacks on the British-led forces. This tactic scared the daylights out of the British and American Loyalist militias. It also led to great successes. In one of the few bright moments for the Patriots over the long, hot summer of warfare, a rifleman from Washington County (formerly the District of Washington) brought down one of Ferguson's key colonels at Musgrove's Mill during a Patriot attack in the Carolina piedmont.

Because of their Cherokee-acquired forest-fighting tactics, the Appalachian guerillas, or Overmountain Men, gained a reputation as natural-born warriors or wild-eyed bands of long hunters, unleashed in the forests to wreak havoc. For many romantic historians today, this portrayal is still common, though etched with a patriotic fervor. A more accurate picture of the mountain rebels, however, is far more complex and remarkable.

Under Shelby's leadership, the Appalachian militias exhibited an exceptional sense of organization, experience, commitment, and awareness of the political machinations of the times. Divided into community regiments, elected officials in the pioneering settlements led the guerillas in highly coordinated attacks; many founders of the District of Washington, for example, served on the front lines as captains. The militia regiments were neither new nor hastily arranged. Virtually all of the mountain soldiers had served in some capacity over the past decade in the grueling campaigns against the Cherokee, Shawnee, and other indigenous groups. They had fought Dunmore's War in 1774, served as the shock troops for the four-state invasion of the Cherokee towns in 1777, and carried out the bitter campaign against Dragging Canoe and his Chickamagua rebels in 1779. Some members of the militia had already served in a rifleman division sent to defend Charleston in 1776.

Despite their seeming distance on the mountain frontier, the Appalachians watched the unfolding events of the Revolution in the lower colonies with great interest and concern. Couriers provided daily updates on the Continental troop movements and plans. As the Revolution ebbed with the increasing misfortunes of the Patriot forces on the battlefield, the southern mountaineers also played host to huge numbers of ousted rebels, including the McDowell brothers and their fleeing piedmont militia, and Georgia militia leader Elijah Clarke and his troops. Hundreds of other refugees, including General Richard Caswell and Governor Alexander Martin of North Carolina, fled for the Southern Appalachians during the worst fighting. At a time when everyone in the nation was struggling to survive, the mountaineers found themselves in a situation of supplying food, lodging, and clothes for a flood of refugees and Patriot fugitives displaced by Cornwallis's brutal southern campaign.

NONETHELESS, Shelby's call to unite the mountaineer militias would have been scoffed at by most military commanders or observers of the period. No one disputed the warring talents of the frontier people. Washington had even famously declared that he would plant his "banner on the mountains of west Augusta, where I will draw around me the brave men who will yet advance our independence," if the British chased him out of the lowlands. Still, few military or political leaders in the American colonies counted on the militias to provide much more than sporadic support. Rarely compensated, often conscripted, poorly armed and maintained, and made up of common farmers and hunters who could ill afford time away from their livelihoods, most militias formed more out of demand than desire.

The disparaging sentiment of their service was underscored by the humiliating role of the Virginia and North Carolina militias at the disastrous battle at Camden in mid-August 1780, where over two thousand militiamen dropped their weapons and hightailed it at the first glimmer of British bayonets. This act completely destroyed what reputation had been earned in blood. Noting the plummeting morale after this debacle, Washington had written Thomas Jefferson to lament the state of the southern militias as "too fluctuating and undisciplined" to confront the British campaign.

SHELBY'S envisioned Southern Appalachian battalion came into reality on receipt of Ferguson's ultimatum. Moving immediately to consult at Sycamore Shoals with John Sevier, who served as colonel of the Washington County militia, Shelby proposed to bring together his North Carolina mountaineers with the Washingtonians and William Campbell's Virginia mountaineer militias just across the border. Other Virginia Patriots and the remaining militia members from McDowell's North Carolina units that had escaped into the Appalachians eventually joined their united force.

The parties agreed to gather at the mountain stronghold of Sycamore Shoals on September 25. Their decisiveness was unwavering. Shelby threw himself into the preparations. Scrambling with Sevier to find the funds to underwrite the needed supplies, the former commissioner of provisions for the Continental army managed to assemble and arm a militia of over one thousand troops within days.

Shelby's initiative was extraordinary on several fronts, but, remarkably, his military decisions, like those of his fellow militia leaders, had no authorization from the Continental army and its commanders. The plans, risks, and ultimate political stakes of their actions rested in the hands of the mountaineers.

THE FATE OF the initiative also rested on a tremendous faith. Summoned by Sevier, Presbyterian minister and educator Samuel Doak delivered a homily for the soldiers on the eve of their departure for battle. Standing in the forest before a thousand troops and hundreds of other family members and onlookers, Doak reached back into religious history and retold the story of a poor Hebrew farmer called on to lead his people against the Midianites. The biblical story of the underdog Hebrews, found in the Book of Judges, resonated among the poorly equipped Patriot forces with its creative twist to war. Sounding their three hundred horns and smashing their three hundred jars, Gideon's overmatched followers destroyed the Midianites, despite the odds.

Calling on the "sword of the Lord and of Gideon" to lead them in battle, Doak sent the mountaineers on their march against Ferguson. The sermon has remained legendary; the soldiers invoked the name of Gideon in their charges.

Doak's involvement in the guerilla campaign adds to the complexity of the Appalachian character in this period. Raised by Ulster immigrants in the valleys of Virginia, he had grown up in a frontier community in Augusta County, Virginia. Eschewing the life of a farmer, he convinced his family to allow him to attend a formal school in the classics. His decision was indicative of the value of higher education and literacy among a great part of the frontier people, especially the Scotch-Irish Presbyterians.

Dating back to the medieval policies in Scotland, the Presbyterian Church had been instrumental in educating its network of local churches to read the Bible. The educational role of the missionaries in Scotland and beyond resulted in one of the highest literacy rates in Europe, a phenomenon that was carried over to the early Appalachian frontier.

By 1773, Doak had enrolled in the College of New Jersey at Princeton, where he graduated in theological studies within two years. Instead of following his classmates into the elite centers of colonial America, Doak returned to Appalachia, teaching at a Presbyterian "log college" that insisted on using Latin as the "habitual language of the school." The children of rugged mountaineers discussed the *Metamorphoses* by Ovid and the "Bucolics" of Virgil. In 1778, ordained as a Presbyterian minister, Doak and his young family set off for the mountain valley settlements of the Shelbys, tucked into the southwestern corner of Virginia.

With the mountain world around him unhinged into warfare, first between the American settlers and the Cherokee, and now between the British Crown and its rebelling colonists, one might question the impact an intellectual, melancholy clergyman could have on his Appalachian flock. How could his emerging log college in the forest teach the colloquies of Corderius in Latin, and courses in religion, philosophy, science, Greek, and Hebrew, in this volatile period? Indeed, Doak had to put down his Bible several times, pick up his rifle, and join his parishioners in their skirmishes with the Cherokee.

More importantly, Doak viewed the unfolding history of the mountain frontier through a biblical lens. He placed the Appalachian struggle for independence within the historical context of Jews in the Holy Land. The clergyman was not alone in this quest for higher education and a higher purpose in Southern Appalachia. Sevier, the commander of the Washington County militia, served as a trustee for the missionary's new college, the Martin Academy, the first such institution in the region. Doak, in turn, became a political fixture in Washington County.

After his sermon at Sycamore Shoals, Doak's students and parishioners loaded up their rifles and marched down from the mountain, imbued with an Israeli fervor to defend the Promised Land.

THE BATTLE against Ferguson did not go quickly. The mountain divisions and their militia counterparts had to traverse extraordinarily rugged parts of the Smoky Mountains. They also needed to locate the elusive Scotsman and his Loyalist militia. Within a few days, their ranks had swelled by 350 more Carolinian militiamen, who had been alerted by couriers. Another column of north Georgia militiamen and South Carolinian backcountry recruits had joined by the end of the first week. Arriving at Cane Creek in the North Carolina piedmont, where McDowell's forces had been routed, the leaders of the multiple divisions of militiamen came to the realization that they needed a symbolic commander to rein in the increasingly unwieldy maneuvers of their growing army. They selected the Virginian mountaineer Campbell to command, though the rest of the militia colonels agreed to make all decisions in a daily council. Most historians believe Shelby remained the driving force behind the rally.

The movements of such a large force through the mountains did not escape Ferguson and his Loyalist spies. Two turncoats from Washington County had escaped from Sevier's command and made it to Ferguson's camp, informing him of the mountain guerillas' march. One of the traitors was related to a District of Washington founder, whose large estate had been confiscated by Sevier's Patriot committee. The size of the force impressed Ferguson; it took him days, however, to request additional troops from Cornwallis. The cat-and-mouse chase proceeded. Nonetheless, following up his first dramatic communiqué, Ferguson issued a general proclamation to the farmers and other settlers in the North Carolina backcountry to rise up, join the British militia, and defend themselves against the coming hordes. Ferguson's missive is infamous:

> Gentlemen: Unless you wish to be eat up by an inundation of barbarians, who have begun by murdering an unarmed son before his aged father, and afterwards lopped off his arms, and who by their shocking cruelties and irregularities, give the best proof of their cowardice and want of discipline; I say, if you wish to be pinioned, robbed, and murdered, and see your wives and daughters, in four days, abused by the dregs of mankind—in short, if you wish or deserve to live, and bear the name of men, grasp your arms in a moment and run to camp. The Back Water Men have crossed the mountains.

Ferguson's appeal failed to sway many bystanders. In the meantime, he directed his command of more than 1,100 soldiers to march to Kings Mountain, just south of the North Carolina–South Carolina border. Still confident of an easy victory over the growing Patriot force, Ferguson wrote to Cornwallis about his movements, adding only in an aside that 300 or 400 good soldiers "would finish the business."

By October 5, the mountaineers and the various militias had pinpointed Ferguson's direction and recognized his plan to hold the small ridge at Kings Mountain. They understood that timing was critical to their attack, especially given the possibility of British reinforcements appearing on the scene. Exhausted by their ten-day tramp through the mountains and piedmont hills, with minimal provisions and weakening horses, the Patriots reorganized their divisions and selected 700 of the top men and horses for a "flying column." Fearful of any delay, Shelby led an essentially forced march.

Reports now emerged from spies in Ferguson's camp. The British commander was only miles away. Joining up with 200 more South Carolinian militiamen, the mountaineer-led division included 120 men from Shelby's North Carolina mountain militia, 120 men from Sevier's Washington County troops, 200 men from Campbell's Virginia mountain militia, and 300 militiamen from various southern states, as well as a small group led by a German colonel. The division broke camp that night and sprinted for Ferguson's trail.

Within fifteen miles of Kings Mountain and facing a downpour and poor visibility, most of the colonels called for a halt to the march. Shelby refused to relent. Recognizing his virtual command, the others pushed on, storming through the forests and farms until they pulled within a mile of Kings Mountain. By midday on October 7, 900 militiamen had encircled the forested mountain, a hill in actuality, which measured no more than six hundred yards at its highest crest. Ferguson's troops had encamped on the top of Kings Mountain, outmatching the Patriots in number and weaponry, including the dreaded bayonet.

Ferguson's so-called British troops included only one British citizen: Ferguson himself. Not unlike its opposing force, the entire Tory force was made up of American Loyalists and backcountry militiamen. This often-overlooked detail in the American Revolution is a startling reminder of the civil-war nature of the Revolution, especially in the south, where sympathies between the Patriots and British Crown divided families as devastatingly as the subsequent Civil War in the 1860s. In fact, to distinguish themselves from one another, the Patriots placed a white piece of paper in their caps, while the Loyalists placed a pine knot in theirs.

Led by their individual colonels, the various Patriot divisions spread out along the base of the mountain. No actual commander in chief existed at this point. Sevier called on all mountaineers to serve as their own guides. The Patriots understood their orders; they had to scale the mountain, surround the enemy, and fire. Shelby and Campbell led their mountain troops in the first wave of attacks, their Cherokee-learned cries of war echoing through the forests. The militias began a slow assault up the incline, maneuvering from tree to tree. The mountaineers had perfected this forest-fighting tactic over a decade of battles with the Cherokee. The eeriness of the "yelling boys," like Gideon's trumpets, immediately unnerved the British-led troops. Under Ferguson's command, the Loyalists launched bayonet charges whenever the militiamen pulled within distance. In the process, aiming down the hill, the Loyalist riflemen tended to shoot over the heads of the charging Patriots.

Within an hour, the mountain regiments had reached the crest of Kings Mountain. Their sharpshooters, relying on slow-loading but deadly hunting long rifles, closed in on the British-led battalion with tremendous accuracy and force. The Loyalists' defense began to crumble. Ferguson had to personally dismantle white flags of surrender that suddenly appeared. Commanding his soldiers to fight on, the Scottish officer blew a whistle for his orders, using a sword with his one functioning arm.

While more than a half dozen men would lay claim to shooting Ferguson off his horse, Essius Bowman, a free African American militiaman from the Virginia Blue Ridge, is most often credited with the decisive shot. Regardless of who killed Ferguson, the rest of the British division surrendered. In little over an hour, the mountaineer-led coalition of forces had delivered one of the Revolutionary War's most stinging defeats to the British command.

THE ASTONISHING triumph of Shelby and his allied militias quickly passed through the horseback networks of news and stirred the beleaguered souls of the American Patriot forces. It was a triumph of the spirit as much as an achievement on the battlefield. The honor, and the pivotal role, of the militiamen had been restored in the minds of the Continental commanders. In the face of an unstoppable British march through the Carolinas, the combined backcountry militias had pursued and outmaneuvered a far better equipped and armed British-led force.

Kings Mountain quickly became a famous location, and a terrifying code word, on the revived American battlefield. Within days, wolves held Kings Mountain, ravaging the shallow graves of the dead. The brutal aftermath of the mountaineers' victory, which resulted in hangings, torture, and the forced march of prisoners, also struck fear into the equivocating Loyalist partisans.

Beyond their fighting prowess and their lightning-quick response to defend their Promised Land at all costs, the mountaineers and their allies gave the American colonies a fine lesson in the dual requirements of coordination and determination. The mountaineers had carried out their self-appointed task without the political infighting, mutiny, or indecisiveness at play in the Revolutionary campaigns, especially in the low country of the south. Without any true commander in chief, their tightly organized regiments, based on years of common experience and interest, had swept across some of the most difficult terrain in the American colonies and devastated the British facade of power. Corresponding years later, an elderly Thomas Jefferson recalled the historic event as the "joyful annunciation of that turn of the tide of success which terminated the Revolutionary War, with the seal of independence."

In real terms, the shock factor of Ferguson's loss compelled Cornwallis to adjust his plans and retreat to South Carolina. The British momentum had been destroyed in one swoop. Cornwallis lost months of gains on the battlefield. The American Patriots redoubled their efforts and soon launched a string of successful attacks. Writing later in his memoirs on the war, Sir Henry Clinton, the British general who had led the siege of Charleston, depicted the Kings Mountain event as "the first link in a chain of evils that followed each other in regular succession until they at last ended in the total loss of America."

On October 17, 1781, almost one year to the day after the Battle of Kings Mountain, Cornwallis surrendered his British troops to Washington and his American and French-allied forces at Yorktown, Virginia.

Chapter Four

THE EMANCIPATORS

✢

The slavery of the Africans in the United States, if continued
a few generations longer, will produce such scenes of misery and
destruction for our posterity to wade through, as have not been
exceeded in the history of man.

—ELIHU EMBREE, *Emancipator,* 1820

IN 1808, as African and African American slaves stumbled through the emerging Ohio River port city of Wheeling, in western Virginia, a teenage saddle-maker stopped his hammering and observed their procession. The drivers had shackled the slaves at the neck, wrists, and legs. The saddle-maker, a young Quaker, felt the iron shackles "enter my soul."

Descending farther down the Great Valley of Virginia into the Carolinas, the slave drivers and their captives had a similar effect on another young Quaker in Daniel Boone's "peaceable" home front on the Yadkin River. Overcome by the desperation of the slaves, this young man appealed to his father to assist in the escape of a kidnapped free African American.

In this same year, a Quaker industrialist in the eastern Tennessee mountains inherited slaves through marriage, forcing him to reconcile their value to his life's work. Spanning across all these communities, from the Ohio River to the piedmont of the Carolinas and the back reaches of the Tennessee Valley, a Quaker minister and an abolitionist crusader embarked on a groundbreaking preaching tour.

All of these Quakers came to the same realization in the early nineteenth century: Slavery was entrenched, widespread, and passionately defended in the Southern Appalachians. It always had been. As a staple of warfare, it had been an aspect of indigenous cultures in the mountains for centuries. In 1681, the Cherokee made their first entreaties to the British to halt the enslavement of their own people by aggressive colonists. African slavery was then dragged into the hills and mountains with the first European and American explorers, the Cherokee, the settlers in the first District of Washington, and the American Patriots who died at Kings Mountain.

By the time these Quakers began to confront the labor realities of their communities, an estimated 17 percent of the population in the region was enslaved. The most well established plantations and slaveholdings ringed the periphery of the mountains in the Shenandoah Valley of Virginia, the piedmont of the Carolinas, and the cotton- and tobacco-growing valleys in lower Tennessee, Georgia, and Alabama.

To equate the African slaveholding experience of Southern Appalachia to its lowland brethren in the Deep South of course overlooks the complexity of the Appalachian region's development and the reality of its geography. The early mountain economy couldn't compete with the lowland's large-scale plantations of cotton, tobacco, and other crops; in the early nineteenth century, the mountain and hill regions had less than one plantation for every five large-scale plantations in the Deep South. Nearly a third of Southern Appalachia's most remote counties possessed extremely low numbers of slaves.

Yet, as the experience of the first Washingtonians in Appalachia demonstrated, an enduring elite in the mountaineer communities, especially among the growing townships and fertile valleys, depended on slave labor. This group relied on slaves for clearing and opening the frontier; for developing their small farms, livestock business, and orchards; for timbering, mining, and cottage industries; and for myriad domestic chores.

No one struggled more with this slaveholding reality than Samuel Doak, the Presbyterian minister who inspired the freedom-loving mountain guerillas at Sycamore Shoals. By 1810, Doak's crusade to bring a classical education into Southern Appalachian forests had emerged as one of the great successes in the region. When North Carolina political leader Zebulon Vance arrived in Washington, D.C., in 1858, he claimed that twenty-two other members of Congress had attended Doak's college in the mountains. Renamed Washington College (originally chartered as Martin Academy), the institution had become renowned for its curriculum and high standards. At the heart of its achievements, Doak, his sons, and his grandson played a tremendous role in shaping the minds and ambitions of several generations of mountaineers.

Doak has often been portrayed by historians as an inspiring but rather humorless teacher; one peer referred to him as an American John Knox, "fearless, firm, nearly dogmatical and intolerant." His inflexible Calvinist leanings compelled him to vote with the Old-Side Presbyterians in the region in 1796, when confronted with Samuel Hopkins's popular "new divinity" teachings that challenged the doctrine of predestination and limited atonement for the selected few. Even more resistant to change, this camp of conservative Presbyterians in the southern Virginia and Tennessee valleys refused to share the growing antislavery views of the Cumberland Presbyterians in the Southern mountains.

Despite his unfair reputation as "The Father of the Copperheads," Doak never closed the door to the dialogue over slavery and emancipation. In fact, he professed to being personally against slavery, welcomed theological debate around the subject, and increasingly found himself surrounded by family members and other people, including former students, who held persuasive abolitionist opinions. Late in his life, the elder Presbyterian would relent and grant his slaves manumission in Ohio.

More importantly, Doak played a dramatic role in challenging his educated elite to become independent thinkers. He purposely built his school in the forests outside the town of Jonesboro, the first capital in eastern Tennessee. Like many other Presbyterian school founders, Doak believed education needed to be an intense intellectual experience devoid of the vices of town life and immersed in the aura of nature. He grounded his philosophical lectures in the belief that God "hast made man rational and formed him for social happiness." The purpose of a student's education was to "enquire after truth," guided by common sense and self-consciousness. To Descartes' dictum *cogito, ergo sum,* Doak responded: *sum, ergo cogito.* "I am, therefore I think." Structuring his classes "without artificial restraint," Doak sought to instill a sense of "independent investigation and vigorous thought." He sent his students into the world to be leading ministers, educators, writers, and politicians.

Many of Doak's students took his sentiments to heart. The school turned out some notable iconoclasts, like David Nelson, a mercurial preacher, college founder, and medical doctor who had a penchant for poetry and who wrote some memorable church hymns and *The Cause and Cure for Infidelity,* a popular religious text for his times. Nelson, though, and several other Washington College students became more important for their contributions to the most divisive trigger issues in the early nineteenth century: the pioneering antislavery movement a generation before William Lloyd Garrison and Frederick Douglass, the rise of Abraham Lincoln, and the irreconcilable currents that led to the Civil War.

BY 1808, the early abolitionist movement that nearly passed an antislavery plank at the Constitutional Convention debates in 1787 had become moribund. Abolitionist godfather Benjamin Lundy declared there were "scarcely any abolition societies in existence" at this point. The societies that had survived, such as those among the Quakers in Philadelphia, tended to be local and religious in scope and irrelevant on the political scene. Girded by the fervent antislavery beliefs of the Quakers, the state of Pennsylvania, on the border of Southern Appalachia, had enacted gradual-emancipation laws in 1780. Vermont had already done so in 1777, and Massachusetts, Connecticut, New Hampshire, and Rhode Island would follow. The Northwest Ordinance of 1787 had banned slavery in future states that arose in the Midwest. "Voluntary emancipation" by slave owners was allowed in Delaware, Maryland, Kentucky, and Tennessee.

In the meantime, while the U.S. Congress officially outlawed the importation of slaves from Africa after January 1, 1808, the cotton boom in the South had accelerated reliance on slave labor on the large-scale plantations. Inter-American slave transactions flourished and proliferated throughout the South and the undeclared western territories.

The Southern slaveholders tightened their grip on the political machines in the South, virtually unfettered by federal laws. The few anti-slavery advocates remaining in this period had divided themselves into those who believed in gradual emancipation and those who believed in immediate. Both camps had followers in the movement for "colonization," a euphemistic term for deporting Africans and African Americans to the recently liberated Republic of Haiti or established colonies like Liberia, in western Africa. Either way, the terms of emancipation were as controversial as freedom itself among gradual and immediate partisans. The various groups argued endlessly over compensation for slave owners, the cost of colonization in Africa, or the social dynamics of incorporating free African Americans into the labor force and broader society. For others in the South, such as Doak, the issue of states' rights over federal authority also remained an unresolved matter.

IN THE WINTER OF 1811–1812, the worst earthquakes in modern U.S. history rumbled across the Midwest into the Southern Appalachians, forming lakes and crumbling edifices in their wake; the Mississippi River reversed its current for a spell. This natural phenomenon, coinciding hauntingly as it often does with changes in social history, precipitated a shift on those same grounds in many respects. For Elihu Embree, the earthquake in his own life that year was equally traumatic and life changing.

A student of Doak's in the eastern Tennessee mountains, Embree had embarked on a spiritual and intellectual journey that had taken him away from his family's longtime commitment to the Quaker faith. Like many upper-class intellectuals of his day, Embree had flirted with the rational views of deism, which sought to supplant religious mythology with concepts of ethics and natural law. Benjamin Franklin and Thomas Paine were notable believers. But the popularity of deism had faltered into the early nineteenth century, as the Second Great Awakening of evangelical Protestant sects and the phenomenon of their camp revivals spread dramatically through the Southern Appalachians. Embree disregarded both trends; his spiritual road to Damascus took him back to the inner light of his Quaker faith. In the process, having inherited a number of slaves from his second marriage a few years earlier, the young businessman's first act of contrition was to free his slaves. This didn't quite work out as Embree had planned.

As one of the early Quaker families to arrive in the American colonies in the mid-seventeenth century, the Embrees, originally of French Huguenot ancestry, had drifted into the colony of Pennsylvania like many others in their faith. The family moved on to Virginia, then the Carolinas, before crossing into the Appalachians. Embree's grandfather Moses, an ironworker, had settled among the early Washingtonians in eastern Tennessee in the late eighteenth century. The family, in fact, eventually married into the rich Sevier clan. Embree's father, Thomas, an ironworker, blacksmith, and entrepreneur, had worked in Pennsylvania, Virginia, and North Carolina before returning to eastern Tennessee to run an iron manufacturing plant. Thomas was not only prosperous but also active in local political affairs as a Quaker. In 1797, as the state of Tennessee was about to celebrate its first birthday, Thomas Embree wrote a letter to the *Knoxville Gazette* newspaper calling for the gradual abolition of slavery in the new state and the formation of an antislavery society for "spirited citizens of every denomination whose patriotic zeal is not limited to those of their own color."

The elder Embree's declaration was no small act; years later, his son Elihu would write that a man's life was at risk at this time, if he "interfered or assisted in establishing the liberty of a person of colour that was held in slavery." Nothing dramatic came about from the elder Embree's prophetic announcement. When Elihu refound his Quaker faith in 1812, at the age of thirty, the antislavery movement in the mountains finally had its mover and shaker.

Elihu did not inherit just his family's antislavery forthrightness. He and his brother Elijah also took over the reins of the family's successful iron business when their father (and a large part of the Embree clan) decided to move north, crossing the Ohio River into the free state of Ohio. The sons prospered. Operating mines, forges, furnaces, and a nail factory, they expanded their holdings over three large mountain counties. Doak's classical teachings had not gone to waste; the Embrees named one of their major ironworks after the Pactolus River of the mythological Greek Midas. In 1820, they purchased the Bumpass Cove iron mines, which had reportedly been utilized to make bullets for the Patriots' war effort at Kings Mountain. At the height of their business ventures, the brothers declared assets of over $120,000. The town of Embreeville was named in their family's honor.

The wealth of these ironworks provided Embree with resources unknown to the limping antislavery activists of the period. The most fervent was Embree's fellow eastern Tennessean and Quaker, Charles Osborn. Osborn, born in 1775 in the North Carolina piedmont, and his family had settled in the upper reaches of eastern Tennessee at the same time that the Embrees were doing so. What the members of Osborn's family lacked in riches, they made up for in passion. By 1809, sanctioned by the Religious Society of Friends (the Quakers' formal name), Osborn had begun to travel the Southern Appalachians as a minister, setting up meetinghouses along the way. His itineraries grew with need and ambition. Within a few years, he had traveled into the Carolinas, Virginia, Pennsylvania, New Jersey, and Ohio, marking over three thousand miles on horseback on one stint alone. Osborn's notorious traveling schedule had even made him "considerably known abroad."

Wherever he preached the Quaker gospel, Osborn sounded off on the one subject that he declared had claimed his attention: the suffering of African and African American slaves and the cause of emancipation. A brilliant organizer as much as a circuit-riding preacher, Osborn set up antislavery societies in numerous regions. The first such society, of course, was formed in his home community in eastern Tennessee. More than a decade after Embree's father's call for an antislavery society, Osborn and a small cadre of Quakers officially founded the Tennessee

Society for Promoting the Manumission of Slaves at the Lost Creek Meetinghouse in Jefferson County, in February 1815. Within a year, thanks largely to the aggressive traveling and outreach of Osborn, over sixteen chapters in eastern Tennessee, claiming hundreds of members, were founded and then brought together under the auspices of the renamed Manumission Society of Tennessee.

While members of the association had their own personal feelings about gradual or immediate emancipation, the Manumission Society cloaked its favoring of gradual emancipation in the language of the Declaration of Independence. The members took their roles seriously; each had to display an advertisement in the "most conspicuous part of his house," declaring the following message:

Freedom is the natural right of all men; I therefore acknowledge myself a member of the Tennessee Society for promoting the manumission of slaves.

Despite the declaration, Embree still had to sort out his contradictory ownership of inherited slaves. He had also purchased a young African American couple and their child. As part of a business agreement in 1809, he had sold many of the slaves, including members of one family, to two different owners. Agonized by his decision to split up the family, he repurchased the slaves a few years later and granted them their freedom. Later admitting to not being "very scrupulous in adhering to what I believed to be right," Embree reminded any critics that the act of manumission had come at "considerable financial sacrifice." He placed their value at $4,000. His economic interests, though, never exonerated his sense of guilt; he resigned himself to "suffer the just judgment" for going astray.

Nonetheless, Embree's status among the Quakers was still not resolved. As a result of proslavery statutes passed by the Tennessee legislature, he could not grant manumission to underage slaves. This meant his "faithful servant and slave black Nancy" and her four children remained his slaves, though he reserved the right to be their designated trustee until emancipation was legally possible. In his will, he set aside

$40 per child to be used for their education. While the Manumission Society confirmed Embree's membership, the truth remained that one of the leaders of the antislavery movement was, in fact, a slave owner.

ANOTHER Doak student and Osborn associate was neither a slave owner nor a gradual emancipator. Born in 1793, John Rankin, who married one of Doak's granddaughters, was a young Presbyterian preacher whose antislavery invective had drawn the censure of conservative church members. Uncompromising, Rankin insisted on immediate emancipation and the assimilation of African Americans into the society. Assisting Osborn with the formation of the nascent manumission societies in the region in 1815–1816, the young firebrand preached at various Presbyterian churches in the mountains until he was reproached for his unnerving sermons. He had dared to use the word *slavery* in the pulpit.

Rankin was not alone. His father-in-law, Adam Lowry, a mill owner and abolitionist, probably convinced the elder Doak to free his slaves. Even so, the restless Rankin departed in 1817 with his family on a horse-drawn wagon. He headed for Kentucky, en route to the free state of Ohio. His work had just begun.

In the meantime, Benjamin Lundy, the young saddle-maker and Quaker in western Virginia, who had witnessed the horrors of the shackled slave gang, crossed the Ohio River during the year of the massive earthquake and set up his own shop ten miles west of Wheeling. With a handful of other Quakers in 1815, he formed the Union Humane Society in Saint Clairsville, the first antislavery society in Ohio committed to gradual emancipation. Within months, the society numbered over five hundred members. Displeased with the ineffective presence of the association in a free state, Lundy, who continued to make periodic trips along the rivers to hawk his saddle wares, began to write articles condemning slavery and its horrors. Either for reasons of timidity or fear of harassment, he published his first appeal against slavery under a symbolic pen name, Philo Justitia.

Lundy's newfound talent as a writer blossomed, and with it came more contacts in the antislavery circles. These connections led him to the traveling Quaker minister Osborn, who ended up transferring from the Southern Appalachians to the nearby southern Ohio town of Mount Pleasant in 1817. At an annual meeting of the Quakers, the two antislavery activists met and exchanged ideas. Osborn had also launched a religious newspaper, the *Philanthropist,* in which he devoted columns to the cause of the abolitionist movement. Osborn, too, had become increasingly more impatient with the gradual-emancipation supporters; he railed against the move to colonize Africa as an antidemocratic sham. Within a short time Lundy became a regular contributor to the weekly. Impressed by Lundy's work and eager to return to his traveling ministry, Osborn asked the young Quaker to take over the editorial duties of the newspaper in 1819. Lundy's traveling life as a salesman, however, prevented him from moving directly to Mount Pleasant.

Lundy and his apprentices soon journeyed down the river highways toward Saint Louis with a new load of goods. Little did they know as they were arriving at the confluence of the Mississippi and Ohio rivers that one of the most historic developments in the antislavery crusade was about to take place.

AS PART of the Louisiana Purchase, the territory of Missouri had started to petition for statehood as early as 1817. The "Missouri question," as it came to be known, delayed the accession into the union of any western territories as the U.S. Congress debated the nuances of the budding state's constitution The issue hinged on whether Missouri had the right to frame its articles without limitations over slavery. By 1819, the twenty-two states in the union were divided evenly by geography over the issue of slavery, with newcomer Alabama balancing the eleven states on the proslavery side. The U.S. House of Representatives, though, in the hands of the Northern antislavery supporters, managed to pass a law that restricted any slaveholding articles that could be written into the proposed state's constitution. The stalemate over Missouri erupted into a bitter national debate, which grew sectional in nature and divisive in tone. Remaining in Missouri for nearly two years, Lundy devoted himself "sedulously" to the "long and severe" campaign.

The Missouri Compromise, with its clear-cut partition of the country over the slave issue, was one of the most important precursors of the Civil War, still a generation or so away. For Southern activists like Embree, the stakes had been raised considerably in the process. Slavery, in Embree's mind, required a national solution, not a state or regional choice. By 1820, the U.S. Senate prevailed in resolving the impasse by proposing to admit Maine as a free state, prohibit slavery in the northern section of the Louisiana Purchase, and allow Missouri to frame its own proslavery constitution. The so-called compromise infuriated antislavery advocates, such as Embree. Lundy left the state in disgust, returning to his home in southern Ohio; he made the seven-hundred-mile journey through the winter on foot. He found that Osborn had moved to Indiana and that the *Philanthropist* newspaper was faltering in the hands of a fellow Quaker.

Yet, the Missouri crisis had lit a fire in the hearts of these Southern Appalachian abolitionists. After making a few unsuccessful appeals to their own slave-owning-dominated state legislature in Tennessee in 1817, Embree and his manumission cohorts had recognized that the festering Missouri controversy required them to take their antislavery crusade to the "world at large." Despite the enduring role of the American Convention for Promoting the Abolition of Slavery, the national association that had been in existence for two decades, the efforts of antislavery societies remained limited and unaware of other regional campaigns. The most concentrated activities had been on the development of the American Colonization Society and its scheme to create Liberia.

On a broader level, Embree felt there was very little public discourse about the moral corruption and injustices taking place in the country over the treatment of slaves. The Quaker industrialist even mocked the Northern Yankees and their indifference to slavery in the South: "We are frequently told that the people of the Northern and Eastern states know nothing about slavery in the South."

The ways to generate attention, however, were even less available.

Outside of a traveling road show, with which the singular Osborn continued to demonstrate great success in the religious communities, and the issuing of "memorials," or public appeals to politicians, the mountaineers realized that the main publishing venues were closed to any advertisements, articles, or examination of the slavery issue from an abolitionist perspective.

With Embree at the helm, the society launched the *Manumission Intelligencer* in the spring of 1819. Published in Jonesboro, Tennessee, the weekly sold by annual subscriptions nationwide for a $3 fee. Operating under the consensus of the society committee, Embree not only edited but also bankrolled the effort. While the publication chronicled the endeavors of abolitionists in Tennessee, the South, and the rest of the nation, it also featured poetry and articles on agriculture, world news, and notable individuals.

The journal couldn't have been founded in more difficult times. The Panic of 1819 resulted in the first major financial and banking crisis in the United States. With the boom years after the War of 1812 coming to a close, the importation of foreign goods on the rise, and the lending practices over land speculation and development reaching a tipping point, the national economy came to a halt. Banks failed, factories closed, and foreclosures ensued. Cotton prices had plummeted. A tide of malaise rippled across the country with its first real economic depression. Unemployment in the cities skyrocketed; when the bills of debtors came due, thousands of violators found themselves jailed. The New York Stock Exchange, still in its infancy, teetered. The "multitudes," wrote one observer, "are in deep distress." In the process, the expense of churning out fifty issues of the weekly *Intelligencer* took a considerable toll on Embree's bank account.

The wealthy iron maker pressed on, despite the fact that one of his importation schemes of products into the Southern Appalachians went belly-up. He wrote that he had spent several thousand dollars "already in some small degree abolishing, and in endeavoring to facilitate the general abolition of Slavery—yet he feels not satisfied without still continuing to throw in his mite." In fact, the most pressing issue for the restless advocate was not finances but freedom. The Manumission Society's democratic process of group approval over written materials prevented Embree from publishing his weekly paper in a timely manner.

EMBREE decided to "throw his mite" one step further. In the spring of 1820, only a month after antislavery advocates had failed to impede the disastrous congressional concessions in Missouri, Embree single-handedly launched the first U.S. newspaper dedicated exclusively to the abolition of slavery. At a dark and critical moment in American history and facing personal economic ruin, Embree showed unwavering determination to keep the lamp burning for the national abolitionist movement, in the words of one of David Nelson's well-known hymns, "Shining Shore."

The announcement of the *Emancipator* came more than a decade before William Lloyd Garrison's legendary *Liberator*, which is often credited as the first abolitionist newspaper. The *Manumission Intelligencer*, meanwhile, transformed into the weekly *East Tennessee Patriot* news sheet. At the same printing house, Embree designed and focused the *Emancipator* on several key areas in the antislavery movement: The monthly publication served as a clearinghouse for information by regional and national abolitionist societies, published correspondence between activists in various parts of the country, reprinted speeches and appeals made to Congress and state legislatures, and provided historical data on the lives and conditions of slaves. Severing his relationship with the manumission society in order to sidestep any issues of censorship, Embree pledged his newspaper to be a "true chronicle" of the organization's proceedings.

Embree started with six subscribers. Within six months, relying on regional Quaker organizations and abolitionists around the country to sell subscriptions for a $1 annual fee, he had over 2,500 national subscribers, rivaling any regional newspapers in the South. The demand compelled him to reprint earlier issues. Such numbers galvanized Embree. He tooted his own horn in defiance, claiming that the periodical met "the approbation of thousands, and [was] patronized perhaps at least equal to any other in the state." His work drew considerable praise at a national meeting of antislavery advocates in Philadelphia.

In the process, Embree and his Tennessee Society friends emerged as the trendsetters for the national abolitionist movement. They used the pioneering publication as an educational tool and as a way of recruiting allies in the community, especially among churches. Their efforts paid off remarkably well for the times; within seven years, Tennessee had twenty-five antislavery societies with over one thousand members, more that any other state; neighboring North Carolina, where Osborn and others often traveled, also ranked high.

Despite these successes, a few historians tend to dismiss Embree and his abolitionist cadre as ineffective or, worse, link them to the advocates who viewed slavery more as a scourge to free white labor and the stability of the Southern economy than as an injustice to African Americans. These arguments, based on Embree's and the Tennessee Society's call for gradual instead of immediate emancipation, overlook the larger impact of their work, the complexity of their circumstances in the Mountain South, and the increasingly radical tendency of their views.

When the *Emancipator* rolled from the eastern Tennessee press, the momentum of any broad antislavery sentiment roused by the Missouri crisis had sputtered once more. Many American civic leaders and politicians, especially in the North, appeared to be content with the "compromise," which effectively banned any further slavery from the western territories. Attention focused again on colonizing western Africa with repatriated slaves and African Americans. The mainstream religious communities remained bitterly divided. No national forum, in terms of publications, existed to exchange ideas or platforms for a renewed antislavery movement. In effect, the South was left to nurse its own misery.

Embree's publication, therefore, provided virtually the only arena for antislavery discourse on a national level. He reprinted letters and articles from activists and friends from across the country. More importantly, Embree, as the publisher and editor, continued to insist on viewing the issue of slavery as a "deeply rooted national disease," not a regional aberration. Missouri determined that it was no longer a "Southern institution."

The backlash against abolitionist activities and publications in the South had forced Embree to defend himself on more than one occasion. Increasingly, most of the Southern states deemed any antislavery materials in the mail licentious and therefore subject to bans and prosecution under decency laws. In one of the most scurrilous attacks, Governor George Poindexter of Mississippi, who had received a complimentary copy of the newspaper (like every other governor in the nation), branded Embree a stooge of "an association of individuals in another section of the United States," as if a true Southerner could not have been capable of pulling off such a publication on his own. The threats were not in print only. In his newspaper, Embree complained about regional post offices that refused to deliver or lost shipments of the publication.

Embree was not unaware of the fine line he had to tread in this tense atmosphere of the South. He recognized his groundbreaking role as a publisher who extolled the First Amendment right to free speech. To his credit, he published missives that were critical of both the antislavery movement and his own contradictory role as a slave owner. Invoking the Constitution, he reminded readers that he avoided using "liberty to a degree that might be deemed licentiousness, and, on the other hand, never to allow myself to be borne down by a squeamish pusillanimity." Whether or not he advocated gradual or immediate emancipation, the Quaker rarely pulled any punches.

The circumstances when Savannah was devastated by a fire in 1820 serves as a good example. The city leaders refused a donation of several thousand dollars from New York City, which had stipulated that the funds be distributed regardless of race. Embree had also contributed to the emergency effort. Outraged by such racism in the face of ruin, the publisher excoriated these "monsters in human shape" and wondered at the mercy of a God that "has not destroyed its proud inhabitants with fire unquenchable."

He was even less merciful with slave traders. He declared in one issue that though he opposed "sanguinary punishments," he believed slave traders would merit "an ignominious death." Setting a precedent that Lundy and Garrison would refine, Embree also published news items or

letters of the most horrific kind, detailing the vicious acts of slave owners. He declared his intention to "shame the perpetrator."

As a Quaker activist, Embree presented much of his work as a moral
charge to fellow Christians to break the "hold of Satan" and, in fact,
geared his publication toward challenging the increasing role of mainstream churches in justifying slavery. He reprinted sermons and state-
ments by fellow Quakers, Presbyterians, and Moravians. He published an
open debate with Poindexter, who claimed that "real Christians" would
not disrupt domestic tranquility in the South; Embree berated the Mississippi governor's manipulation of religion, concluding that the Apostle
James would have cast a "low opinion" of such faith.

The industrialist's obsession with the abolitionist cause did lead to
bankruptcy in the end. It also took his life. After his second wife died of
tuberculosis in the summer of 1820, only months after he had launched
the *Emancipator* on his own, Embree found himself in charge of his seven
children (from both marriages) and dealing with massive debts from a
merchandising scheme that had failed to pan out and a struggling iron
business. Overworked and overcome by the turmoil of the affairs, he collapsed out of nervous fatigue and succumbed to fever. The thirty-eight-
year-old Embree died on December 4, 1820. He had published only seven
issues of his remarkable newspaper. Despite the family's considerable
assets, Embree's brother had to appeal for emergency relief from the
Tennessee state legislature in 1821.

Had Embree survived, we might be recounting a different chronicle
of the early abolitionist movement. His sudden loss was met with shock
and admiring eulogies in newspapers across Tennessee, the South, and
eastern Quaker centers like Philadelphia. His final issue, in fact, had
become more radical in view. He published an extremely critical analysis
of the more popular colonization groups and their "chimerical" attempts
at relocating Africans and African Americans.

THE FRUITS of Embree's labor did not go to waste, nor were they
ignored. Informed by Embree's father of the publisher's death, Benjamin

Lundy recognized the "Almighty Disposer of events" had called him to take up the antislavery torch in print. Having returned to his base in southern Ohio, Lundy, in fact, had already considered launching his own abolitionist sheet and printed the first issue of the emphatically named *Genius of Universal Emancipation* a month after Embree's death. Lundy had been an admirer of the Tennesseean. He announced that his newspaper would "rise like a Phoenix from the ashes of the late 'Emancipator'" and hoped his work might "supply its place." He also planned to relocate to the eastern Tennessee mountains. Packing up his load again, the traveling saddle-maker journeyed eight hundred miles on foot and boat, finally settling in the Tennessee Society's hometown of Greeneville.

To Embree's passion and plundered wealth, Lundy added his honed talents as a traveling salesman. Within a few years, despite the continual postal disturbances and physical threats by local slaveholders, the fleet-footed Quaker fashioned a monthly newspaper that was truly national in scope and circulated in every state. It remained religious in tone, but political in vision; by 1824, Lundy had chronicled the presidential election closely and encouraged his readers to vote for opponents of slavery. To support his work, the Quaker activist also published a general newsweekly and an agricultural sheet. Following in Embree's footsteps, Lundy also attended the national antislavery meetings in Philadelphia, speaking and organizing manumission societies along the way. With the first lines of the Declaration of Independence at the top of its masthead, the *Genius of Universal Emancipation* remained the only abolitionist newspaper in the period.

Lundy, like Embree, favored gradual emancipation. He also became interested in the prospect of allowing African slaves to emigrate to the independent Republic of Haiti. In 1824, Lundy made the first of many visits to the Caribbean, escorting freed slaves with him. The Quaker's association with colonization groups, however, was tenuous; Lundy believed Africans and African Americans had a right to remain in the country as citizens, and only raised his "feeble voice" in agreement with colonization efforts that were part of universal emancipation.

Within three years, the publisher packed his bags and set off across the Appalachians on foot for Baltimore, lecturing and delivering his newspaper along the way. He declared that the East Coast held the most potential for an extensive campaign that linked national antislavery movements. He also recognized the growing uncertainty of the Southern postal service in distributing his publication.

Lundy may have left the Southern Appalachians, but his hard-won experiences in the mountains would soon lead him to an even greater legacy.

THE DEPARTURE of so many antislavery advocates from the Mountain South, as well as the untold waves of settlers who fled from the slave-holding Deep South in general, had frustrated diehard Southern activists like Embree, who was convinced that, under the right circumstances, a majority opinion of non-slaveholding citizens could have prevailed in the South. He had chided his fleeing Southerners for turning their backs on "seeing the cruel oppressor lacerate the back of his slaves." Embree wrote about this phenomenon of the flight of "first-rate citizens" from the slave states. Whether Embree was deluding himself over the abolitionists' ability to unhinge the grip of the slave-owning elite in the South is secondary to the consequence of this mass migration of illuminated thinkers. In effect, the Midwest, East Coast, and western territories inherited more than one generation of progressive thinkers and activists. Southern Appalachia provided these regions with some of the most outspoken leaders of the antislavery movement.

The expatriated roles of Benjamin Lundy, Charles Osborn, David Nelson, John Rankin, and Levi Coffin remind us of the Southern Appalachian influence on the abolitionist movement in the country. Rankin, for example, after holding down a parish in northern Kentucky for a few years, crossed the Ohio River on an icy cold New Year's Day in 1822 and settled in Ripley, Ohio. He immediately became active in the local antislavery group. His home turned into a key hideout on the Underground Railroad. But it was his theological writings, sharpened for the process of critical inquiry by the teachings of the elder Doak, that launched Rankin onto the national stage in 1824.

He began to write a series of public letters to his brother, who had recently purchased some slaves in Virginia. Rankin's correspondence appeared in a Ripley-based newspaper, the *Castigator,* over twenty-one issues. "Shall I suffer sin upon my brother?" he asked. The law of God forbids it, he answered himself. He announced that his letters would address the injustice of enslaving Africans. In truth, Rankin's letters were the subtext for a greater purpose: Beyond an in-depth cataloging of the brutal and inhumane treatment of African slaves and the religious context of sinful complicity of Christian believers, the young Presbyterian sought to analyze the devastating repercussions of slavery on the psyche of the nation. For Rankin, slavery not only oppressed the slave, but irreparably damaged the makeup of the slave owner. His writings soon became recognized as one of the first thorough reckonings of the toll of slavery on the conscience of the country.

A publisher in Ripley reprinted Rankin's letters in book form in 1825. Nearly half of the thousand copies immediately went up in smoke after the printer's warehouse across the river in Maysville, Kentucky, was torched. Yet, the book prevailed, passing through hands from one avid reader to the next, and was eventually reprinted by a Quaker publisher in New Jersey in 1830. Another edition soon appeared in England. Within the next two decades, nearly twenty more editions cropped up across the country, transforming Rankin's *Letters on Slavery* into a critically important and much-referenced text in the antislavery movement.

About the time Rankin's letters had been published as a book, another Southern Appalachian abolitionist crossed the Ohio River. Establishing himself in Newport, Indiana, for twenty years, Levi Coffin became a crucial link on the Underground Railroad, eventually earning the informal title of president. Some historians credit Coffin with sheltering over three thousand escaped slaves. As a young Quaker, Coffin had been impressed by the visits of Osborn and Embree at his meetinghouse in North Carolina. He also read Lundy's *Genius of Universal Emancipation* with great interest. Moving to Cincinnati in 1847, a critical underground junction on the northern side of the Ohio River, Coffin set up a business network that sold products from free laborers. As one of the leading spokesmen in the abolitionist movement, Coffin also founded orphanages, schools, and training centers for African Americans.

David Nelson and Gideon Blackburn, both Doak students at Washington College, also played key roles in the antislavery movement. Nelson, a Presbyterian minister and college president who had to flee from the slave state of Missouri after his incendiary sermons resulted in a lynch mob, became a leading voice for the abolitionists in Illinois. Blackburn, an itinerant preacher and military chaplain throughout the Southern Appalachians and the rest of the South, and one of the first Presbyterian missionaries among the Cherokee, also relocated to Illinois and served as a college president and antislavery spokesman in the Midwest.

LUNDY'S departure from the Mountain South was not a final adieu, nor would he disappear into anonymity in the East Coast cities. Reestablishing his fugitive printing operations in Baltimore, he announced in the *Genius* in 1827 that one-fifth of the abolitionist societies in the nation resided in his former stronghold of eastern Tennessee. With this new coastal launching pad, Lundy expanded his circulation and continued to speak throughout the Atlantic coast and New England at a merciless pace. His increasingly harsh attacks in print, including his infamous "Black List" of slave owners, drew violent repercussions. The publisher was severely beaten in the streets of Baltimore by one offended slave owner. Nonetheless, Lundy remained defiant and indefatigable and insisted on making additional trips to free slaves in Haiti and Mexico. In the spring of 1828, addressing a religious gathering in Boston, Lundy's reportedly pitiful speaking style had a dramatic impact on an intense young editor, William Lloyd Garrison.

Arguably the most important and controversial white social figure to emerge from the abolitionist movement, Garrison had felt little more than intellectual discomfort at the fate of African slaves before meeting Lundy. Then, he declared, the Quaker's "unconquerable spirit of reform" converted him. The Massachusetts printer and editor, who was then running a fledgling newspaper in Vermont, was not a self-possessed or indifferent Boston Brahmin; he had been raised in poverty by a God-fearing Baptist mother. Lundy's detailed analysis of slavery struck Garrison. It cast a spell on him with the urgency of emancipation. He hailed the *Genius* as the "bravest and best attempt in the history of newspaper publications." Within a short time, Garrison joined Lundy in Baltimore, serving in the apprentice role Lundy had once played under Charles Osborn.

Allowing the Quaker time to travel and lecture, Garrison took over the editorship of the *Genius* with the fervor of a recent convert, pushing the publication to new limits. Garrison refused to soften his terms for the sake of moderation. In 1830, he and Lundy were saddled with a libel suit when Garrison accused a local Massachusetts shipowner of kidnapping and slave trading. Whether or not Garrison had all his facts in order, he was found guilty and fined $50. Unable to raise the money, the young abolitionist served seven weeks in jail until a New York philanthropist came to his rescue. The incident, however, compelled Garrison and his mentor, Lundy, to part ways. They had already split over their visions for the antislavery movement. Garrison insisted on advocating immediate and complete emancipation; he disparaged the colonization movement as a mockery.

By 1831, Garrison had returned to New England and founded his own newspaper, the *Liberator*. His debut issue was unambiguous: "I do not wish to think, or speak, or write, with moderation. I am in earnest—I will not equivocate—I will not excuse—I will not retreat a single inch—And I will be heard." As the founder of the American Anti-Slavery Society and considered one of the most dangerous men in the nation by the slaveholding South, the radical abolitionist printed 1,820 issues of the newspaper over the next thirty-five years.

Lundy would not be the only Southern Appalachian influence on Garrison. The New Englander reprinted every one of Rankin's legendary letters to his brother in 1832 and praised the Presbyterian preacher as "my anti-slavery father," claiming that Rankin's book "on slavery was the cause of my entering the anti-slavery conflict."

As Embree had predicted in 1820, the Appalachian range divided into inevitable ruin during the Civil War. His grandson of the same name even fought for the Confederacy. As a precursor of the region's doomed fate, John Brown led his historic 1859 raid on the federal arsenal at Harper's Ferry in western Virginia; he was intent on triggering a slave rebellion that could base itself in the Mountain South. Brown met his fate on the gallows in Charleston, in today's West Virginia. The mountaineers did not rally to his defense.

Amid the devastation in the mountains, the prophetic voices of the pioneering Appalachians remained even more important. In one of our country's most distressing periods of history, a small but courageous group of abolitionists in the Southern mountains kept the light of our nation's conscience aflame, eventually passing its leadership to the North. Beseeching his own Southern mountaineers to embrace their legacy of antislavery sentiment, Elihu Embree cast his terms in a prayer:

> That you live and act, not only for the present, but for generations to come; and for eternity. And that on this act of yours depends the slavery, the freedom—the happiness, the misery of thousands. O! that you may incline your hearts to wisdom—your ears to the cries of the poor and oppressed. And may a peaceful conscience, and that happiness which you secure to others, be your portion.

Chapter Five

ALL THE NEWS THAT'S FIT TO PRINT

✦

It is only in the mountains that I can fully appreciate my
existence as a man in America, and my own native land. It is then and
there my soul is lifted up, my bosom caused to swell with emotion,
and I am lost in wonder at the dignity of my own nature.

—MARTIN DELANY, Letter to Frederick Douglass, 1848

IN THE SUMMER OF 1829, the latest gossip about a trial in Washington, D.C., dominated the parlor rooms across the country. For the first time in American history, a citizen was being tried as "a common scold," an offense of inappropriate public behavior plucked from old English laws.

At first glance, Anne Royall, the charged woman, would have seemed an unlikely wrongdoer; she was a demure, squat, graying woman in her sixties. Andrew Jackson's secretary of war had testified in her defense. Brimming with confidence in the seat of the accused, Royall was no stranger to controversy. She had already been pushed down a flight of stairs in New England, horsewhipped in Pennsylvania, and chased out of towns and inns on the Atlantic coast. Her self-published travel memoirs and social critiques—the insufferable *Black Books*—had made her famous.

Royall's defense did not hold up well. She claimed the trial was part of a conspiracy of Protestant churches to "overwhelm the land" with a new

Inquisition. It had nothing to do with her behavior, she said, but only with her writing and her right to free speech. In many respects, Royall was right; her antichurch diatribes had made her the target of religious activists. Her infamous toast to the "blueskins—may all their throats be cut," still resonated in the rafters of untold congregations. Nonetheless, the older woman had taken her opponents' bait. After chiding a local congregation of evangelical Presbyterians from her neighboring house, she had been drawn into a stone-throwing brawl with children in the streets. Branded "the widow with a serpent's tongue," Royall had berated the kids and "blackcoats" with profanity. The police arrived and arrested her.

The Circuit Court of Washington, D.C., took only a few minutes to find her guilty of being a "common scold." Or, rather, "an uncommon scold," as reported by the amused press. A public nuisance. The judge spared her the proscribed penalty: "ducking" by water, despite the public clamor to give the "old woman a cold bath." Instead, she was fined $10, a sum immediately paid by a pool of journalists on Capitol Hill. Humiliated, but most likely humored by the affair, Royall left town for another fact-finding trip as a travel writer.

Our nation's capital had not finished with Royall, or more accurately, Royall was not finished with the nation's capital. The payment of the fine by the journalists foretold the writer's new mission. She returned to the capital in 1831 and launched the first newspaper written, edited, and published solely by a female journalist in Washington, D.C.

Royall took her place among other Southern Appalachians in the forefront of pioneering newspapers. Charles Osborn, Elihu Embree, and Benjamin Lundy left their mark in the field of abolitionist journalism in the early 1800s, and Sequoyah and the Cherokee launched the first bilingual indigenous newspaper in the country in 1828. Along with Royall, two other journalism pioneers, Martin Delany and Adolph Ochs, were shaped in the hills by tenacity, self-determination, and an extraordinary regimen of autodidactic study. These three trailblazers would carry on their Appalachian achievements at the national level over the next century.

THERE ARE FEW American iconoclasts as colorful as Anne Royall. Born in Maryland in 1769, she and her family moved into the western Pennsylvania frontier in the 1770s. A questionable story of captivity among the indigenous mountain tribes became a part of Royall's childhood mystique. Still, her upbringing was one of pioneering drudgery and warfare, with a self-proclaimed diet of cornmeal and jerked venison instilling a sense of hardiness that would serve the mountain girl well. When her Tory-leaning father died, Royall's destitute mother found work as a maid for a wealthy Revolutionary hero and slave-owning plantation landlord on Peters Mountain near Lewisburg, in today's West Virginia.

Major William Royall, who served under Washington and Lafayette in the American Revolution, had fled his prestigious Tidewater family ties for the serenity of the Southern Appalachians. Like the young Embree, he had a penchant for the deists and supported the Freemasons. He loathed the Anglican Church; he championed Thomas Jefferson's attempts to divide state matters from organized religion. The plantation owner opened his vast mountaintop library to the maid's teenage daughter and immersed her in the intellectual wonders of the Greeks, Shakespeare, and Voltaire and other Enlightenment philosophers. In turn, she became a voracious reader and student. She roamed the mountain settlements for more books.

The aged patrician wooed his maid's daughter in more than the classics. After a decade of hushed romance, Royall, well into his fifties, married Anne in a quiet ceremony. She was twenty-eight years old. The time of tranquility as a plantation owner's wife was short-lived. Lofty thoughts aside, her husband's love of brandy ruptured whatever peace occurred on their mountain near Sweet Springs. He died in the winter of 1812, leaving his wife to sort out a hornet's nest of intrigue and demands on his estate. His Tidewater family members challenged a hastily scrawled will that had left the bulk of Royall's fortune to his young wife; they dismissed her as a concubine.

Impervious to the family dispute, which would languish in the courts for years, Anne sold some properties in Charleston, packed up a wagon, plucked three slaves as traveling servants, and embarked on a journey over the Southern Appalachians to the warmer province of Alabama. The Appalachians were beautiful to view, she declared, but she had "suffered too much among the mountains ever to love them."

Royall's career as a chronicler emerged on this trip. She corresponded frequently with her lawyer, Matthew Dunbar, filling her letters with colorful details of her travels. Her background in history informed her observations; she reveled in her descriptions of the Southern elite. Operating as if her funds were unlimited, Royall also racked up significant debts. When the Royall estate was finally adjudicated in the courts, she was stunned to learn that the final will had been struck down, and the judge had granted her a small settlement. Her remaining funds barely covered her debt. She lost her slaves and an affluent lifestyle in the process. She fled Alabama in fear of being imprisoned as a debtor and an imposter.

Left penniless, her health failing, Royall first lived off the favors of her husband's Freemasonry connections, until she ventured to Washington, D.C., to seek a war widow's pension. A legislative clause that excluded Revolutionary War widows married after 1794 compelled Royall to file a special petition for her husband's pension. The quick-witted woman was not without options; she had already announced her intentions to publish a book on her travels in the South. She went directly to the secretary of state, John Quincy Adams, who took pity on her case. He also became one of the first paying subscribers for Royall's promised book on her travels in Alabama and other parts of the South. This pioneering form of book advances saved Royall. While forced to wait years to sort out the technicalities of the pension dispute, she collected enough subscriptions for her forthcoming book to underwrite a new fact-finding journey to Pennsylvania, New York, and New England.

When she was fifty-seven, Royall's *Sketches of History, Life and Manners in the United States, by a Traveller,* was printed on credit at the office of a New Haven newspaper in 1826. In many respects, it counterbalanced the "nauseous flattery" of early-American ways in Scottish-born Fannie Wright's own travel memoir, *Views of Society and Manners in America,* published in England in 1821. Royall's work stretched along the full chain of the Appalachians, from Alabama to New England, drawing occasional praise and complaints from every region. Local characters and their etiquette, more than picturesque scenes, interested her. Beyond any travel narrative of descriptions, facts, and personal observations, the book included a series of idiosyncratic portraits of the famous and unknown, and "manners" Royall had encountered along her way. These sketches were a preview of her take-no-prisoners approach to writing.

If anything, the mixed reviews established Royall's name in the public arena. The *Boston Commercial Gazette* praised the nuances of Royall's observations: "Here is a first view of everything—politics, literature, history, biography, rivers, mountains, men, women and children. . . . She marches on speaking her mind freely, and unpacking her heart in words of censure or praise, as she feels." The *Hampden Journal* responded that the work had emerged from "a poor, crazy vagrant," who should be committed to a "Home of Correction." Outraged mostly by Royall's frank exposés of family life, the *New Yorker Advertiser* found it a contemptible book.

Remarkably, *Sketches* withheld any comment on Royall's pet project: castigating the political and social role of the Protestant churches in America. This would come in due time. Encouraged by the reception of her first book and outraged by the disparagement of her detractors, Royall announced her next travel volume would be named the *Black Book*, as a chronicle of the "black deeds of evil doers." She published a novel, *The Tennesseans*, in the meantime.

DESPITE her peripatetic existence, Royall always considered herself part of the "backwoods folk." She frequently employed a vernacular from her mountain past, even to the extent of referring to one American president as a "Gee-Gaw" in one of her last newspaper columns. Whether or not her affair with the mountaineers endured, she was one of the first modern writers to view Appalachia as a republic on its own, "every way different from any people" in the lowland South. She referred to the mountain region as "my Grison republic," drawing parallels with the cantankerous, independent canton in the Swiss Alps. She made notes of language differences and Shakespearean nuances. She loved the "sweet melodious" voices.

Her view, a half century before Northern travel writers and historians like Teddy Roosevelt perfected the pure Anglo-Saxon stereotype of the mountain frontier, was equally select in its ethnic praise. She found "a serenity of countenance altogether peculiar" among the emerging mountain towns and villages, while dismissing the German settlers, blacks, and remote Scotch-Irish backwoods farmers as lacking "arts, taste and refinement."

The primary bane infiltrating the mountains, and the nation, infuriated the writer and encouraged her to pick up her pen. Royall despised missionaries and evangelicals in America. Her vantage point as a Southern Appalachian had been sharpened by experience. The surge of religious reevaluation and worship, galvanized by the massive camp revivals of the Methodists, Baptists, and numerous other Protestant sects, had swept through the Mountain South around the turn of the nineteenth century. In turn, the Awakening's populist and emotional treatment of universal salvation in the region had provided the nation with one of its most critical opponents. Royall vented her wrath especially on the reactionary forces of a group of Presbyterians and their attempts to enter American politics. She invoked Robert Burns's poetic satire of the "Holy Willies."

By 1827, the outspoken Presbyterian minister Ezra Stiles Ely in Philadelphia had announced a move to create a Christian Party. His interdenominational followers launched a campaign to elect Christian politicians, with a less-than-secretive plan to amend the Constitution with a declared national religion. Royall found Ely to be a "monster." Dedicating a large portion of her first *Black Book* to the machinations of "missionaries"—Royall's word, essentially, for all Protestants—she described revival meetings in severe terms and attacked Ely's new American Tract Society as a front for treasonous behavior. The missionary's object, she declared, "is to plunge mankind into ignorance, to make him a bigot, a fanatic, a hypocrite, a heathen, to hate every sect but his own, to shut his eyes against the truth, harden his heart against the distress of his fellow-man and purchase heaven with money."

Royall never shirked at confronting the religious activists. A newspaper in Montgomery, Alabama, praised her campaign "in opposition to fanaticism." She made appearances in cities and inns that had threatened her life in advance. A "blueskin" merchant pushed the sixty-year-old gadfly down a flight of stairs in Burlington, Vermont, giving her a broken leg and concussion. She would get her revenge in her next *Black Book*.

Mastering the form of the "pen portrait," Royall went straight to her opponents and solicited interviews, or "sittings." According to one reviewer in Baltimore, her portraits may be "hideous of many," but they reminded readers of the "pride and haughtiness among men of our country, whom fame and public employment have designated as prominent citizens." In the process, she became one of the first writer-journalists in the United States to employ quotations for her interviews.

After her "common scold" trial in Washington, D.C., fearful of the rise of the anti-Mason sentiment in the early 1830s and probably fatigued by a rigorous decade of travel, Royall found that her books were not enough for her prodigious writings or for her crusade to keep separate the church and state. She had published ten volumes, including her *Letters from Alabama* and a largely panned novel, within five years. She returned to Washington, D.C., to launch an independent newspaper, *Paul Pry*. Her reputation, of course, both from the trial and from her writings, preceded her with the dark shadow of locusts. Her *Black Books* became prize possessions, if only for the delight of their callous descriptions. Innkeepers, booksellers, politicians, and newspaper people sought out her company or boarded their doors to her arrival. John Quincy Adams hailed Royall as the "virago errant in enchanted armor."

ROYALL was not the first woman journalist or editor in the United States, as is occasionally suggested. Fannie Wright, the wonderful free spirit and radical thinker much admired by Royall, coedited the *New Harmony Gazette* at Robert Owen's commune in Indiana. The *Gazette* evolved into the

Free Enquirer newspaper, which Wright coedited with Owen's son in New York City in the late 1820s. A generation before both of these innovators, Mary Katherine Goddard had written for and edited her family's newspapers in Providence, Philadelphia, and Baltimore before taking the reins of her own newspaper in 1775. *Paul Pry,* though, was the first Washington, D.C.–based newspaper written, edited, published, and fully owned by an American woman and aimed at the heart of the nation's political elite.

Named for a popular English theater icon of the day, *Paul Pry* was determined to emulate its busybody namesake in the world of journalism. In the celebrated play in London, the mischievous Paul Pry would often leave his umbrella behind, as a way of returning and eavesdropping on his latest victims.

Assembling the remains of an old Ramage press, discarded type, and a staff of two orphans as printer's devils, Royall printed the first issue of *Paul Pry* from her kitchen in 1831. Her stated mission was hardly modest. The newspaper declared its independence in patriotic terms: "The welfare and happiness of our country is our politics." It issued a headlong assault on the rise of evangelicals and the fear instilled by Nat Turner's slave rebellion, which had occurred only months before: "As for those cannibals, the Anti-Masons, the co-temporaries of Negro insurgents, we shall meet them upon their own ground. That of extermination. Let all pious Generals, Colonels and Commanders of our army and navy who make war upon old women beware. Let all pious Postmasters who cheat the government by franking pious tracts beware. Let all pious booksellers who take pious bribes beware." Royall's wit wasn't lacking. She concluded her benediction with an appeal: "And let all old bachelors and old maids be married as soon as possible."

Paul Pry delighted most in its discovery of government graft. Becoming a self-appointed whistle-blower on Capitol Hill, Royall attended congressional meetings, haunted government buildings, and interviewed low-level employees, always in the search of fraud. She became obsessed with the inner workings of the Post Office Department. Her pen portraits shifted toward office holders and Washington socialites; she would interview every American president over the next twenty years.

By 1832, the newspaper was a veritable though still debt-ridden success, with subscriptions nationwide. While her fans and zealous Mason connections cushioned a lot of the ridicule, Royall's detractors continued to be merciless. The *New England Religious Weekly* referred to her as an "old hag" who printed all the "scum, billingsgate and filth extant."

Royall was not alone in this arena of newsmakers and newspapers. *Paul Pry's* public castigations in the press emerged during a dramatic period of transition in American journalism. A new readership had bloomed with prosperity across the country. The rise of the penny press in the early 1830s had led to a proliferation of rumor-hawking sheets in every city, perfected in Benjamin Day's *New York Sun* and Scottish-born James Gordon Bennett's *New York Herald*. Both papers claimed readerships in the thousands, obliterating the stranglehold of the more elite or politically affiliated press on the country's growing literate population. They specialized in stories about "broken heads, broken hearts and broken bones." Improvements in the printing process, cutting the cost and time in half, allowed an army of ragged delivery boys to hit the streets with daily headlines that competed over the intrigues of murder and scandal. This journalistic trend crept in the direction of a century of yellow journalism.

Royall's mixed brew of politics had been shaped on Peters Mountain in the Southern Appalachians, under the auspices of her Freemason husband and refined by her own personal experience. The role of religion in daily life affected all her views; the separation of church and state remained a graph in nearly every column. She was antislavery, but supported states' rights and viciously opposed the Christian rhetoric of abolitionists; she hated alcohol, but ridiculed the religious element in the temperance movement. She advocated public schooling, to keep any education efforts out of parochial hands. While a fair-weather supporter of Andrew Jackson's administration, Royall railed against his treatment of Native Americans. The "aborigines," she declared, were the most virtuous people on the globe, until they were "contaminated" by the missionaries. Thoroughly nationalistic in spirit, Royall detested the "America for Americans" anti-immigrant movement of the period and called it a "despotic" plot by Protestants.

As a singular woman publisher in Washington, D.C., and often a solitary female among the male elite, she was never concerned with the early proclamations of the suffrage movement or socially proscribed "women's issues." Instead, she dealt with the bread-and-butter battles of the times, such as the monopoly of the Bank of the United States, which controlled much of the revenue of the country, or the monopoly of the beef industry. She praised the nascent labor union movement.

After five years of traipsing up and down the halls of politicians in search of evildoers and still struggling to keep the wolf from her publishing door, Royall decided to put *Paul Pry* to rest and launch a new Washington paper geared more toward "amusing tales, dialogues, and essays upon general subjects." The Washingtonians had not heard the last of Royall. *Paul Pry*'s departing admonition was haunting: "Let no man sleep at his post. Remember, the office holders are desperate, wakeful and urgent."

It took less than three weeks for the first issue of the *Huntress* to appear. A quote from Thomas Jefferson rested below the masthead: "Education, the Main Pillar, which sustains the Temple of Liberty." Named in jest for Royall's reputation on Capitol Hill, the *Huntress* was a kinder, gentler version of *Paul Pry*, perhaps less strident in tone, but no less passionate in spirit. With her hand firmly on the editorial rudder, she published an eccentric mix of personal narrative and editorial rant, part attack dog and part crusader, still a muckraker of corruption, though dedicated to more poetry and excerpts from novels. She would still "put the rod to both parties [Whig or Democrat] when we think they do wrong." The "we" referred to the aging Royall, her longtime assistant Sally Stack (a tall "widow's daughter"), and a generation of orphan helpers.

The newspaper continued as Royall's personal lobbying board for pet projects. One of those, in fact, made history. As an early supporter of Samuel Morse, the elderly publisher had actively lobbied members of Congress for years to provide funds for a stretch of telegraph wire to test the invention. When Congress finally allocated $30,000 in 1843, Royall managed to attend the demonstration of the invention to Congress. The first message sent to Baltimore in the telegraphic code became historic: "What hath God wrought?" The operator added that Royall was in the room. The reply to Morse's phrase swelled Royall's sense of importance among the politicians: "Mr. Rodgers' respects to Mrs. Royall."

After years of petitioning Congress to the point of being considered a crank, Royall was finally granted a widow's pension in 1848 for her husband's service in the American Revolution. She was eighty years old. Her final victory was for naught. Royall's heirs took a sizable share; the rest went to the publisher's debt.

With or without funds, operating often on credit and the goodwill of subscribers, Royall and her crew managed to turn out their weekly newspaper for eighteen years without fail. Only one issue was suspended, when Royall announced a reprieve "to fix up our wardrobe which is getting shabby." By 1854, however, the paper's format had shrunk to a diminutive six-by-eight inches. Nevertheless, the heroic and independent tone of the muckraker remained clear: "Our object is [to] expose, strip the mask off hypocrisy—defend the innocent, detect treachery, and hold the traitor up to public view. . . . We look after the great enemy of our country—despotism."

Later that summer, the eighty-five-year-old publisher failed to pay her rent for the first time in three decades. Her attire had become noticeably ragged. Royall announced in the paper that she possessed "thirty-one cents in the world." Nonetheless, she declared Dr. Morse's Invigorating Elixir had enlivened her health. With an eye on the future, she addressed Congress with three prayers, ending with a plea that foreshadowed the Civil War. Despite her longtime states' rights tendency, she called for the Union of the States to remain "eternal."

Royall died on October 1, 1854. Newspapers made only a brief mention of her passing; one Washington journal praised her "strict integrity." Buried in an unmarked grave in the Congressional Cemetery, one of America's pioneering muckrakers was quickly forgotten.

ROYALL'S final departure from the western mountains of Virginia in the 1820s coincided with the flight of another future journalist and iconoclast out of Southern Appalachia: Martin Delany. While their writings and roles in American society couldn't have been further apart, the two shared a similar fate as self-proclaimed agitators, stinging social critics, and ultimately disregarded antagonists. Their dispatches as travel writers were incredibly unique for their times. They were lifelong supporters of Freemasonry, though for entirely different reasons. Their strongly held belief in the power of education and literature would have been an unshakeable bond.

Born in today's Charleston, West Virginia, in 1812, Delany paid a huge price for his education, four decades before African American spokesman Booker T. Washington would develop his "intense longing to read" in the same Appalachian mountains. Delany's mother, a free African American, had secretly purchased a *New York Primer* from a traveling peddler. A Virginia law passed in 1806 prohibited any blacks, free or enslaved, from receiving an education. The penalty was severe: imprisonment and probable re-enslavement. Delany's mother had already been forced to defend her free status in court. Her husband remained a slave on a plantation near today's Martinsburg, West Virginia. Under their mother's guidance, the children became literate quickly, and often played school in the forests.

Delany's older brother Samuel even developed a special hand at forging travel passes for slaves. When a local white official became suspicious of the children's literacy in 1822, he made a surprise visit and disingenuously questioned their reading and writing abilities. The kids joyfully admitted their achievements. After returning home and hearing about the exchange, Delany's mother packed up a rented wagon and announced that the family was relocating to Martinsburg, to be closer to her enslaved husband.

She feared, of course, an immediate indictment. A sympathetic banker assisted her move. Departing during the day, in order to not attract any suspicion of their motives, they didn't stop their wagon until it had gone sixteen miles beyond the southern border of the free state of Pennsylvania. By 1823, Delany's father, known in western Virginia as an indomitable figure who had openly defied his master's whip, managed to purchase his own freedom through his wife's aid and joined the family in the frontier black community of Kernstown, outside Chambersburg, Pennsylvania.

In later years, the Delany family's dramatic escape into Pennsylvania lent itself to his own version of an American Moses and his search for a "Black Israel." Of course, the lists of modern-day Moses figures abound, but few could stake a claim for a life as prodigiously inventive and dynamic. A pioneering journalist, editor, author and novelist, medical doctor, school principal, African explorer, Civil War military leader and political figure, Delany crossed more than one historic river in the nineteenth century.

SUPPORTED by his determined family, Delany attended school until the age of fifteen, at which point financial necessity forced him to take up manual labor in Cumberland County. His yearning for education never waned. In 1831, the epic year of Nat Turner's slave rebellion in Virginia and the launching of William Lloyd Garrison's radical abolitionist newspaper in Boston, the nineteen-year-old Delany decided to venture to nearby Pittsburgh on foot to further his studies.

He first enrolled in classes in the basement of an African Methodist Episcopal church, falling under the guidance of noted black thinker Lewis Woodson, an advocate for self-help and education. Working his way through school, Delany later took courses in the classics, Greek and Latin, at Jefferson College. During an outbreak of cholera in the area, he found work as an apprentice to a doctor. In 1836, the young Delany opened his own medical studio as a "cupper and leecher," featuring "good, healthy, active leeches." Within a few years, continuing his medical studies under abolitionist doctors in the area, the young doctor added "galvanizing" to his repertoire.

Delany's quick rise to prominence in Pittsburgh in the field of medicine came during a period of significant transformation in the abolitionist movement. The gradual-emancipation tendencies of Lundy and

Embree had largely been rejected by the immediate-abolition and anti-colonization efforts of Garrison and black abolitionists like David Walker, whose "Appeal," a pamphlet distributed widely in 1829, called for rebellion and the end of slavery.

By this time, African Americans had begun organizing national conventions to discuss the course of the abolitionist movement as well as emigration options to Canada and elsewhere abroad. In 1833, under Garrison's leadership, the American Anti-Slavery Society was formed at a convention in Philadelphia as a historic interracial gathering. Demanding immediate emancipation without compensation for slaveholders (compensation being a detail that had held back many of the gradual-emancipation proposals), the society issued its call for "the overthrow of prejudice by the power of love—and the abolition of slavery by the spirit of repentance."

In his early days in Pittsburgh, Delany once wrote, the Northern white abolitionists had made his "tender heart leap with anxiety in anticipation of the promises then held out by the prime movers in the cause of our elevation." A Pennsylvania law prohibiting free African Americans from voting in 1838 devastated these sentiments. It completely destroyed whatever faith Delaney had entrusted in the abolitionists and "free state" politicians.

In his book *The Condition, Elevation, Emigration, and Destiny of the Colored People of the United States, Politically Considered,* published in 1852, he would refer to this time as a tipping point in his views: "Denied an equality not only of political, but natural rights, in common with the rest of our fellow citizens, there is no species of degradation to which we are not subject. . . . [T]hose of their descendants who are freemen even in the nonslaveholding States, occupy the very same positions politically, religiously, civilly and socially, (with but few exceptions), as the bondman occupies in the slave States."

For Delany and a new generation of black abolitionists, many of whom had escaped from slavery, a decade of virtuous but empty promises and increasingly racist and paternal rhetoric among emancipationists had resulted in little gain. He declared that the African Americans' dependence on whites had made blacks "doomed to disappointment," relegating them to a "mere secondary, underling position." Acts of violence and kidnappings of free African Americans were on the rise; riots had broken out against blacks in numerous cities, including nearby Philadelphia. The market demands for slaves had grown in the South and the slaveholding Republic of Texas. Stricter laws and punishment had been meted out against slaves, fugitives, and antislavery advocates.

Unlike white abolitionists, of course, Delany's views had been informed by real-life experience. He had grown up the free child of an enslaved father. Seeking a better understanding of the country at large, he had even made a risky trip by boat down the Ohio and Mississippi rivers in 1839, arriving in New Orleans. Armed only with his "free papers," he ventured into the Choctaw Nation in Arkansas and then over to the independent plains of Texas. Delany's fact-finding journey served many purposes: It generated the details of a future novel, provided the social activist with a firsthand view of the slaveholding Deep South and Texas, and gave a glimpse of possible land tracts for Delany's growing interest in creating a "Black Israel."

The journey also came at a critical time of soul-searching for Delany. He began to formulate his ideas and notes on black independence and the insufferable consequences of white control. He would later write: "We must have a position, independently of anything, pertaining to white men as nations. . . . I am heartily sick of whimpering, whining and sniveling at the feet of the white men."

Back in Pittsburgh, he found his fellow antislavery advocates stuck in a rut of despair. Responding to calls for an independent black wing of the abolitionist movement, another convention of black social figures proposed to launch a new African American newspaper in 1840. The initial investment and economic uncertainty of such a venture, however, delayed any move. Most viewed journalism schemes as laudable but disaster-prone, especially in raising capital and advertising revenue from black merchants. The convention advocates doubted that a critical mass, defined as one thousand subscribers, could be found. The pioneering efforts of black journalists Samuel Cornish and John Russwurm dampened any enthusiasm.

Their landmark African American publication in New York City, *Freedom's Journal*, had failed to attract enough support in 1827; Russwurm ended up emigrating to Liberia and founding the *Liberian Herald*, while the more conservative Cornish, a Presbyterian minister, edited two more incarnations of the newspaper over the next decade. His last journal, the *Colored American*, collapsed in 1842.

By 1843, there was no exclusively African American newspaper in the country. Amid an air of hopelessness and financial morass among black abolitionists and their supporters, the restless Delany decided he could no longer wait on the reluctant advocates.

ENDOWED with a handful of promises and a surplus of personal energy, Delany published the first issue of the *Mystery* in Pittsburgh in the fall of 1843. The newspaper's motto trumpeted its unequivocal commitment to African heritage and self-reliance: "And Moses Was Learned in All the Wisdom of the Egyptians." Like Embree, Lundy, and Royall, Delany was *the* staff, serving as writer, editor, and publisher; the newspaper, as such, was his personal organ. Ads for his medical practice even ran on the front page.

Far from being an advocate of black separatism at the time, however, despite Delany's misgivings about white abolitionists and the free-state politicians, the *Mystery*'s opening statement couched its pious mission in terms of universal equality: "The paper shall be free, independent and untrammeled and whilst it shall aim at the Moral Elevation of the Africo American and African race, civilly, politically and religiously, yet, it shall support no distinctive principles of race."

For the next year and a half, the *Mystery* defied the economic odds and rose in distinction as the nation's only African American newspaper. "Far west" in the Alleghenies, it remained an important reference point in the antislavery movement until Delany's departure. Charging an annual $1.50 fee, it drew subscribers from around the country; it became an institution in the black communities in Pittsburgh and Philadelphia. Most importantly for Delany's sense of integrity and success, his articles reappeared in other abolitionist and mainstream newspapers. His chronicles of the Great Fire in Pittsburgh in 1845 were even republished in a few proslavery newspapers. His relentless investigations of kidnappings and slave stealing in the border states commanded attention as well and occasionally ran as news items in other Pittsburgh and Pennsylvania newspapers. The *Mystery*'s success compelled the other Pittsburgh newspapers to finally recognize the news and events among its sizable black community and Delany's role as an intellectual and public spokesman.

Garrison, especially, reprinted untold articles in his Boston-based *Liberator*, including an often-quoted piece Delany had written on the "long gestation of high culture." When confronted with the challenge that African Americans had not produced a sufficient number of intellectuals and artists to justify equal treatment, Delany recalled Thomas Jefferson's defense of the Americans when they were charged with the same by the British:

> *The American statesman quickly replied that, when the United States had been an independent government as long as Greece was before she produced her Homer, Socrates, and Demosthenes, and Rome, before she produced her Virgil, Horace, and her Cicero; or when this country had been free as long as England was before she produced her Pope and Dryden, then he would be ready to answer that question. . . . With this cursory view of the subject, then, all that we have in conclusion to say is that if we produced any equals at all, while we are in the present state, to say the least of it, we have done as much as Greece, Rome, England or America.*

The *Mystery* reached a personal high, and a closing chapter, when two of the most outspoken abolitionist leaders of the age, Garrison and Frederick Douglass, arrived in Pittsburgh. Douglass had reached celebrity status in America and abroad. Having escaped from slavery in Maryland in 1838, he quickly rose to become one of the great orators and writers of the abolitionist movement. Joining up with Garrison, Douglass drew large crowds on his and Garrison's tour through Pennsylvania in the summer of

1847. The crowds were not always favorable; the two abolitionists had to flee for their lives after being attacked in Harrisburg. The reception in Pittsburgh, however, was "electrifying," according to Garrison. They were most impressed by Delany, who had spoken on the same platform. Douglass declared that Delany was one of "the most open, free, generous and zealous laborers in the cause of our enslaved brethren." The famous abolitionists did not flatter the Pittsburgh speaker in words only. They invited Delany to join their lecture tour in another city.

In defending Douglass in the *Mystery,* he wrote of the "injury, insult and degradation, concomitant with Slavery . . . sanctioned by the Constitution and upheld and supported by the Union." In this reality for blacks, he declared, "No union with slaveholders—Perish the Union or any Government rather than to be upheld by the forfeiture of the liberties of the people." Over the course of his life, Delany thrust the ideals of the American Constitution and its self-evident truths into the face of prejudice; he invoked the country's founding fathers as exemplars.

The meeting in Pittsburgh was providential. Quietly formulating a plan by themselves, outside the purview of the dominating figure of Garrison, Douglass and Delany agreed to join forces and launch a new African American newspaper.

Later that fall, Delany sold the *Mystery* to the African Methodist Episcopal Church association. He framed his departure from Pittsburgh, hardly a risk-free and dauntless transition for his family and medical practice, as a duty "we must obey." His newspaper had essentially fulfilled its purpose, serving as a bridge for a new generation of African Americans and abolitionists. Over the course of the *Mystery*'s four years of publication, Delany proudly noted that eleven more abolitionist newspapers had emerged in the country.

DELANY'S first assignment as coeditor for the *North Star* highlighted his role as a Southern Appalachian. From Douglass's perspective, Delany was a westerner who understood the ways and wiles of those on the frontier. He asked Delany to make a western tour across the Appalachians and

Ohio Valley to drum up support for the newspaper and to file dispatches of his lectures and observations.

During the journey, Delany had one of his most spiritual, even mystical moments, in crossing the Southern Appalachians. In a letter to Douglass, Delany confessed, "It is only in the mountains that I can fully appreciate my existence as a man in America, and my own native land."

It would be an overstatement to assert that the West Virginia–born Delany considered himself a Southern Appalachian mountaineer; the urbane gentleman had firmly cultivated his sense of place in the river city of Pittsburgh and its sophisticated, urban black upper class. But his West Virginian mountain roots, with their conflicting origins of freedom and terror, forever shadowed his view of the possibilities of emancipation in the United States. While always reminding his audiences that he had been "born free" to a courageous mother in the Mountain South, Delany often recalled the "torture of knowing his father to have to serve fifty four years of his life in Virginia slavery, and was now only free of his will, having walked away."

The western tour for the *North Star* churned out some of the most fascinating and informative portraits of travel writing by African Americans in the mid-nineteenth century. Few other writers ever gained Delany's insights into the successes of black communities or described the horrific accounts of slavery and prejudice in their daily lives. Traveling across Kentucky, Ohio, and Michigan, Delany detailed the achievements of African American merchants and free farmers in the various towns and prairies. Any sense of hope, however, succumbed to the reality of unremitting prejudice. Attacked physically on more than one occasion, Delany recorded abolitionist activities in the areas and increasingly became more inured to the limits of black advancement in an age of "black codes," laws that prevented African Americans from voting, defending themselves in court, or participating in the local economies. Toward the end of his journey, chronicling the case of fugitive Kentucky slaves who had found refuge in Michigan only to have the judge rule in favor of the fugitive-slave hunters, Delany wrote angrily that "every colored man in the nominally free States . . . is reduced to abject slavery."

DELANY'S joint venture with Douglass did not last long. Delany left the newspaper within eighteen months. While the two men would disagree bitterly on a number of issues over the next two decades—most importantly on the role of white abolitionists in the antislavery movement, integration versus black separatism, and the cause of black-led efforts for emigration to Africa and elsewhere abroad—their split at the *North Star* was probably over the economic challenge of the two men maintaining a livelihood through abolitionist journalism.

Delany fell into a secondary role in the abolitionist movement at this point. The newspaper was soon renamed *Frederick Douglass' Paper* and helped to solidify Douglass's high profile in the nation.

DELANY did not simply vanish from the national scene. Wishing to ground his medical career in the advances of modern science, he entered the Harvard Medical School in 1850. The white students protested, however, and within a short time Oliver Wendell Holmes, the dean of the faculty, approved Delany's dismissal.

Left distraught and angered by the Harvard experience, Delany drifted to New York City. His resentment had been exacerbated by the passing of the Fugitive Slave Act, which opened the gates to bounty hunters for escaped slaves and resulted in terrorizing free blacks across the country. Delany sat down and quickly wrote his first major book, *The Condition, Elevation, Emigration, and Destiny of the Colored People of the United States, Politically Considered.* Published in Philadelphia in 1852, the book shattered any precepts of white benevolence, questioned the possibility of political and social equality for blacks in American society, and called on African Americans to assume a larger role for their own welfare at home and abroad. It issued a pioneering manifesto for black separatist thought in the United States. Delany threw out a challenge to Douglass and other black abolitionists: "Have we not now sufficient intelligence among us to understand our true position to realize our actual condition, and determine for ourselves what is best to be done? If we have not now, we never shall have, and should at once cease prating about our equality, capacity, and all that."

As a clarion call for black independence, and with the author more convinced than ever that emigration orchestrated and led by African Americans, not whites, provided the only means for equality, Delany's work became the primary voice against Douglass's integrationist ideas. The book also functioned, in some respects, as a preemptive gesture to the growing commotion over Harriet Beecher Stowe's *Uncle Tom's Cabin,* published that same year. Delany excoriated Stowe for the novel's depiction of irresolute and deprived blacks in need of white assistance.

After serving as a doctor in another cholera outbreak in Pittsburgh in 1854, Delany finally packed up and relocated to Chatham, Canada. He attended John Brown's secret meeting at Chatham in 1858, where the revolutionary unveiled plans that would lead to the raid on the federal arsenal at Harper's Ferry the next year. Delany, like most black leaders at the convention, was sympathetic to Brown's mission, but leery of his plan.

In the meantime, Delany had been writing his own version of a slave rebellion in novelistic form, driven in large part by his response to Stowe's novel. First serialized in the New York–based *Anglo-African Magazine* in the early spring of 1859, several months before Brown's raid, *Blake; or, The Huts of America,* chronicled the exploits of an alter ego, Henry Blake, an African American insurgent who travels through the South, Canada, across the seas to Africa, and then back to Cuba in a crusade to stir a revolt. Like Brown, Blake views the Southern Appalachians as a possible place of guerilla warfare for the slaves. Unlike Brown, who was convinced that the mountaineers would rise up in support, Blake's sense of white support is a cynical one, based more on corruption than a change of heart: "Money alone will carry you," he tells one slave, "through the white mountains." Nonetheless, he envisions a "day of deliverance" for the African slaves. His parting words are unforgiving: "Woe be unto those devils of whites, I say!" Delany published more chapters in 1861–1862, though the novel itself, one of the earliest fiction achievements by an African American, did not appear in book form until 1970.

While Brown led his small company on its suicidal mission at Harper's Ferry in 1859, Delany undertook a commissioned journey for the Canadian Emigration Convention and sailed to West Africa. After meeting with African and colonization leaders in Liberia, he ventured deep into today's southwestern Nigeria and then led an expedition along the Ogun River into Yoruba territory. At the Egba capital of Abeokuta, Delany made a formal agreement for a future settlement of free African Americans. Delany's motivation, of course, was not only emigration, but the self-appointed role of bringing "Christian civilization" to the African natives. He published a scientific report on his explorations in the Niger Valley, ending with the appeal, "Africa for the African race, and black men to rule them." After making a highly publicized lecture tour through Great Britain, Delany returned to Chatham.

The Civil War brought Delany back to the United States. While he would never abandon his Niger Valley emigration project, which failed to generate enough financial support, Delany championed the war as a last chance for redemption in the country. After rejecting a number of appeals for the development of black military units, in 1865 President Abraham Lincoln finally appointed Delany—whom he referred to in a letter as a "most extraordinary and intelligent black man"—the first African American major in the Union forces, instead of Delany's long-time rival Douglass.

Despite the prestige of the appointment toward the end of the war, Delany's star on the national scene failed to rise. His campaign to be appointed ambassador to Liberia never materialized. His relocation to South Carolina as a military leader and then as an official with the Freedmen's Bureau led to a career in real estate and politics that became mired in the machinations of Reconstruction. Fed up with the abuses and delays of the Republicans and their Reconstruction policies, Delany even supported a former Confederate for governor in 1874. The tactic backfired, ultimately leading to violent attacks by other blacks when he was on speaking tours. Further alienated by politics, Delany returned to his emigration schemes and authored a rather skewed but inventive book on racial and genetic differences in 1879.

By the time Delany had crossed the Appalachians again to join his family in Ohio in the 1880s, his ideas of black separatism and African ascendancy curried little favor in the country. The projects of a young black leader, Booker T. Washington, who had risen from the salt-packing houses and coal mines in the mountains of West Virginia, would soon command the nation's attention for his mix of industrial education and nonconfrontational assimilation.

Delany's death in Wilberforce, Ohio, in 1885 passed with little notice. It took nearly a century before a new era of black nationalists rediscovered his writings and life story.

No one understood the immense changes taking place in the South in the 1880s better than a young newspaperman in the Southern Appalachian stronghold of Chattanooga. Sympathetic to the politics of the conservative Southern Democrats, Adolph Ochs would have approved of Delany's harsh critique of the Republicans and their Reconstruction plans. The rest of Delany's black nationalist and emigration ideas, however, would have fallen on deaf ears.

Ochs, though, was no stranger to African Americans. He railed against the lynchings and "mobocracy" that occurred in his town and surroundings; he supported the establishment of public schools for blacks, though strictly through segregationist efforts. The ambitious publisher shared the muddy streets of the emerging industrial river town in the lower Tennessee Valley with over seven thousand black inhabitants, who made up one-third of Chattanooga's residents. Two African Americans ran his paper's first printing press.

Like Royall and Delany, Ochs had his eyes on a national arena. Before the century's end, he walked the streets of New York City as one of the most important publishers in the world.

Born in Cincinnati to Jewish immigrants from Germany in 1858, Ochs's Southern Appalachian story begins after the Civil War, when his father, a Bavarian linguist and Union soldier who had briefly been a teacher in Mount Sterling, Kentucky, drove his family in a covered wagon across the Cumberland Gap into the Tennessee mountains in 1864. Ochs's father was a compassionate polyglot whose intellectual interests somehow derailed any financial success. His mother came from a Confederate-leaning New Orleans family that had fled Germany during the revolutionary upheavals in the mid-nineteenth century. The family settled in Knoxville, an Appalachian town still raising itself from the dust after the brutal Civil War campaigns.

The Jewish experience in Southern Appalachia remains another hidden chapter in American history. Although waves of Jewish immigrants arrived in the Mountain South's coalfields and townships during the great migrations of Eastern Europeans to the United States in the 1880s, Jewish pioneers had already been crossing into the Appalachian frontier for nearly a century. The first synagogue in Wheeling was founded in 1849. By the end of the century, synagogues appeared in all the major towns and cities; nine synagogues dotted the rural coalfields in southern West Virginia, Virginia, and Kentucky. In Knoxville, Ochs's father served as a substitute rabbi, assisting in the formation of that town's first synagogue.

Despite his active role in the public affairs of Knoxville, Ochs's father never quite earned enough to support his family. At the age of eleven, Adolph had to drop out of school and find work as an office boy at the *Knoxville Chronicle* newspaper. He never lacked for ambition; he cleaned the offices "so methodically" that he was promoted to delivery boy. Ochs's publishing destiny was cemented at the age of thirteen, when he became a printer's devil, a jack-of-all-trades position that gave him firsthand experience with the entire publishing process.

Ochs hadn't completely abandoned his studies. Although he attended classes at the Hampden-Sydney Academy and eventually took night courses at the local university, he described the newspaper office as his "high school and university," falling under the tutelage of editor William Rule, a high-minded Republican. Afraid of walking home at night in the dark, Ochs spent the late hours at the newspaper's printing room, waiting for an escort. In the process, he became immersed in the trade.

Nonetheless, as a restless teenager, Ochs wanted to throw his newspaper experience to the wind and venture to California. He made it as far as

Louisville, Kentucky, where he found work as a printer at a local newspaper. Homesick and disheartened by the move, he returned to Knoxville in less than a year, where he took a job as a printer and reporter for a competing newspaper, the *Knoxville Tribune*. The change was propitious. Colleagues from the Knoxville paper had plans to launch a daily in Chattanooga; they sent Ochs to the Southern river town to serve as the advertising solicitor in 1877.

Despite its company's Knoxville experience and resources, the newspaper failed to survive the rough economy of the emerging town. The competing daily, the *Chattanooga Times,* was also deep in debt. Left penniless by the move, Ochs remained in Chattanooga. In search of a foothold, he assembled and sold a business directory. When the *Times* announced its intentions to close, Ochs, who had developed his contacts in the business community, somehow managed to convince the publisher to sell him the paper for $800, assuming $1,500 of debts. Too young to sign the deal himself, Ochs had to summon his father to town. With no funds of his own, and banking on the supportive contacts he had made through the town directory, Ochs ended up borrowing $300 to buy a controlling share of the paper.

At the age of twenty, too young to vote and growing a dark mustache to mask his inexperience, Adolph Ochs became the publisher of the *Chattanooga Times*. The newspaper, Ochs declared, "was utterly dilapidated, demoralized, and publicly and privately anathematized." But it was his.

THE WASHBASIN settlements of the Cherokee and other tribes in Chattanooga had been founded for their pivotal place along the Tennessee River gorge. The settlements had first been called Ross's Landing, named after a Cherokee trading post. Mountain summits ringed the area like tabletops, providing a view deep into the Appalachian forests. The Creek had referred to the most auspicious mountain as the "rock that comes to a point," while the Cherokee term for the area translated into "mountains looking at each other."

Over the years, American frontier people and militias used those facing mountains in the brutal removal of the Cherokee and Creek. A generation later, Union soldiers gained the upper ridges by 1863, in a crucial Civil War battle in the Southern Appalachians. The city's first college, the Lookout Mountain Educational Institute, laid its foundation on the summit in 1866.

Ochs's tenure in Chattanooga corresponded with the birth of the New South agenda, marking the leap into an industrial economy and heralding a massive change taking place in Southern Appalachia. In the aftermath of the Civil War, Northerners (many of them Union war veterans), outside corporations, and longtime pioneering families had trundled into Chattanooga to embark on a campaign to exploit the vast natural resources of the mountains and valleys. The river city itself, described by a *Harper's Magazine* travel writer as "a brown and white mound of smoke and steam," became a hub on the ABC (Atlanta–Birmingham–Chattanooga) axis for the vibrant steel and iron industry in the New South.

With Knoxville and Chattanooga serving as two key launching pads for speculation, agents for absentee lumber and coal barons based in the northeast swept into the Mountain South and set off a frenzied industrial boom. The mountains had become "a country of infinite wealth-creating possibilities," according to one agent. In the forefront of this plunder, newspapers trumpeted "resources great enough to enrich empires."

Private empires in the timber, coal, and cotton mills rose within a generation, leaving an entirely different Southern Appalachia in their wake. "A huge compulsive greed had been at work," North Carolina novelist Thomas Wolfe declared. "Something had come into the wilderness, and left the barren land." In his landmark analysis of industrialization's impact on Appalachia in this period, historian Ronald Eller concurs with Wolfe:

The industrial wonders of the age promised more than they in fact delivered, for the profits taken from the rich natural resources of the region flowed out of the mountains, with little benefit to the mountain people themselves. For a relative handful of owners and managers, the new order yielded riches unimaginable a few decades before; for thousands of mountaineers, it brought a life of struggle, hardship, and despair.

Ochs viewed this disparity between progress and poverty in a different light. He was part of a new breed of Appalachian capitalists. He had come of age in Knoxville amid the machinations of the Reconstruction policies of President Andrew Johnson, a transplanted Appalachian himself from the nearby eastern Tennessee town of Greeneville. Deep into printer's ink, Ochs had witnessed Knoxville's rise as a key industrial and railroad depot for the Southern mountains in the volatile decade of the 1870s.

He declared in his own newspaper that he had "become a citizen—a man," celebrating his twenty-first birthday in Chattanooga. In his first issue of the *Times,* he announced that the paper would be an "organ of the business, commercial and productive, of Chattanooga, and of the mineral and agricultural districts of Tennessee, North Georgia and Alabama." In less than two years at the helm of the fledgling newspaper, Ochs sounded the bell for Chattanooga's plan to become the Pittsburgh of the South. "Go ring your bell and fire your gun, shout for glory," the *Times* announced, as the last tie for a new railroad line was hammered into existence in 1880. "The Boom has come."

From the muddy streets and open sewers that first had met the young teenager, Chattanooga flourished in the Gilded Age, doubling its population within a decade. With the boom came underground sanitation, paved streets, public hospitals and schools, railroads, electricity, mills, and factories. The scope of economic transformation in Tennessee in these years was breathtaking: By 1890, the state produced $72 million in manufactured goods, compared to $700,000 during the Civil War era.

As a self-proclaimed progressive businessman in the New South, Ochs and his *Times* promoted virtually every campaign for urban growth and development in the city. He launched an additional business publication, the *Tradesman,* to advance industrial schemes in the region. Ochs did not merely sit aside as an observer; he invested heavily in real estate and business ventures. He also served on the local school board and joined various fraternal organizations.

With the city's progress, the *Times* grew in readership and ambition. The original four-page sheet had a circulation of 250. Ochs managed to turn a profit within the first year. His brothers joined the staff within a short time, expanding the newspaper and its sections. Readership grew to the thousands. In less than two years, Ochs purchased the remaining shares of the *Times,* though this time he had to pay $5,500 (as compared with his initial $250).

By 1892, the *Times* had become one of the most influential and widely read newspapers in the South; the paper's success led Ochs to construct an imposing building—aptly named the Times Building—in the city for his printing operations. Ochs must have been overwhelmed by the city's dedication; over ten thousand attended the ceremonies for the six-story tower.

As a keynote speaker at the National Editorial Association in Saint Paul in 1891, the young Southern Appalachian publisher challenged his fellow journalists to raise the standards of their newspapers. While falling in line with the conservative Southern Democrats of his age, Ochs had made a significant departure in his paper's reporting of the news. "The day of the organ," he admonished the crowd in Saint Paul, "if not past, is rapidly passing. A journal conducted as a newspaper [with the emphasis on the news] is the newspaper of the future."

Since his first issue of the *Chattanooga Times,* Ochs had made his editorial intentions clear. "Your only policy," he told his editor in chief, "is to have no policy—no policy, that is, except to be right." In the *Times* prospectus, Ochs announced his refusal to be a front for the pet project schemes of publishers like Royall or the editorial crusades of journalists like Delany. The *Times* would make "no appeals, but rely upon that sense of propriety and justice which must teach every intelligent citizen that the obligation between himself and the paper is a mutual one . . . in short, we shall conduct our business on business principles, neither seeking nor giving 'sops' and 'donations.'" And while it could be argued that Ochs's business principles, functioning as an indispensable organ for commerce, propagated its own New South agenda, his obsession with getting the news story right was notable for the period.

This sense of journalistic integrity did not go unnoticed. National political and literary figures, including President Grover Cleveland, courted Ochs and paid visits to Chattanooga. Joined by his wife, "Effie" Wise, whose father had founded the Hebrew Union College and became a rabbinical leader in the Reform Judaism movement, Ochs emerged as one of the New South's most prominent publishers and Jewish figures.

Harry Alloway, a *New York Times* business reporter, made his own visit in 1890. Ostensibly in the region to investigate the growth in industrial development, Alloway struck up a close friendship with Ochs, who served as his host. In a casual conversation, Ochs had mentioned his admiration for the *New York Times* and its potential market.

Alloway never forgot the discussion. Six years later, as the *New York Times* struggled financially, its circulation having plummeted to less than nine thousand readers (with twenty thousand copies a day), Alloway and other business associates alerted Ochs to the paper's troubles. The Southern Appalachian quickly ventured to Manhattan by train. Despite his ambition and success in Chattanooga, the thirty-eight-year-old publisher first assumed he was not big enough for the task of taking over the *Times*. Still reeling from the effects of an economic depression in 1893 and unable to compete with the penny presses of William Randolph Hearst's *Journal* and Joseph Pulitzer's *World*, whose rivalry of the newspaper titans had begun to make headlines of its own, the *Times* was losing $1,000 a day, with thousands of dollars in debt. Pulitzer even referred to the *Times* as moribund. The paper had the lowest circulation in the city.

Recalling his own daunting task to resurrect the *Chattanooga Times*, Ochs couldn't resist the challenge in New York City. But he first had to convince the *New York Times* management that a small town Southern Appalachian publisher could rescue the paper. He called on all of his past acquaintances, including President Cleveland, for support. One of the main political questions of the day, the debate over the gold standard, had actually thrust Ochs into the company of prominent Republicans in Washington, D.C., and on Wall Street.

While the interviews and negotiations went favorably, Ochs turned down an initial offer to manage the *Times* syndicate. He wanted to run the paper on his own terms. Within six months, assembling a group of backers, Ochs invested his entire savings, mortgaged his Chattanooga assets, and borrowed enough money for his investors to gain an absolute majority of shares. On August 19, 1896, Ochs introduced himself to the *New York Times* readers as the new publisher.

The Chattanoogan brought his Southern Appalachian style of journalism into the national arena, vowing to "conduct a high-standard newspaper, clean, dignified and trustworthy," directed toward "thoughtful, pure-minded people." The paper would continue as a nonpartisan entity, with a "devotion to the cause of sound money and tariff reform, opposition to wastefulness and speculation in administering public affairs." It would "assure the free exercise of a sound conscience."

In the face of the incredible circulation of the *Journal* and the *Herald*, which fed off each other's flamboyant headlines, Ochs provided the newspaper with its new motto: "All the News That's Fit to Print." His plan was not limited to pious phrases. Against the advice of his colleagues, Ochs took a tremendous risk in 1898, during the newspaper battles over the Spanish-American War in Cuba, by lowering the price of the *Times* to one penny. As a symbolic gesture of his refusal to wallow in the wildness of yellow journalism, which tended to write its scandalous headlines before finding the news stories, Ochs also announced that he would publish a Sunday magazine instead of comics. This gesture, in fact, was more than sheer symbolism: Yellow journalism had taken its name from an extremely popular cartoon strip, *Yellow Kid,* which had first appeared in Pulitzer's paper in the advent of color comic sections. In 1896, the same year Ochs took control of the *Times,* Hearst had managed to buy off the cartoon's artist and bring him over to his stable. Undaunted by the ploy, Pulitzer continued to run the *Yellow Kid* cartoon with another artist. The celebrated Sunday book section of the *Times* soon appeared, though it initially ran as a Saturday *Review of Books and Arts.*

Ochs's success at the *New York Times* has been chronicled by many and needs little additional praise. By 1900, he had turned the newspaper into a profitable venture and became the majority stock-owner. Under his dominating personality, the *Times* emerged as one of the most respected and relied-on journals in the world; circulation surpassed 100,000 by the turn of the century. It boasted nearly 700,000 readers by the time of Ochs's death, three decades later. Following his own example in Chattanooga, Ochs left an architectural legacy as well, constructing the newspaper's new building headquarters, and subsequently the Annex, in today's Times Square.

OCHS's wife, when first learning of his success in taking the reins of the *New York Times,* reminded him that he was still "the little boy that had tramped the streets of Knoxville." Over the course of his forty years in New York City, in fact, Ochs continued to refer to Chattanooga as his home.

That sense of home occurred on many levels for the publisher. For one, the Southern Appalachian river city had rarely roiled in the muck of anti-Semitism. Some of Ochs's worst racial detractors had come from Hearst's New York newspaper, which reveled in spreading theories of Jewish conspiracy and once portrayed the publisher as "an uneducated . . . oily little commercial gentleman." Nonetheless, speaking in later years to a Jewish congregation in Chattanooga, Ochs encouraged the people to "live quietly, happily, unostentatiously," adding that they should not demonstrate "knowing too much." Ochs's brother George, on the other hand, officially filed to change his surname to Oaks in 1917, after an anti-German rage swept across the United States. George, who had twice served as mayor of Chattanooga, was living in Philadelphia at the time, where he had formerly run the *Philadelphia Ledger,* another Ochs newspaper.

Lookout Mountain, overlooking Chattanooga with its reminder of the Southern Appalachian range, forever served as the symbol of the region and the nation's unity, for the publisher. As early as the 1890s, Ochs had purchased part of the "sacred ground," where Civil War veterans and tourists flocked for the panoramic views, as a part of a longtime campaign to create a park. Even after his departure for New York City, Ochs and his brothers continued to campaign for the preservation of the mountain from reckless development plans. Their dedication eventually resulted in the establishment of the country's first national military park, on Lookout Mountain.

Adolph Ochs died in Chattanooga in 1935. He had "ascended into the hill of the Lord," according to one newspaper tribute.

Chapter Six

THE GREAT AMERICAN INDUSTRIAL SAGA

+~+

This is what I want you to do. I want you to hide your disgust, take
no heed to your clean clothes, and come right down with me—here, into the
thickest of the fog and mud and foul effluvia. I want you to hear this story.

—REBECCA HARDING, "Life in the Iron Mills," 1861

IN THE SPRING OF 1861, the country on the verge of fracturing into
civil war, a short story appeared in the *Atlantic Monthly*. The tale stunned
the nation's most elite readership with its unwavering descriptions of
labor conditions in the iron and cotton mills in western Virginia. The
narrative was audacious; it mocked the dilettante ways of its affluent
readers; it challenged the "Egoist, or Pantheist, or Arminian, busy in
making straight paths," to stop what he or she was doing. For the
unsigned author hailing from the "back hills of Virginia" (according to
her patrician New England editors), "there is a secret down here in this
nightmare fog, that has lain dumb for centuries: I want to make it a real
thing for you."

Six years before French novelist Emile Zola's epics among the working class ushered in an era of literary naturalism, "Life in the Iron Mills"
leaped from the most prestigious pages of the literary world as a
groundbreaking American fiction endeavor. For the first time in the

legendary Boston magazine's four-year history, readers encountered a lyrical and often scolding account of the wretched conditions of immigrants and the underclass trapped in a subterranean world. Written from the perspective of a woman tucked behind the curtains of Southern protocol, the story shattered the constraints of the fainthearted morality tales that cluttered the literature of the "feminine fifties" and launched the young author, and her Appalachian base, into the front ranks of American realism.

"Life in the Iron Mills" tells the story of two Welsh immigrants, Hugh, the iron puddler and sculptor, and his cousin Deborah, a cotton mill worker, who inhabit a western Virginia river town. They are emaciated figures in their teens, deformed by their labors. Life revolves around the hellish furnaces at the mills and their moss-ridden hovel in a basement. These characters are not just window dressing for a greater romance. The narrator depicts Hugh and Deborah with souls and intellects and whose aspirations are no different from those of the rich. "The note is the same," the narrator tells us, "be the octave high or low." When lovesick Deborah takes Hugh his meals during the night shift, we get a glimpse of the "devil's place," and the mill's inferno aura.

Enter a journalist (perhaps a young Adolph Ochs), the mill owner's son, a doctor, and a Northern visitor, whose tour of the factory has been prolonged by the outside rain. Biding their time for the storm to pass, they examine Hugh and in the shadows, his sculptures, which have been carved from korl, the waxen refuse of the pig iron. They admire the Welshman's talent and eye for anatomy, especially in a statue of a nude woman with a "wild, eager face." They ask Hugh to explain his work. "She be hungry," he says. Not a hunger for food, he adds, but something "to make her live, I think—like you." The visitors are more amused than moved, and dismiss Hugh's thoughts. They launch into a philosophical bantering over the "lives of the wretched" and the possibilities of social reform.

"Be just," the narrator scolds. She holds the visitors, not completely devoid of empathy, to their words. Impatient with the talk, the mill owner's son throws up his hands and declares, "I wash my hands of all social problems—slavery, caste, white or black." The doctor sighs in disbelief. The journalist has vanished.

"You have it in you to be a great sculptor, a great man," the doctor tells Hugh.

"Will you help me?" the Welsh puddler responds.

"I have not the money, boy," the doctor says.

Money, declares the Northern visitor in his cynical way, is the cure for "all the world's diseases." And while he continues a philosophical repartee peppered with French and Latin, Hugh and Deborah take him for his word. In the end, the Northern provocateur dismisses the doctor's talk of reform and concludes, "In this lowest deep—thieves, Magdalens, negroes . . . some day, out of their bitter need will be thrown up their own lightbringer—their Jean Paul, their Cromwell, their Messiah."

The visitors toss coins to the mill workers and depart, but we soon find that Deborah, hovering like the apparition of the korl woman in the shadows, has picked the Northerner's pocket and stolen a fortune that could forever change their lives. She presents the bill to Hugh as a gift to another future. The mill worker staggers through the town in agony, clutching the bill as if it is a ticket to freedom, tortured by the moral cost of thievery to rectify his position in society. His decision is made for him; he is arrested and tried for robbery, and is given nineteen years of hard labor, a sentence that mirrors his age and labor in the mills. "Serves him right," the once caring doctor grumbles.

Deborah lands in jail as an accomplice and is sentenced to three years. Even worse, she witnesses Hugh's final act as a sculptor, as he takes his own life in the neighboring prison cell. Beyond reform or revolt, the answer for Deborah lies in the touching words of a Quaker visitor, who motions to the Appalachian range as her refuge, telling Deborah, "[Begin] thy life again—there on the hills."

THIS WAS Rebecca Harding's vision of industrial Appalachia, and it was an incendiary one. It served as her first offering to the outside world of another Appalachia—a modern geographical term, of course, not yet in vogue, but soon to be conjured in a "discovery" of a "strange land and peculiar people."

In the eyes of Harding and subsequent generations of many Appalachian women writers, Appalachia was not simply a literary curiosity or a remote travel destination. It was the burning ground of industrial America; the region's coal, at the time of her first story, literally fueled the nation's mills and factories. Her pioneering work placed the Southern mountains at the forefront of the industrial upheaval taking place in nineteenth-century America. The region became the setting for many important and classic American stories in our country's struggle over brutal labor practices and dramatic acts of resistance.

Far from peopling the region with Appalachian-clad Rip Van Winkles or rubes, Harding set the standard for a century of chroniclers in shattering the stereotypes of the mountaineers and hill folk. Her work reminded the country that Appalachia was not a foreign land, but a vital American crossroads of numerous immigrant groups, blacks, and courageous women, all of whom were playing a significant role in our nation's industrial saga.

WHEN the young Rebecca Harding received her first copy of "Life in the Iron Mills" that spring, the muddy towns in western Virginia were in the throes of great turmoil. April, truly, had been a cruel month; in the same days that the story circulated among the literati on the East Coast, Wheeling served notice of its separation from the Confederate brethren in lower Virginia, launching the Wheeling Convention Movement for the establishment of the mountain state of West Virginia. The first shots would soon be fired at Fort Sumter.

Wheeling had been in a state of change for as long as Harding could remember. In the course of her twenty-five years of growing up in Wheeling—born in Alabama, Harding had moved to the river town at the age of five—it had been transformed from a "silent and empty" frontier outpost on the National Road to a highly strategic industrial boomtown in the Ohio Valley. Living near the town market, this daughter of an English businessman had witnessed the massive influx of capital and immigrants into the town, as rolling iron mills and glassworks sprouted along the Ohio.

As a precursor to the industrial phenomenon of coal camps and mill towns that would sweep across the Southern mountains a generation later with Ochs and his New South industrialists, thousands of skilled and unskilled workers from various parts of England, Wales, Poland, Germany, France, and Ireland, along with African and African American slaves, arrived at Southern Appalachia's northern crossroads. By 1861, over thirteen thousand inhabitants, a third of them foreign born, pounded out the nails and iron products and loaded them onto boats for the markets that had arisen with western settlements. In this same period, the workers churned out the materials for more than thirty thousands miles of railroad draped across the growing country.

As the *Emancipator* publisher Elihu Embree demonstrated in eastern Tennessee, the iron industry had been one of the first large-scale industrial economies across the Mountain South. From settlements in northern Virginia to the Carolinas and lower Tennessee Valley, ironworkers had heated and hammered the converted ore into nails, tools and plows, pots and pans, guns and bullets, and numerous other needs long before the American Revolution. Wheeling's industrial rise was related, in many respects, to the nearby mountain deposits of iron ore, coal, and timber required in the rolling mills.

After the decades of boom, Harding's river town had crept through an economic depression in 1857. Cloaked by clouds of smoke—"the idiosyncrasy of this town," Harding wrote—there were "masses of men, with dull, besotted faces bent to the ground, sharpened here and there by pain or cunning; skin and muscle and flesh begrimed with smoke and ashes; stooping all night over boiling caldrons of metal, laired by day in dens of drunkenness and infamy; breathing from infancy to death an air saturated with fog and grease and soot, vileness for body and soul."

The rolling mills lent themselves to otherworldly descriptions. They were cities of fires with "tent-like roofs," according to Harding. Flames of every sort writhed "in tortuous streams through the sand; wide caldrons filled with boiling fire, over which bent ghastly wretches stirring the strange brewing; and through all, crowds of half-clad men, looking like revengeful ghosts in the red light, hurried, throwing masses of glittering fire."

UNLIKE Anne Royall, Harding came from a privileged past that kept her from the hardship of frontier drudgery. Her father was a quirky patrician Englishman, an émigré similar to Ochs's German father, who placed his financial dealings on a secondary level with his intellectual and social interests. The family's house was full of books; Harding's father had a penchant for medieval tales and regaled his daughter with fanciful stories of chivalry. Her mother, however, who came from nearby Washington, Pennsylvania, on the other side of the river, was an independent thinker for her times. Under her tutelage, Harding read Shakespeare and Hawthorne at the age of eight and studied with private tutors. In her mid-teens, she was sent to a private school for girls in her mother's hometown, only to return to the dismal cesspool of Wheeling's streets after her graduation.

The narrator of "Iron Mills" hints at the sheltered life of a young woman whose view of the outside world never veers from behind the curtain of her upstairs window. Her future appears to be as limited as those manacled to the mills. While half of the female workers of her period in Wheeling were foreign-born mill workers or maids, or slaves, young women in Harding's class languished in idleness until their duties of matrimony, a duty Harding spurned until after her literary success in her thirties.

This seclusion made the publication of "Iron Mills" and its biting narrative all the more remarkable. Some critics saw her depictions of the gritty inner workings of the iron mills as a near-miraculous literary effort that should have been outside the purview of her eyes. How did she know? How did a young woman ever glimpse such a wicked place, let alone write about it?

In truth, while the protocol of the times most likely prevented Harding from walking the back warrens of factories alone or hovering in the shadows of whiskey dens, she was wiser in the wiles of Wheeling than we can imagine. Her family's residence was in the heart of the iron mill district, flanking boardinghouses and businesses. She would have been privy to the encounters and stories of her father's dealings—he even served as town treasurer at one point—and his nightly descriptions of "vulgar American life."

Harding also wrote in the late 1850s for the region's largest newspaper, the *Wheeling Intelligencer.* She was not a reporter by any means; she turned in reviews, poems, and editorials for the newspaper. Her interactions with the editor and reporters, however, put her in touch with the daily scandals and crises on Wheeling's changing waterfront. This contact didn't leave her unaffected. Though the editorials of the newspaper were unsigned in this period, some of the writing on the conditions of the poor and living conditions employed a prose style hauntingly similar to that found in "Iron Mills."

All experience aside, Harding's success in getting the mill story accepted by the *Atlantic Monthly* is almost as astonishing as its content or impact on its readers. This was the most prominent journal of the age, the hallowed arena of Ralph Waldo Emerson, Henry David Thoreau, Harriet Beecher Stowe, and Oliver Wendell Holmes, among other luminaries. Harding would later write, "I went to Concord, a young woman from the backwoods, firm in the belief that Emerson was the first of living men." When an envelope from Boston arrived at Harding's home in Wheeling in January 1861, she carried it around unopened for most of the day, convinced it was a rejection letter. Instead, the journal praised her story for its remarkable urgency and writing, promised to publish it, and included a check for $50.

The magazine payment was a tremendous amount for the times, of course. A subsequent letter from the editor offered $100 for the next story. Overwhelmed by the offer, a stunned Harding turned down the advance, preferring to work on her next story without any monetary pressure. Her only request was to remain anonymous. When the editor suggested using a different title for the story, Harding countered with "The Korl Woman."

Fan mail somehow found its way to the western Virginia town. A letter arrived from the legendary Nathaniel Hawthorne himself, quite possibly the most important living American author at that point, requesting a visit during one of his tours to Harper's Ferry. Only a few years prior, Hawthorne had written to his same editor at the *Atlantic Monthly* and complained, "All women, as authors, are feeble and tiresome. I wish they were forbidden to write, on pain of having their faces deeply scarified with an oyster-shell."

The outbreak of war, however, precluded a rendezvous with Hawthorne or any other admirers, for that matter. The "transcendental coterie" had been desperately trying to get its new star writer to New England for a visit. Instead, ensconced in a Union town that would eventually fall under martial law during the Civil War, Harding wrote another story about mill life for the Boston magazine. This time the magazine editors rejected it on the grounds that it was "too gloomy." Appending a sunny ending, Harding resubmitted the story, "Margret Howth," about a young woman bookkeeper in a mill, and "this common every-day drudgery," among men and women in a mill town, "crippled in the slow, silent battle, in your alleys." Set in a frontier town in Indiana, the story was serialized later that fall in the *Atlantic Monthly* and then published in book form to rave reviews.

Harding's debut appeared to be no fluke. One magazine praised her as an American Charlotte Brontë, the English author of recent *Jane Eyre* fame. The *Continental Monthly* recognized Harding's foray into "a new field, right into the rough of real life, bringing out fresher and more varied forms than had been done before." Her focus on common people, namely, industrial workers, impressed the *Continental Monthly* for an understanding that "few, especially in the Atlantic cities, know what becomes of culture among men and women who 'work and weave in endless motion' in the counting-house, or factory, or through daily drudgery and the reverses from wealth to poverty."

According to author Tillie Olsen, who rediscovered the story in a torn edition of the *Atlantic Monthly* in a junk store in Omaha nearly a hundred years later and then set in motion a literary campaign to recover Harding's work, "Life in the Iron Mills" was an event for the times and a literary landmark in modern literary history. Its provocative style startled readers. As one of the first stories to chronicle the misery of mill workers and working-class immigrants in detail, far from any other patronizing portraits found in the era, it shocked the magazine's readership with its "terrible tragedy" of "living death." "In the consciousness of literary America, there had been no dark satanic mills," Olsen wrote. "When industry was considered at all, it was as an invasion of pastoral harmony, a threat of materialism to the spirit. If working people existed—and nowhere were they material for serious attention, let alone a central subject, they were 'clean-haired Yankee mill girls.'"

In effect, Harding's writings about industrial lives had established a new American literary form. The *Continental Monthly* reviewer was right: With "Life in the Iron Mills" and *Margret Howth,* Harding's work emerged as a literary harbinger, foreshadowing the human wreckage of the industrial revolution in Southern Appalachia and the country as a whole. It set the standard of social realism nearly a half century before Upton Sinclair and *The Jungle* heralded an era of muckraking writing. Her uncompromising literary style, especially in "Iron Mills," presented American readers with a riveting account of a previously unknown way of life.

With the country dissolving around her, Harding's writing career had been launched. As the Union's mountain garrison took control of Wheeling, she immediately turned to writing about the war, mountaineers, and rebellious slaves.

THE FETED tour of Boston finally came in late 1862. Hosted by James Fields, the editor of the *Atlantic Monthly,* Harding went from one dining affair and parlor room to the next, meeting Emerson, Holmes, and a timid Louisa May Alcott, who quietly acknowledged Harding as her role model. It must have been a bewildering but gratifying experience for the young writer, on her own for the first time in her life. Removed from the provincial mores of wartime Wheeling, she found herself surrounded by free-spirited transcendentalists and even women who exhibited their "desire for men." Alcott's renowned father, the eccentric philosopher—or "sage of Concord," according to Hawthorne—had made a visit himself to meet Harding. He was anxious to know "what kind of human beings come up from the back hills in Virginia."

Whether or not he was speaking in jest—out of all the transcendentalists, Alcott was the only one who had spent any considerable time in the South, including a stint as a peddler in his teens in Virginia and the Carolinas—his comment reflected a view by outsider writers of the inhabitants of Southern Appalachia: the coven of the back-hills creature.

In 1863, Harding married Clarke Davis, a Philadelphia editor and abolitionist who had originally contacted her with a fan letter about "Life in the Iron Mills." She became Rebecca Harding Davis. Her career over the next five decades included a dozen novels and hundreds of stories and essays, many dealing with the dispossessed women of her times. Her star faded over the years, however. The quality of her work was irregular at best. Nonetheless, as a pioneer in American realism, she played a key role in writing about "life in the commonplace," which was often overlooked or chronicled in tawdry romances. Her fame became secondary to that of her son, Richard Harding Davis, who emerged as a celebrated novelist and journalist in the gilded era of Teddy Roosevelt.

In Harding Davis's lifetime, the industrial reality of the "Iron Mills" would be replicated across Southern Appalachia on an unprecedented level. Coal and timber camps and cotton mill towns rose, completely transforming the makeup of the mountaineers and their environment. Hundreds of company towns—townships formed under the control of single coal or timber corporations, most of which were owned by outside interests—had filled the hollows and valleys by her death in 1910, outnumbering independent towns in some areas by five to one.

The age of the high, lonesome dirt farmer, in a region where 75–90 percent of the land was owned by absentee landlords and outside companies, had come to an end. In 1907, the *Raleigh Register,* a small-town newspaper in the coal country of West Virginia, captured the turn-of-the-century shift in Appalachia that virtually all outside writers had casually overlooked:

Towns and cities are springing up where before stood dense forests or waving fields of grain; thousands of coke ovens gleaming along the pathway of the iron horse and clouding the noon-day sun with their endless streams of smoke; armies of men collected together from every quarter of the globe to dig his vast treasures from the mines; heavily loaded freight trains plunging through mountain fastnesses, fording great rivers and spanning wide canyons to carry to the world its precious supply of fuel.

Long after her debut publication, Harding Davis's determination to "tell this secret down here" remained an exception among most chroniclers during an explosion of magazine writing and stories about the Mountain South. The secrets gave way to stereotypes. In their haste to conjure the exotic and embellish the preindustrial and romantic ways of the mountaineers, most authors rejected Harding Davis's sophisticated view of the growing urban reality in the region. Immersed in nostalgia and condescension, writers were commissioned to go in search of Alcott's question: Who on earth would live in the back hills of Southern Appalachia? Or, as one of the first headlines that appeared in 1873 in the popular *Lippincott's Magazine* put it, "A Strange Land and Peculiar People."

During the golden age of travel writing in the 1870s and 1880s, magazines such as *Lippincott's, Harper's,* and the *Atlantic Monthly,* which had provided space for Harding's groundbreaking stories, became a venue for some of the most ridiculous and uninformed depictions of people in Appalachia and other "remote" corners of the earth. In one often-quoted piece, Southern mountaineers led lives as "unfamiliar to us as the dweller in a wheeled house on the Scythian steppes."

I n 1899, educator and author William Frost published a seminal essay in the *Atlantic Monthly.* "Our Contemporary Ancestors in the Southern Mountains" made one of the first important references to "Appalachian America." Frost's naming of Appalachia and its slumberous inhabitants, living "in the conditions of the colonial times," culminated three decades of "discovery" and travel in the region. It also added an air of rescue to the mission.

To be fair, Frost's romanticization of Appalachia was not malicious. He struggled to correct the more vicious portraits of gun-toting feudists, moonshiners, "white trash," and lazy "hillbillies" (the term officially given birth in the New York media in 1900). In an era of post-Reconstruction hand-wringing, he sought to depict a pro-Unionist Southern Appalachia that could serve as a bridge for national reconciliation. In fact, serving in the 1890s as president of Berea College, a pioneering school founded as an abolitionist institution in eastern Kentucky, Frost embodied the late-nineteenth-century missionary spirit that desperately championed the Union-supporting "mountain whites," a supposedly singular ethnic population left behind by progress and "beleaguered by nature."

This sentiment, of course, presented a curious paradox for the times: At precisely the same moment that Southern Appalachia was being irrevocably altered by widespread industrialization and immigration, social reformers and travel writers insisted on depicting the region as a remote outpost inhabited only by rawboned and coon-capped Anglo-Saxon-Celtic (today's Scotch-Irish) mountaineers.

Harding Davis published a short story in 1875 in *Lippincott's Magazine* that excoriated these fulsome travel writers of her age, while attempting to depict the healing powers of the mountains and their war-torn people. Loaded with symbolism over the Civil War, the new tourist industry, and the role of nature, "The Yares of Black Mountain" tells the story of a Northern Civil War widow and her ailing baby and their journey to the North Carolina mountains. Arriving near the tourist hub of Asheville, where a tourist from Detroit establishes the outsider's view that "civilization stops here," they are joined by a New York travel writer, a hilarious woman by the name of Miss Cook, who is working on a book, *Causes of the Decadence of the Old South*. Instead of the picturesque, however, Cook finds mountaineers dressed in "dirty calico wrappers" and the panorama lacking grandeur. After a short tour of the town, she has "done the mountains and the mountaineers." She adds in the wonderfully affected parlance of the travel writers of her era that she doesn't need to do any research or backwoods journeys, because she possesses the "faculty of generalizing." Cook's story is over; the stereotypes for her readers will remain intact.

Harding Davis's story of the young mother and baby, instead, heads into the mountain refuge of the Yares family, in search of the healing pines. In the process, they learn the "terrible history" of the Civil War in the mountains. Having sided with the Union forces, more for national unity than any antislavery sentiment, the Yares have paid a high toll of ostracism and poverty. While the males of the clan want to regale the young woman with their Davy Crockett tales of bear hunting, the reader soon learns that the true heroic role belongs to the women of the family, who served as scouts and guides through the mountains for Union soldiers and Confederate deserters.

Nature is not "beleaguering" for the Yares and their Northern visitor. In great detail about the flora and fauna of the area, Harding Davis presents a powerful image of the Southern Appalachians as a curative and nurturing world. Despite their poor living conditions, the Yares hold to the mountains not as a romantic refuge, but for a sense of community, even humanity. And for a matriarchal sense of family. For the young widow, the Yares are the first people to transcend their apparent social position in class or education, "to go straight to something in her beneath all of these things."

Harding Davis's view of the mountaineers was not one of romance, but resistance, to the "terrible history" of the times. It was also a Southern Appalachia led by women.

NOT FAR from the Yares in the Carolinas, as the tracts of timber and coal veins were being carved from the Appalachians, another industrial phenomenon was taking place in the New South era: the rise of the cotton mills. Whereas Harding Davis had already introduced us to the plight of Deborah, the hunchbacked Welsh cotton mill worker in 1861, it took another sixty years before one of the great uprisings of young female mill workers against their own "terrible history" would sweep across the Appalachian hills and mountains.

These "disorderly women," wonderfully described by social historian Jacquelyn Dowd Hall, would surprise us today with their fearless acts of resistance, their modern habits and sexual mores, and their keen sense of fashion. They had come a long way since the era of the slavish Deborah. Far from the stereotypical portrait of demure mountain mill girls—dumbstruck, barefoot, and topped with sunbonnets—they gamboled along the picket lines like the flappers of their jazz age. They were outraged and outrageous. They stared down the rifle barrels of the National Guard. In the process, their protests triggered a series of historic mill strikes across the Appalachians and into the Southern lowlands.

Cotton mills, of course, were not a uniquely Southern Appalachian or Southern invention. Long before Deborah's act of thievery to rectify her plight in society, Lowell, Massachusetts, reigned as the classic bastion of children and women mill workers scrambling like dancers in front of the great spinning frames. Dramatic strikes took place there in 1834 and 1836. An uprising of young female cotton workers erupted in the Allegheny mountain communities in Pennsylvania in the 1840s.

In the aftermath of the Civil War, though, the South's cheaper labor pool and access to cotton spurred a shift of the cotton mill workforce from New England. While the profits rang from timber and coal extraction like a battle hymn for outside corporations, entrepreneurs in the reemerging New South "tied their hopes for prosperity to the whirring of spindles and the beating of looms," according to historian Hall, in her collaborative landmark study, *Like a Family: The Making of the Southern Cotton Mill World.*

With these whirring spindles and beating looms came a transformation in the mountains on a par with the coal and timber camps. Mirroring the urbanized phenomenon of the timber camps and coal company towns, where workers lived, shopped, socialized, and worshipped in tightly clustered villages owned and operated by the same company that determined their employment and wages, 92 percent of the Southern mill workers lived in company mill towns. As a federal labor report noted in 1907, the company (often a Northern-based entity) not only regulated the daily affairs, but "controls everything, and to a large extent controls everybody in the mill village."

The villages were fed by Southern Appalachians, as hill folk and mountaineers yielded to the increasingly difficult realities of subsistence farming. With the virgin forests and their lumberjack communities exhausted by the end of World War I, and much of the best farmland owned by wealthy interests or outside speculators, many small mountain farmers struggled to make a living off the diminished land left in the wake of deforestation and widespread erosion. A new pool of distressed workers poured by the thousands into the mines and timber camps, and then into the piedmont and lowlands, offering themselves as sharecroppers and mill workers.

Far from any Rip Van Winkle existence, a large part of Southern Appalachia was either on the move or in a continual state of being invaded by outside forces. Again debunking the misperceptions of isolation or the contemporary travel writer's sense that "civilization ends here," even the most remote parts of the mountain region had been linked with the outside world through the railroads for decades. But railroads were not the only modern convenience to appear in the hollows or within sight of that classic lonesome cabin on the ridge. Sears & Roebuck and Montgomery Ward catalogs of the latest fashions and other goods stood alongside those burnished copies of the King James Bible. Traveling medicine shows and minstrels appeared on a regular basis.

By 1922, WSB radio in Atlanta began to crank up its volume, sending out the first radio programs in the region. Within a decade, scores of radio stations, reaching millions of listeners, showered the Appalachian valleys and mountain range with dramas, music, news, and a relentless barrage of commercials and corporate sponsors and their new array of products.

The radio exchange worked both ways. Just as urban American modernity wallpapered the most forlorn mountain shacks with the latest trends, the most traditional elements of Appalachian music and life furnished the backdrop and soundtrack for the era's most important invention. Appalachian musicians waltzed in and out of urban and small-town

American kitchens and living rooms on a daily basis in commercials. The contexts of Southern mountain lives became story lines in radio dramas, songs, advertisements, silent pictures, and talking films.

Even before Fiddlin' John Carson, a former mill worker, became in 1923 the first person to record a country, or "hillbilly," record in Atlanta, female Appalachian cotton mill workers had seen themselves on the big screen as celebrity protagonists. Blending fact with fiction, one literary and film portrait in particular presented the outside world with a ground-breaking view of the avant-garde ways and abilities of the young moun-taineer women.

Long before the free-spirited Daisy hopped behind the wheel in *The Great Gatsby*, as historian Elizabeth Engelhardt has pointed out, a moun-tain girl and cotton mill worker by the name of Johnnie Consadine was barreling down the steep back roads of Southern Appalachia in an auto-mobile "contraption," intent on saving the life of her lover. As the pro-tagonist in the popular novel *The Power and the Glory*, by Grace MacGowan Cooke, which was published in 1910 and turned into a silent film by Hollywood director Lawrence Windom in 1918, Johnnie's charac-ter is the very antithesis of the archetypal hillbilly girl image that would appear in so many stories and cartoons. She is smart, pleasant-speaking, cool-headed, and fully grounded in her Appalachian culture and ways. She has walked out of the mountains and into a cotton mill town in the lower Tennessee Valley to fill a yearning to "have more" and "make a chance for the children." The backwoods life, however, has not sheltered her from modern inventions and troubles; newspaper accounts of a mill girl's suicide have been passed "from hand to hand in the mountains." Like everyone in her hollow, she recognizes the makes of the nascent automobile industry, because "illustrated magazines go everywhere these days." She always has her "face in a book."

Instead of being devoured by the industrial furnaces as Hugh and Deborah were in "Life in the Iron Mills," Johnnie tackles the horrific working conditions of the mills by inventing a safety device, works against the polluted water sources and decrepit housing, leads a charge to bring an Appalachian sense of greenery to the mill town, and eventually woos the mill owner into marriage. She also dodges a lot of bullets and turmoil in the adventures connected to her uncle's pursuit of a lost mine.

The living and working conditions in *The Power and Glory,* in some respects, are no less frightening than those in "Life in the Iron Mills." A mill worker laments, "Cain't you see that a cotton mill is bound to either kill or cripple a child? Them that don't die, sort o' drags along and grows up to be mis'able, undersized, sickly somebodies." Pellagra, the scourge of malnutrition, is rampant; diseases like typhoid fever and diphtheria flourish. With most of the closely stacked houses lacking sanitation and clean water, "the very sight of the village is a horror." Inside the mill, working at least fifty-five hours a week, the largely female and underage workforce loses limbs and lives in the face of the dangerous machines and suffers from the devastating effects of byssinosis, or brown lung, a respiratory disease caused by long-term exposure to cotton dust.

Turning to the genre of historical romances to chronicle the morass of the mills and its town of "sewerage," MacGowan Cooke's novels and other stories established a Southern Appalachian viewpoint in the forefront of the labor reform movements at the turn of the century. MacGowan Cooke's father had been an editor for Ochs's *Chattanooga Times.* While she would leave the Mountain South in her forties, setting off on a bohemian life that brought her into the communes of Upton Sinclair and Sinclair Lewis, the settings and players of the region remained at the heart of her work.

Her writing, while praised by the *New York Times* and national literary journals for its "undeniable charm," did not possess the sense of urgency or the stylistic mastery of someone like Harding Davis. Nonetheless, her depiction of Appalachian women characters, like that of Johnnie portrayed by Hollywood silent film star June Elvidge in *The Power and the Glory,* was an important and groundbreaking event for American women, especially in presenting mountaineers as capable of change and rebellion and on the cutting edge of modern times. Not only do Johnnie and her fellow mountain girls wish to earn their daily bread among decent working conditions, but they aspire to wear beautiful blouses, lacy neck-bands, fancy shoes, and the frivolous hats of the rich. They also understand the "laws of attraction."

Therefore, when a German company announced the opening of a rayon mill in Elizabethton, Tennessee, in 1925, in the same meadow where the first Washingtonians announced their defiance of British rule in 1772, its managers probably didn't realize they were about to encounter their own raging fashion show for justice. The mill needed a legion of workers to wind, reel, twist, and otherwise process the yarn used in making stockings for the flappers kicking up their heels in the Jazz Age. Mirroring a phenomenon that had already dragged mountain families into the lowlands of the Carolinas and Georgia, Elizabethton boomed, tripling in population in less than a decade, drawing mountain farmers and their families from around the region. Others commuted daily from their nearby hollows. Similar to Deborah's time in the "Iron Mills" story of Wheeling in 1861, over a third of the workers were teenage girls. Canny, self-possessed, and sharp, these Southern Appalachian young women shared Johnnie's burning need to earn their own keep, work under fair conditions, and regain "their wings of desire."

THE FIRST walkout happened on March 12, 1929. Young mill workers were outraged by their low wages—a situation worsened by the town leaders who had courted the German company with promises that the mountaineers were so desperate and dull they would accept wages at a fraction of what was paid in the North. From 1880 until the stock market crash in 1929, Southern workers earned less than 60 percent of the wage paid for the same mill job in New England. The young women also resented their exposure to toxic chemicals in the spinning process, as well as regulations that had kept them from wearing makeup or taking private bathroom breaks. The teenage mill girls revolted, leading the strike in an atmosphere of a festival.

Their defiance mocked the mill owner's power. Underscoring their options as mountain farmers, they reminded the town leaders that they hadn't "forgotten how to use a hoe." As more mill workers, both men and women, joined the ranks, the strike and its confrontation with strikebreakers led to the arrival of the National Guard. Draping themselves in the American flag, a large contingent of the young women led the vanguard in confronting the soldiers and their rifles. The workers chartered a union and organized the daily tasks of the strike and support committees. They flirted with and taunted the soldiers; they harassed the strikebreakers. Turning the tables on the middle-class protocol of "respectable women," they shouted down men and marched in rallies in stylish clothes and high heels.

Despite the carnivalesque feeling surrounding the town, the times were not all fun and games. With machine guns stationed on top of the mill, violence erupted at various roadblocks, gun battles ensued, and the town water tank was dynamited.

News of the strike spread across the mountains in the same way Johnnie sought to save her loved ones in MacGowan Cooke's novel: behind the wheel of the Model T. Brigades shuttled messages from mill town to mill town in Southern Appalachia and then into the piedmont hills and lower Carolinas. Young women made fund-raising trips and strike speeches in nearby Appalachian centers like Knoxville and Asheville and as far as Nashville. Defying the image of helpless and disorganized "lint-heads," a common slur against the cotton mill workers, these disorderly young women presented themselves, according to Hall, in "their own version of a brash, irreverent Jazz Age style." Within weeks, the infectious spirit of their strike, with young women marching in "their Sunday best," led to walkouts by thousands of mill workers in South Carolina and North Carolina.

Nowhere did the strike of 1929 become so infamous as in Gastonia, North Carolina. As in Elizabethton, young women also took a lead role in organizing a strike at the Loray Mill in Gastonia, the center of the textile industry in the piedmont South. Swelled by mountain workers from around the region, the mill towns in the Gastonia area had grown to over thirty thousand inhabitants; by the time of the strike in 1929, nearly 1.2 million spindles churned daily, making the county the third most important mill producer in the nation. The typical mill worker, however, earned less than $16 for a fifty-five-hour week. The same job in the North paid $21.49 for a forty-eight-hour week. Beyond the poor wages and living conditions, the Loray Mill—owned entirely by a Rhode Island corporation—also showcased the first techniques in the South to "stretch out" the mill worker's duties, augmenting the number of machines the worker was responsible for and hence the workload.

Ella May Wiggins, a mountaineer whose family had drifted among the logging camps in Tennessee and the Carolinas, became one of the key mill organizers in the area, largely because of her ability to turn mountain ballads and popular tunes into union songs. Depicted variably by fellow activists as "Slavic looking" or with "Galician" or "Polish" origins, Wiggins defied the typical descriptions of the Scotch-Irish or white mill girl. She rose as an admired symbol of the rebellious and fearless women willing to take on the mill town on her own terms. She had lost four out of her nine children from various diseases and malnutrition; after her husband had abandoned the family, she eschewed marriage altogether, reclaimed her maiden name, and championed the role of the women as the wage earners and community leaders. In open defiance of racial mores, she moved into a black neighborhood and eagerly sought out black support for the union.

Wiggins's most famous ballad, "Mill Mother's Lament," emerged as the anthem for cotton mill workers and spread from the Southern region to New England. Sung to one of Fiddlin' John Carson's tunes that had aired on the radio, the ballad recast the modern-day mill mothers in the role of sole providers for their kids, forced to choose between serving the company or their family's needs. The stanzas captured the dilemma over the traditional role of a mother, the company's disregard for families, and their entrapment in the mill:

> We leave our home in the morning,
> We kiss our children goodbye,
> While we slave for the bosses
> Our children scream and cry.

How it grieves the heart of a mother,
You every one must know.
But we can't buy for our children,
Our wages are too low.

Within two weeks, the company and town leaders managed to crush the strikes around Gastonia. They refused all the demands of the strikers or recognition of their union. Strikebreakers had been shipped in under police protection. Despite widespread support from the communities near Elizabethton, the strike also collapsed in that mountain town after six weeks, resulting in no improvements in wages or working conditions.

In the end, the mill girls garnered the most national and international attention in the aftermath of their uprisings. In June, with the mill towns still simmering, the police chief of Gastonia led a raid on the offices of the radical National Textile Workers Union. A gun battle took place, cutting down the police chief in the process. When the trial over his murder resulted in a mistrial, a mob went on a rampage in the area, burning down the union offices and attacking known union supporters. Riding in the back of a pickup truck, en route to a union rally, Ella May Wiggins was shot to death. As a sign of company town justice, seven union activists were eventually retried and convicted of second-degree murder in the police chief's death; the murderers of Wiggins were acquitted.

The revolt of 1929 did not go unnoticed. The powerful impact of the young women reverberated across the country. With dramatic accounts appearing in national newspapers and magazines, astounding readers with brutality and lawlessness, the revolt inspired a generation of "new women," as Hall depicted the Elizabethton mill workers, "making their way in a world their mothers could not have known but carrying with them values handed down through the female line." It also took a heavy toll on the young women. Many strikers were blacklisted and forced to search for other work around the region.

Wiggins's ballads took on a life of their own, joining the pages of popular labor songbooks; she emerged as one of the mythic figures of the era and as a heroine for leftists and radicals. The Gastonia strike itself inspired six major novels and plays during a dynamic era of "proletarian literature" in the 1930s. These works included Grace Lumpkin's best-selling *To Make My Bread* and Appalachian author Olive Dargan's *Call Home the Heart.*

It would take a chaotic general strike in 1934, the great labor reforms of the New Deal, and the aftermath of World War II before the cotton mills in the South saw any recognition of unions. By then, with machines rapidly taking the place of workers in the factories, the mill villages had become a part of the region's forgotten history.

LIKE THE murder of Wiggins and the strikes over the cotton mills, the staggering level of bloodshed and labor uprisings in the coal mines and cordoned-off company coal camps in Southern Appalachia startled both mountaineers and outside observers with the perilous state of affairs. The industry itself was in a constant state of flux, booming and busting over the decades with the capricious demands of the world market and the largely merciless feudal policies of the coal companies. Appalachian coal had fed the nation's great furnaces for industrial progress. In the process, Appalachia's prized mineral wealth, buried under the mountains like gold, had triggered some of the twentieth century's most important clashes between the nation's key industrialists and labor figures.

As the last battlefield for unionism in the face of King Coal, Appalachian miners, in particular, quickly became the tragic symbols of a dark and terrifying underground industry taking place outside the norm of reality. In the eyes of many observers, their coal-black faces and crooked backs had sunk to the lower depths of human existence. Regions in the mountains emerged as infamous and bloody blemishes on the American landscape, as if lying beyond the scope of everyday life. Harlan County, Kentucky, for example, was eventually branded the homicide capital of the rural counties in the nation; over a dozen people were murdered in the labor conflicts of the 1930s. For most people, the unrelenting images of battles between companies, laborers, and various labor unions had presented a backward region in a continual state of war.

In the early stages of mining, the dismal working conditions for the miners reflected a truly warlike scenario. According to one historian, a U.S. soldier in World War I had a better chance of surviving on the field of combat than did a miner in a West Virginia mine. That particular mountain state had a higher casualty rate among miners than American soldiers killed in the Spanish-American War. Since 1900, over 104,500 coal miners have reportedly been killed in the mines across America. In 1907, more than 3,000 mine workers lost their lives; 361 men were killed in one explosion in Marion County, West Virginia. Tens of thousands of others have been maimed in accidents or suffered the fatal consequences of black lung, various other diseases, and malnutrition.

Far from being enslaved mules or ghostly souls who acquiesced to their damned fate, coal miners in the region launched some of the most dramatic rebellions in American history. Without assistance or guidance from "outside troublemakers," operating entirely on their own initiative and infrastructure of command, Appalachian coal miners turned the Battle of Blair Mountain into the largest armed insurrection in the United States since the Civil War.

IN 1921, a handful of counties in eastern Kentucky and southern West Virginia remained as the last bastion of nonunion coalfields. Seemingly cut off from the rest of the nation by its geography, this mountainous neck of the region had been a focal point in national union and coal-mining interests. The counties churned out extraordinary amounts of coal, much to the chagrin of the United Mine Workers of America, which sought to solidify its nationwide negotiation powers.

The key acts of resistance, though, took place locally. Outraged over the "massacre" of a union-supporting sheriff and his associate on the steps of the McDowell County Courthouse by Baldwin-Felts security guards in the summer of 1921, thousands of West Virginia miners formed themselves into armed divisions and marched across the mountains in the spirit of the revolutionary Overmountain Men at Kings Mountain. Their mission was clear: to liberate two southern West Virginia counties that had literally been blocked off by armed company guards from any union organizing. In the eyes of the union miners, the defenders of the coal companies had their own ghastly Ferguson figure (the leader of the British militia): Logan County Sheriff Don Chafin, who had carried out the antiunion sentiments of the coal companies with a reign of terror with his own private army of "special deputies."

Such a war, of course, had been brewing for years. A rehearsal march had been performed two years prior, only to be turned back in the face of the state militia. Gunshots and dynamite attacks had occurred on either side for months. Martial law had been invoked on various occasions. This time, however, the miners' patience had been worn down to the quick, simply awaiting a flame to ignite their rage. The situation had gone beyond desperation. The miners had reached a stage of revenge. Hundreds of families were displaced in tent camps along the hollows and mountain valleys, harassed and terrorized by Baldwin-Felts guards and scrounging to find enough food to eat. Many were blacklisted from working in the mines or were battered by lowered wages and the company's brutal practice of shortchanging its workload. Because the miners were paid by the ton or amount of each load of coal, a frequent scheme by the coal company was to falsify the weight of the load by using tampered-with scales.

Therefore, once the news of the murders of the union supporters in broad daylight had spread, thousands of primed miners took up their arms as a last resort. They believed the only way to free the nonunion Southern counties from the grip of the company and its henchmen was through all-out warfare.

The miners were veterans in many respects. Some actually donned their World War I uniforms and helmets, as if placing a patriotic element into their act of liberation. Marchers talked openly about similar battles in the forests of Argonne. This time, however, the hills and the risks were even steeper. Others had served in the Spanish-American War. By the time former war correspondents from the nation's most important newspapers had arrived at the "front," comparisons were being made with the battles in France and Belgium.

An estimated ten thousand armed miners tramped through the back roads and trails or rode the sequestered coal trains into the back counties, in an image hauntingly similar to the bands of Pancho Villa's infamous armed rebels utilizing the rails for their campaigns. Knowing he was outnumbered, Sheriff Chafin and his well-armed company forces decided to make their stand at the watersheds around the barrier of Blair Mountain in Logan County. Laying land mines and setting up machine-gun outposts, they equipped Blair Mountain like a fortress. In a situation that recalled the divided sentiments of the Americans at the Battle of Kings Mountain, the two sides on the mountain battlefield were distinguished by a simple piece of fabric: The revolting coal miners tied a red scarf or bandanna around their necks, while the company supporters wore white scarves.

Covered by newspapers around the country and the world, the "war raged on a 20-mile front" over a week as the disparate divisions of the "redneck" supporters sought to overwhelm the ramparts of Blair Mountain. Private planes had been hired by Chafin to drop homemade bombs on the guerilla forces. An estimated twenty miners and company guards fell to their death in battle, though no official number was ever recorded; hundreds were wounded. Mountain families fled like refugees into neighboring counties. While pushing beyond the lines of Chafin and his defenders at one point, the "redneck" rebellion ultimately failed in organizing the unwieldy divisions into an effective invasion of Logan County.

After his proclamation to end the fighting had been soundly ignored by the armed miners—the guerilla forces had been warned they would be charged with treason—President Warren Harding dispatched General Henry Bandholtz, a hero of World War I, to take control of the situation. Defiant as ever, the miners had called on their "constitutional right to bear arms—about the only right left to us." Within the week, federal troops had arrived from bases in Kentucky, Ohio, and New Jersey. War hero and pilot Billy Mitchell led a squadron of airplanes, many of which crashed before arriving in the mountain valleys.

Faced with fighting against U.S. soldiers, the miners and their revolt came to a quiet end. In disarray and lacking supplies, thousands of redneck insurgents surrendered or hid their guns. Hundreds were arrested and taken prisoner. Despite Chafin's desire to keep the renegades in his Logan County jails, the trials for murder and "treason against the state of West Virginia" were transferred to the county courthouse in the capital of Charleston. While a number of miners would be convicted and imprisoned for murder charges and eventually paroled in 1925 by the governor, only one rebel was convicted for treason. He skipped bail and disappeared.

With the whole world watching the treason proceedings at the Jefferson County Courthouse in Charleston, the historic parallel with another trial did not go unnoticed. Abolitionist John Brown had been tried and convicted for treason—the last such trial—at the very same courthouse sixty-two years before, as a result of his armed raid of the federal arsenal at Harper's Ferry, in western Virginia. Some of the union miners invoked Brown's name and his prophetic mission at the doomed raid. Responding to the questions of a "war correspondent" from New York about the realistic chances of the union forces at Blair Mountain, one miner had responded: "Well, John Brown started something once at Harper's Ferry, didn't he?"

Like Harper's Ferry and the abolitionist movement, the Battle of Blair Mountain would go down in the history books as a disastrous defeat for the unions and for coal miners in the Southern Appalachians. The memory of the battle, though, much like the mill strikes at Gastonia and Elizabethton in 1929, did not merely disappear into the mountain fogs or fail to influence the nation's view of the realities in the coalfields. Accounts of the uprising reached miners and union workers across the country. Prompted by the rebellion, newspapers, magazines and follow-up U.S. congressional hearings exposed the horrific working conditions for coal miners and their families in Southern Appalachia, setting the stage for future labor reforms and more confrontations.

In 1931, another battle returned Appalachia to the front pages of the national newspapers, when the issue over unions and strikes polarized a mining community in Harlan County, Kentucky. A downturn in work had resulted in layoffs, increasingly unfair working conditions, and desperation among miners and their families. The times were indeed shocking. In nearby Straight Creek, thirty-one babies, beset with pellagra, tuberculosis, and bloody flux, died in the arms of one midwife that autumn. With an iron grip on the mining towns tucked into the hollows, the coal companies redoubled their resistance to any concessions to unions and employed a legion of armed guards, most of whom had been brought in from other states. In turn, many of these hired guards often became deputies under the local sheriff, John H. Blair.

Making one of their periodic raids on the home of a union activist, and upturning the rooms and paltry furniture in the process, the armed raiders crossed the line for one miner's wife. Outraged by their illegal intrusion and unabashed ruthlessness on behalf of the company, thirty-one-year-old Florence Reece ripped a sheet from a calendar off the wall and began to scribble down a song. She hummed the words to an old Baptist hymn. The lyrics poured out in the defiant challenge of a union organizer. When Reece, who had been born and raised in coal camps in eastern Tennessee, finally performed the song for a local group, she had no idea it would go on to become the most widely sung anthem of the labor movement and would be used in strikes and organizing meetings across the nation; it also would be passed on to the civil rights and student movements in the 1960s. In that historic moment of outrage, the young woman had captured the ultimate stand of the unions with the undaunted and inspiring words of a true believer:

> *Which side are you on,*
> *Which side are you on?*

> *If you go to Harlan County,*
> *There is no neutral there,*
> *You will either be a union man,*
> *Or a thug for J. H. Blair.*

> *Which side are you on,*
> *Which side are you on?*

Coal mining, of course, after two centuries of dramatic personal accounts, media reports, novels, poems, plays, and films, has generated a treasury of industrial sagas. One of the best novels, *Storming Heaven,* by West Virginia author Denise Giardina, chronicles the labor march on Blair Mountain. As Reece demonstrated, the coal industry has also created its own soundtrack and some of the most important labor songs in American history. Quite possibly the first labor anthem to be disseminated on a national level was "Solidarity Forever," written by radical labor activist Ralph Chapin, during a strike in the coal mines in West Virginia in 1915. As a Southern Appalachian ambassador from eastern Kentucky, singer and midwife Aunt Molly Jackson toured the country in the 1930s with the status of a cause célèbre, beguiling the nation's leftist circles and literary elite with her heart-wrenching songs about coal miners and the need for unions. She became the "pistol packin' mama" of the coal region. Placing her in the hallowed circles of American folk music, Woody Guthrie hailed Jackson as the "female Leadbelly" of her times.

THE MINERS at Blair Mountain were ultimately vindicated a decade later. When President Franklin D. Roosevelt signed the National Industrial Recovery Act into law in 1933, granting miners, mill workers, and all other American laborers the legal right to belong to a union without any repercussions, "a wave of enthusiasm of mountainous proportions" swept through the coal fields of Southern Appalachia. The *New York Times* reported on a historic union meeting in Charleston, West Virginia, that summer. The meeting celebrated the "veterans of the 1921 pitched battle in Logan, Mingo and 'Bloody McDowell' counties" in the state.

AFTER the Blair Mountain rebellion of 1921, a U.S. Senate committee conducted hearings, which chronicled the brutal conditions in Logan County. One witness amazed both the participants and the press with his story. His name was George Echols; he was a miner who had been dismissed in the mines after serving as the vice president of his local union. He had also been a slave in Virginia.

"I was raised a slave," he addressed the chairman of the committee. "My master and my mistress called me and I answered, and I know the time when I was a slave, and I felt just like we feel now."

Echols's presence at the hearings recalls a commonly overlooked chapter in Southern Appalachian history, especially in the coalfields; a sizable African American population not only took their place in the mines as laborers, but also played an important role in the integrated union leadership. One war correspondent at the Battle of Blair Mountain estimated that black miners made up 20 percent of one column of marchers he shadowed along a road. In truth, 30 percent of the miners in McDowell County at the time, in southern West Virginia, were black. From 1890 until the passing of the National Industrial Recovery Act in 1933, African Americans represented roughly 20 percent of the workforce in the state's mines. The United Mine Workers had been an integrated union since its founding.

With the labor demands rising around the turn of the nineteenth century, African Americans had migrated in the thousands to the Appalachian coalfields in Tennessee, Kentucky, and West Virginia. As early as the 1880s, nearly half of the miners in some coal-mining towns in Perry County, Kentucky, for example, were black. Immigrants from Italy and Eastern Europe also poured into the mountain region and the mining workforce. According to one study, West Virginia had "a foreign-born plurality in its mining population" prior to World War I. While black and recent immigrants were frequently manipulated into the roles of strikebreakers, they often joined or even led union activities, such as the rebellion at Blair Mountain. In the coal town of Boomer, West Virginia, for example, Italian anarchists led an uprising in the 1920s.

Booker T. Washington, who founded Tuskegee Institute and became the nation's most prominent African American spokesman at the turn of the century, worked in the salt mines and coal mines in West Virginia in the late nineteenth century. He attributed his dreadful prospects in the mines as part of his "burning desire" to become literate. Another African American miner in West Virginia, Carter Woodson, who went on to launch a landmark academic journal, published numerous nationally acclaimed textbooks, and became "The Father of Black History," often credited his early backroom discussions and readings among black miners in Appalachia as the inspiration for his pioneering movement to recognize African American History.

WASHINGTON and Woodson were not the only two miners, African American or otherwise, to take their industrial experience from the Southern mountains into other states. One of the most fascinating books in recent Appalachian studies recounts the gatherings of the Eastern Kentucky Social Club, an informal network of black Appalachian miners who reorganized themselves in Chicago, Dayton, and Detroit to celebrate their mountain roots and customs.

Author William Demby foreshadowed this migration in his classic coming-of-age novel, *Beetlecreek,* which was set in a middle-class black Appalachian community in Depression-era West Virginia. Escaping the provincialism of the small town, the African American protagonist and his sophisticated lover are astonished to find so many "hillbillies standing motionless" at the bus station and heading with them to Detroit.

Why were so many Southern Appalachians lining up for the bus to Detroit? Just as the timber, coal, and mill industries had thundered across the region in the late nineteenth and early twentieth centuries with a tremendous demand for labor, the decline or outright collapse of the industries by the Great Depression led to an exodus of mountaineers from the Mountain South. Between 1940 and the end of the 1960s, an estimated three to five million Appalachians left the region in search of work. With the rising wartime and postwar demands in the automobile, tire, and steel industries, these mountain people flooded into the booming cities of Detroit, Flint, Chicago, Gary, Akron, Cincinnati, and Baltimore.

In some respects, the great migration from Appalachia might be the region's most important contribution to industrial America. Beyond its natural resources, Southern Appalachia literally peopled the midwestern factories and other corners of the nation's industries with its very inhabitants and their mountain culture—and their traditions of labor battles and resistance, independence and resiliency, music and literature.

Nowhere was this geographical upheaval and displacement of the mountaineer better portrayed than in Harriette Arnow's 1954 novel, *The Dollmaker*, which chronicled the struggles of a Kentucky mountain family in wartime Detroit. Eventually hailed by novelist Joyce Carol Oates as "our most unpretentious American masterpiece," *The Dollmaker* was short-listed for the National Book Award in 1955, losing out to William Faulkner's *Fable*. Arnow's book remained for weeks on the best-seller list. Jane Fonda adapted a film version of *The Dollmaker* in 1984.

Born in eastern Kentucky in 1908 to a fifth-generation mountain family, Arnow personally moved to Detroit in the 1940s. Thrusting her Appalachian *Dollmaker* characters into the "smotheringly crowded" environment of a Northern city, Arnow tells her story of Gertie, an iron-willed mountain woman who must perform a roadside tracheotomy on her baby at the beginning of the novel. Despite her longing to remain a farmer in the mountains, having nearly raised enough money to buy her own land, Gertie follows her husband into the steel mills in the North. Faced with relentless pressures, including murder, death, the roar of an industrial machine that devours its workers, and a union strike that leaves them in debt, Gertie declares her husband and family life would "be better off in th' war than in one a them factories!"

As a mid-twentieth-century version of "Life in the Iron Mills," powerful and unnerving in its prose and mountain dialect, the *Dollmaker* characters encounter an unforgiving Detroit with its festering discord over ethnic and class divisions, the insatiable demands of the industrial powers, and the daily turmoil of beleaguered laborers trying to survive in a concrete world where flowers fail to grow. It is only through her mountain wood-carving traditions and sense of self-reliance that Gertie and her family are able to weather the upheavals of the mercurial city.

ONE FAMOUS Detroit autoworker's real-life migration experience began in Wheeling, West Virginia, where the scenes in "Life in the Iron

Mills" had first shaken the nation. Into those same iron mills in 1899, a German immigrant by the name of Val Reuther had joined his brothers in search of work. Living in a South Wheeling neighborhood populated by immigrants from Germany, Ireland, and Poland and other Eastern European countries, Reuther eventually found work in the mills as a relief heater. The discrimination against the immigrants, though, stunned him. Losing his job after a failed strike at the mill, Reuther became a wagon driver for a brewery company. After he joined the International Brewery Workers Federation, the union, according to his son, "was the major interest of his life."

Along with a love of Goethe's poetry, Val Reuther's commitment to the unions and to socialism was not lost on his sons. When Socialist Party activist Eugene Debs was imprisoned in West Virginia for advocating resistance to the draft during World War I, Reuther made sure his sons accompanied him on a visit to meet the famed labor leader at the prison. At the age of twenty-three, Reuther had served as head of the Ohio Valley Trades and Labor Assembly. On his frequent journeys in the coalfields of West Virginia, Reuther would often recount to his family stories of child labor and the perilous labor conditions. At one family gathering, Reuther recorded an experience in a small town in southern West Virginia, where he saw "a child twelve years old leading a mule into the mine. I saw them bring that child out, his body crushed and mutilated from falling stone."

In 1923, one of Reuther's sons, Walter, left school after his sophomore year to take a job at a Wheeling machine shop. By the age of seventeen, he had already lost a toe in an accident. The low pay at the mill, however, kept the young man from falling into line. Within four years, hearing about the burgeoning auto industry in Detroit and its higher wages, he left behind his urban Appalachian base and joined the first ranks of migration. He took his Southern Appalachian heritage of union struggles with him.

Walter Reuther eventually rose in history as the president of the United Auto Workers and became one of the most powerful labor leaders in the world. He would even travel to Europe as a special representative, at President John F. Kennedy's behest. While he was operating in the heart of "the world's most influential industrial unit in forming the life patterns of the machine age," the General Motors plant, his controversial efforts on behalf of the autoworkers also earned him the title "the most dangerous man in Detroit."

When Reuther finally gained control of one of the largest labor unions in the country in 1946, he brought his West Virginia father onto the stage and introduced him as "an old rabble rouser in the ranks of labor" and made him an honorary lifetime member of the United Auto Workers. He proclaimed himself in the "vanguard in America."

More accurately, nearly a century after the toiling laborers in "Life in the Iron Mills" had confronted the nation with their saga, the Appalachian vanguard had arrived in Motown.

Chapter Seven

WE SHALL OVERCOME

+∿+

Myles Horton just washed away and melted a lot of
my hostility and prejudice and feeling of bitterness against the white
southerner because he had such a wonderful sense of humor. People were
trying to make it seem impossible to have that type of living that he had
organized and established at Highlander. There was a great thing about
black and white people sitting down to the same table eating.

—ROSA PARKS, "The Mother of the Civil Rights Movement"

ON A HOT summer evening in 1959, taking a break from an all-day community leadership training session among mostly black students, a few women stepped outside the Highlander Folk School farmhouse to freshen up in the night air. Even on the Cumberland Plateau in the eastern Tennessee mountain town of Monteagle, where the folk school was located, the temperature had risen to an uncomfortable level. The heat, in every respect, was about to soar. The women noticed the lights of several cars barreling down the forest road. The rest of their associates were inside, watching a documentary film, sharing punch and cookies.

Plainclothes police officers first emerged out of the cars. They immediately rounded up the women. Other police and state troopers stormed the main room, where forty or so students were viewing the film. Confusion ensued. Screams erupted. A graying sixty-one-year-old African

American woman, Septima Clark, the leader of the workshop, was presented with a warrant to search the school for liquor. The staunch teetotalist educator's amusement was most likely tempered by her outrage at the assault. Within the hour, Clark and three other associates, including the staff's young music teacher, Guy Carawan, were arrested for possession of liquor (a small amount of rum, gin, and moonshine was found in the private residence of the school's director, who was out of the country), drunkenness and disorderly conduct, and resisting arrest (a charge issued after a request to call a lawyer).

The rest of the students had been forced to wait in the dark while the police ransacked the schoolrooms and dormitories, desperately in search of any alcohol or contraband. In the blur of the strange raid, the students began to hum, then whistle and sing an old labor and gospel song they had learned earlier that day from Carawan: "We Shall Overcome." A young teenager from Montgomery, Alabama, reacting to the bullying tactics of the police, quietly added a new verse:

> *We are not afraid, we are not afraid*
> *We are not afraid today*
> *Oh, deep in my heart, I do believe*
> *We shall overcome someday.*

The fear probably resonated more among the pistol-packing intruders than the young students, many of whom had already faced down hostile thugs and bomb attacks in their efforts to desegregate schools across the South. Several had participated in or watched their parents take part in the historic bus boycott in Montgomery, Alabama. Clark, the composed veteran teacher from Charleston, South Carolina, realized at once that the trumped-up liquor charges were simply a front for the longtime efforts of ardent segregationists to shut down the school. Like every other Highlander staff member, she had been expecting court action any day. The police officers, in fact, had been dispatched by a district attorney, empowered by the Tennessee legislature to "smoke out subversion" and gather evidence of Highlander's role as a "public nuisance."

The public nuisance, as everyone knew, had nothing to do with alcohol consumption. Since its inception as an interracial center in 1932, the Appalachian mountain school had courted controversy in its dauntless mission for racial and social justice. Terrified by "the upsurge set off by the Montgomery Bus Boycott," according to Southern writer Anne Braden, and the widespread changes ensuing from the Supreme Court's desegregation decision in 1954, several Southern states had targeted Highlander as the nerve center for the emerging civil rights movement. The mountaintop school was the command center, according to one dramatic report, of "the four horsemen of racial agitation."

There were more sober views, of course. In 1957, at the school's twenty-fifth anniversary celebration, a young minister from Montgomery, Alabama, Martin Luther King, Jr., declared that Highlander had "given the South some of its most responsible leaders in this great period of transition."

MYLES HORTON, the cofounder of the Highlander Folk School, missed that bizarre raid, because he was attending an adult education seminar abroad, but he returned home to take part in court proceedings likened by the *Chattanooga Times* to a modern-day Scopes trial. The educator knew the storm in the Cumberlands had been collecting for some time; he had even taunted the Tennessee officials to set foot on the school grounds. Over the past few years, Horton and his school had faced down the Southern counterparts to Senator Joseph McCarthy's now infamous "un-American" witch-hunt hearings. They had temporarily lost their nonprofit tax status and had defended themselves against attacks from local segregationists and violent Klan elements, Georgia and Arkansas investigation committees, and a Tennessee legislature obsessed with "the intermingling of the races." Highlander had long been branded "the Communist training school."

It had been a rocky road for Horton and his Highlanders. Born in 1905 and raised in the township of Savannah, in the eastern Tennessee mountains, Horton and his family had enjoyed a longtime base in Southern

Appalachia. He could trace one of his ancestors back to the original gatherers at the Watauga Association's declaration of independence by the first Washingtonians. In the shadows of Samuel Doak's missionary work, Horton's family had been members of the Cumberland Presbyterians, whose congregations had been early abolitionists in the Appalachians. His parents were freethinking schoolteachers who openly supported integration.

This progressive Appalachian tradition of education, equal rights, and social justice had new implications for the mountain boy in the 1920s. While studying literature and religion at Cumberland University, Horton taught Bible school classes for kids in Ozone, Tennessee. In the evenings, he also held meetings among the parents, most of whom were poor mill workers and small farmers, who discussed ways of resolving their community's problems. The experience stunned Horton with its potential; no matter how demoralized or inarticulate, common people impressed him with their yearning and ability to "talk out" the causes of and solutions to their own problems in the mountains.

The issue of race relations always simmered in the background for the young man. After a disheartening experience working for the YMCA in Tennessee and unable to garner support for interracial activities or economic initiatives for the Southern mountaineers, Horton followed the urging of a local minister and decided in 1929 to attend Union Theological Seminary in New York. He never intended to become an ordained minister. He viewed his studies at the seminary as a stepping-stone for what would evolve into an international pilgrimage of adult education experiments.

At the same time that Horton ventured to New York City, another mountain boy had enrolled at the School of Divinity at Vanderbilt University in Nashville. A year younger than Horton, Don West had been raised in the north Georgia mountains. His family passed on an ancestral legacy of activism no less rooted than Horton's in the Southern Appalachians. West's grandfather, a Radical Republican in the Reconstruction era, raised his children and grandchildren on Appalachian tenets of independence, self-sufficiency, racial unity, and Baptist righteousness. Members of his family had openly supported the Union and antislavery efforts in the Mountain South. In his mid-teens, West protested the showing of the notorious *Birth of a Nation* silent film and its glorification of the Ku Klux Klan, while studying at Berry College, a unique school set up by a missionary for indigent mountain children. After defending a faculty member in a subsequent controversy, West left the school without a diploma, eventually hitchhiking to Lincoln Memorial University in the Cumberland Gap of Tennessee with less than $2 in his pocket. The college, established in the mountains after the Civil War, had been part of a promise by Northerners, so the story goes, to recognize the mountaineers' role in support of the Union army.

West quickly earned a reputation at Lincoln Memorial as a sports star, a promising poet, and a political rebel. He led a campus protest over what he considered paternalistic rules, leading to his expulsion. Due to West's popularity among the student body and faculty, however, the university was forced to reinstate him. Offered a scholarship to continue his studies, he entered the School of Divinity at Vanderbilt University in 1931.

AS THE FALLOUT of the Great Depression swept across the nation, Horton's and West's early adult lives crossed paths in fascinating ways. West fell under the influence of Social Gospel advocate and ethics professor Alva Taylor at Vanderbilt. The professor called on his students to question the implications of industrial capitalism and sent them on social service missions into the mining and mill communities in the Southern Appalachians. Horton studied under the auspices of Christian theological titan Reinhold Niebuhr, whose book *Moral Man and Immoral Society* would become an influential text for a generation of seminarians on the machinations of capitalism, the shortfalls of liberal Social Gospel idealism, and the need for spiritual awakening and consciousness among the working class.

Neither Horton nor West could be held to the corridors of academia. During their school breaks, they traveled to historic sites of reform and radicalism; they witnessed the violent mine and mill strikes in eastern

Tennessee and North Carolina and the garment strikes in New York; they visited labor colleges and schools in Chicago and throughout the Deep South. Amazingly enough, drawing from different sources of inspiration and information, Horton and West journeyed separately to Denmark in 1931 to visit that country's renowned folk schools.

Commonly considered one of the most successful adult education programs on a national level, the Danish folk schools had been inspired in the mid-nineteenth century by the philosophies of theologian N. F. S. Grundtvig. Recognizing that a majority of the rural peasant population had lost touch with their own cultural traditions, language, and, ultimately, their role in the civic duties of society, the residential folk schools emerged as a place for adults to improve their literacy skills and learn about modern agricultural techniques and cooperative societies, while discussing their cultural contributions and possibilities in Danish society. The "schools for life" placed an emphasis on the "living word," celebrating song and oral traditions. In an attempt to bring the displaced peasants into the inner workings of the liberated country, the curriculum stressed the wisdom of common people and land-based agricultural societies and cooperatives, education through life experiences, and learning through informed and lively discussions. Within a generation, Denmark had witnessed a remarkable revival, thanks in many respects to the schools.

Riveted by their experiences, Horton and West envisioned the Danish folk-school model fitting well among their own displaced Appalachians. The two men were not the only proponents of the folk schools. A decade before their trips to Denmark, John C. Campbell, a midwestern educator who had worked in Appalachia for two decades on behalf of the Russell Sage Foundation and various other institutions, had written a study on the makeup of the mountaineer and the potential role of the folk schools in the Southern mountains. In his now classic book, *The Southern Highlander and His Homeland,* published in 1921 after his death and still considered today a remarkably insightful study on the region, Campbell concluded that the folk schools "might be adapted readily to meet the changing and varied needs of this land." Their implementation, however, rested on the "difficulties of finding persons possessing the proper spirit and personality" to conduct the folk school's ambitious mission.

No one would have agreed more with this assessment than Horton and West. They eventually dismissed the programs at the school named in Campbell's memory, the John C. Campbell Folk School in North Carolina, as a more romantic than realistic endeavor in dealing with the concerns of poor Appalachians. According to West, the Campbell school was inattentive to the region's racial problems and stuck on a curriculum more intent on preserving rather than invigorating cultural traditions. Both men interpreted the "folk" definition in its strictest sense of representing the aspirations of common people in dealing with their daily challenges, not in maintaining a quaint and apolitical, folkloric tapestry in the mountains.

In truth, the two young mountaineers had traveled across the states and the world like pilgrims. They returned to their mountains to ignite a revolution.

When Horton and West met at a conference in North Carolina in 1932, they inhabited a Southern Appalachia that had long been plunged into the depths of the Great Depression. The mills and mines were ablaze with turmoil and labor strife. The timber industry, which had clear-cut its way through the entire Mountain South with devastating results, had collapsed by the early 1920s. Agriculture, textiles, and bituminous coal—the backbone of the mountain economy—as historian Ronald Eller has noted, had stumbled years before the stock market crash of 1929. A massive change in the Southern industrial economy had dragged a generation of families down the mountains into the lower mill towns and coal camps. Now, with industries languishing in trouble, untold thousands of displaced mountaineers wandered back to their dirt farms or huddled in the urban areas in search of work or relief.

Another phase of Southern Appalachia had emerged: postindustrial and transient. According to an official report from the U.S. Department of Agriculture in this period, an irreversible historical shift had taken place in the region:

Our work shows how necessary it is to revise old ideas of the Southern Appalachians as a static region where life goes on unchangingly, a land exclusively occupied by the tall mountaineer with his lanky wife and shock-headed children. The past thirty years have been a time of rapid transformation. Population in the region has increased about 56 percent. This is almost wholly due to the great transforming influences—the growth of cities and the development of rural industries, especially mining.

When an elderly teacher and social reformer in Monteagle, Tennessee, an exceedingly poor area in the region, offered the two young men her large home and farmland for their proposed school in 1932, Horton and West merged their ideas and founded the Highlander Folk School. They relocated to an area mired in deforestation, closed mines, and subsistence farming; the locals harbored a profound distrust of outsiders. The founders' ambitions reflected the uncertainty and hope at the beginning of what would become the "angry decade" of social protest and federal intervention and relief. They announced the school would "train rural and industrial leaders for a new social order," rooted in their Appalachian legacies, "to conserve and to enrich the indigenous cultural values of the mountains." From its first day, Highlander also announced its deep commitment to interracial endeavors.

Untold utopian educational experiments in Appalachia, the South, and the rest of the nation, of course, had gone the route of burning enthusiasm into the dismal ashes of a disillusioning reality in a short time. In fact, Highlander did flounder in its first years before gaining a foothold in the region. Only one student signed up for the school's first classes. The school was forever afoot with a begging cup for donations. Its approach, however, influenced by the Danish model and the young men's own experiences, never wavered: Common people possessed the knowledge among themselves, if analyzed within a group and their social contexts, to solve their own problems. The school's role was to serve as the catalyst in providing the necessary support, courage, and, ultimately, training.

Contrary to the outside missionary viewpoint of "saving" the mountain communities, as if they were deficient, Highlander stood out as a unique institution that recognized the ability of mountaineers to determine their own fate in volatile times. Beyond its classes and discussions on labor history and tactics, unions and collective bargaining, economics, journalism, philosophy, religion, public speaking, and cooperatives, the Highlander experience was equally important in its relaxed and informal, residential nature. It created a microcosm of an interracial and vibrant community. All adult students, from whatever job sector or ethnic group, shared in the cooking and cleaning, socialized outside discriminatory circles and pressures, and took part in singing, dramas, and dances. The educational process, or "diploma" in one sense, consisted of meeting, talking, and exchanging and then going back to the student's community as an activist.

One of the school's first experiences added to the complexity of the region for Horton and West. Joining Taylor and his Vanderbilt cadre of students and faculty, along with other regional activists, in supporting a bitter coal mining strike in Wilder, Tennessee, in 1932, the Highlander staff witnessed the lawlessness and heartbreaking violence in the coal camps.

The outside-owned coal companies in Wilder had declared that they would not recognize any new contracts or negotiations unless the miners took a 20 percent cut in pay; the miners were already trapped in a wage system that paid less than $2 a day for a sixteen-hour shift. Announcing that they preferred to "starve out in the open than starve to death in the mines," the miners went on strike. Gun battles raged through the company town and on the back roads. The National Guard arrived, just as in Gastonia, in an attempt to keep the peace. Within the year, with the nation's spotlight on the conflict, the local union leader was shot in the back by hired company guards. According to the *Chattanooga Times,* the town soon dissolved into "a ragged Wilder, hungry Wilder, desperate Wilder."

Horton was briefly arrested and detained in Wilder for being an outside agitator. Despite national attention, the strike faltered in the spring of 1933. As foretold by Horton, none of the company gun thugs implicated in the murder of the union leader were ever convicted.

Horton and West, along with other Vanderbilt students and faculty, participated in the funeral. Instead of preaching a eulogy of despair, both men marked the occasion as an irreversible turning point in their commitment to social change in Appalachia and the South.

IN THE FACE of such brutal realities in the mining and mill communities, Highlander sought to strengthen its contacts among labor unions and offered the school's services as a training center. The unions responded; they asked Highlander to host workshops and classes for their leaders and members.

In 1938, Hollywood filmmaker Elia Kazan produced a distinguished documentary, *People of the Cumberland*, which highlighted Highlander's success in organizing "the lonely and forgotten people" in the South. Horton took part in the campaign drives of the Congress for Industrial Organization (CIO), traveling throughout the South in the late 1930s as an organizer in the textile mill areas. In the 1940s, Highlander's staff grew, allowing the school to set up scores of labor training programs throughout the South.

Horton's approach of cultivating the rank-and-file leadership flew in the face of many authoritarian labor leaders in the period. He preferred the school's role as a "percolator," instead of being a "drip-down" organ of information. He also agreed to work with anyone, whether left wing or conservative. Disgruntled by the divisions in the labor movement and the Red scare in the CIO, which persecuted and kicked out any organizers affiliated with the Communist Party, the mountain school decided to shift its focus to Southern farmers and farmworkers. Most of all, the school staff had been disillusioned by the refusal of many organized labor leaders to accept Highlander's interracial approach.

Throughout this period, the school had never ignored the issue of ethnic unity and cooperation on a political level. Highlander's fame circulated throughout the South as the singular mountaintop school where both whites and blacks could meet, in defiance of a 1901 Tennessee law forbidding interracial gatherings in the state. A black professor even taught occasionally at Highlander in the 1930s. As early as 1935, the school hosted a session of the All Southern Conference for Civil Rights and Trade Union Rights, which had been chased out of its original meeting place in Chattanooga.

In 1940, Highlander announced a school policy stating that it would refuse to assist any unions that discriminated against blacks. As part of this policy, the school featured interracial dormitories and bathrooms, as well as dining areas, as a groundbreaking institution. According to one African American participant at a Highlander summit for the United Auto Workers in 1944, which drew leaders from around the South and the rest of the country, the communal living was a far more life-changing event than the business meetings. It gave the union a chance to "carry out its constitution . . . in the mountains."

Horton's matter-of-fact approach to interracial efforts confounded a lot of people with its effortlessness. Years later, when asked by reporters how he managed to bring black and white leaders to the same dining table in the South, Horton responded with an often-quoted formula. "First, the food is prepared," he said. "Second, it's put on the table. Third, we ring the bell."

THE TWO founding personalities of the school eventually came to a parting. Despite their common vision and background, Horton and West had completely different operating styles. More militant in his approach, West left Highlander in 1933, setting off on a peripatetic path as a radical labor and political organizer—a path that would make him a legendary revolutionary figure in the South and Appalachia. His bona fides were impressive: He was wanted "dead or alive" during an underground campaign to defend a radical black activist who had organized hunger marches in Atlanta in 1934; he became a best-selling poet and literary phenomenon courted by the Greenwich Village literary circles; often jailed and beaten, he served as a labor organizer in North Carolina mill towns and Kentucky mining camps in the late 1930s; as a one-time Communist activist hounded during the McCarthy era, West even had to shoot his way out of a lynch mob organized against him in the 1950s in Georgia. An internal memo at the FBI hailed him the "most dangerous man" in the South at one point. After years of threats and cross burnings, the Klan burned down his family farm, library, and heirlooms. He founded another folk school in West Virginia in the 1960s and served as a mentor for a new generation of Appalachian activists and writers.

West and Horton continued to correspond and meet throughout their lives. Highlander, as their joint creation, would have an impact on the South and Appalachia far beyond their wildest dreams.

In 1953, the Highlander board announced that the new emphasis at the mountain school would be one of school desegregation. The executive council, in answering its own question—What is the most pressing problem for the people of the South that Highlander can tackle?—declared that the school would seek to conquer "meanness, prejudice and tradition" by becoming a place where educators and community members could "learn the art, practice and the methods of brotherhood."

Such a declaration was not as artless as it may have sounded. Highlander's plunge into desegregation emerged from a longtime experience that the "time for action had come." Horton and his crew based their programs on the feedback of their former students. Over the past twenty years, the institution had trained or hosted nearly ten thousand adults and children at its school and workshops on various issues, sending them back to their communities to take action.

Desegregation efforts by Highlander-trained people, in fact, were already under way in eastern Tennessee communities like Knoxville, Oak Ridge, and Chattanooga and numerous towns in South Carolina, Alabama, Arkansas, and Georgia. Closer to home, Highlander operated on the notion that the public schools in the Appalachian region would be a litmus test for the South in making a smooth transition to integration. Otherwise, as one of the board members noted, if "East Tennessee successfully resists integration, there is going to be a long and tedious history of resistance elsewhere."

Seeking to function as a microcosm of society to discuss and rehearse potential problems and interactions, the school actively sought out people from around the region. A broad array of students—elementary school teachers, professors, ministers, farmers, judges, bus drivers, barbers, businesspeople, and homemakers—began to make the journey to the mountain school. Thrust into an interracial residential experience, black and white educators and other leaders from around the South converged on Highlander to recount their experiences in their own segregated schools and communities.

Through this process of exchange, Highlander drew up the first experimental curriculum in the South to prepare teachers and community members for the transition to integration and launched a series of workshops entitled "The Supreme Court Decisions and the Public Schools." As the word passed among black communities around the region about Highlander's role as the "one place where blacks and whites could meet and talk over problems," attendance at the residential workshops rose dramatically by 1955.

One influential person to emerge from these meetings was an African American public school teacher from Charleston, South Carolina, Septima Clark, who had been active with the National Association for the Advancement of Colored People (NAACP). After being fired from her job for attempting to unionize teachers and attending NAACP meetings, Clark joined the staff at Highlander as the director of education in 1955 and served as a mentor and an adviser for a generation of civil rights leaders.

For Horton and Highlander, the development of African American leaders grew to be the underlying focus of the workshops. The mountain activists recognized early on that an undeniable distrust and tension simmered among blacks and well-meaning white liberals, which often kept supportive campaigns from happening. In response to a crisis situation, the school announced in one of its newsletters, "progress or chaos results, depending upon the leadership. The Negro, barred from the usual places of leadership training, desperately needs leaders among his own people." Another activist with the NAACP was also under pressure in her local community of Montgomery, Alabama. She traveled to Highlander in the summer of 1955 and became the symbol of Highlander's vision.

Rosa Parks, often hailed as "The Mother of the Civil Rights Movement," has been immortalized in many chronicles for her heroic act that set off the Montgomery Bus Boycott and, ultimately, the rise of Martin Luther King Jr. and the civil rights movement. One aspect of Parks's life, however, tends to be overlooked in the mythology of her fame; having joined the NAACP during World War II, the forty-two-year-old seamstress had been a longtime activist, secretary of the local NAACP association, and a youth worker in her community. She had been involved in an earlier altercation at a bus stop, refusing to enter from the back door, a decade before. Her attendance at a workshop at Highlander, in fact, came on the heels of her work to bring a controversial Washington-based Freedom Train exhibit to Montgomery, which prohibited segregated viewing. In a rare occurrence, schoolchildren from the Montgomery schools, black and white, had attended the exhibit together.

A prominent white Southern activist, Virginia Durr, had prompted Parks's involvement with Highlander. Durr's husband, Clifford, was a leading civil rights attorney in Montgomery; her brother-in-law, Hugo Black, served on the U.S. Supreme Court. Durr knew Parks as a seamstress and called on her often for work. As a longtime supporter of Horton and Highlander, Durr encouraged the NAACP activist to attend one of the leadership workshops in the Tennessee mountains. It wasn't until Durr actually wrote Horton and obtained a scholarship that Parks made the trip to Highlander.

Clark, who had been vital in transporting carloads of African American activists from around the South, found Parks an extremely timid and reticent participant. Others referred to her as the "quietest" one in the group. Parks feared that her job might be in jeopardy for attending the interracial workshop, and pleaded with another Montgomery teacher not to inform others of her presence. Nonetheless, the daily workshops and discussions drew Parks out; Clark cajoled her into recounting the Freedom Train events.

Highlander's interracial residential experience astounded Parks. She took part in the dancing and singing with white and black students. In a later interview with radio commentator Studs Terkel, Parks recalled how the Highlander experience had been a first in her life, "where we all were treated equally and without any tension or feeling of embarrassment or whatever goes with the artificial boundaries of racial segregation."

Horton's role in the workshop was crucial. Parks found the Highlander director to be the "first white man" she could trust. Speaking at a gathering thirty-five years after their meeting, she recalled Horton's ability to "strip the white segregationists of their hardcore attitudes and how he could confuse them, and I found myself laughing when I hadn't been able to laugh in a long time."

Horton, who would always downplay any influence or role he held in the civil rights movement, concluded the workshop as he had done at all workshops with a session called "Finding Your Way Back Home." He urged all the participants to picture how they might utilize the workshop discussions in their own communities. "You have brought these problems here," he told them. "We have been a sort of catalyst in a process that makes a little bulge in your education. Now, are you going to keep on learning? Highlander will continue to relate to you in terms of this process when you get back. So you are not going back alone. We will work with you if you get in trouble."

Parks's vision of the Montgomery situation was dismal. She described a fractured and intimidated community in the "heart of the Confederacy," where few blacks were willing to challenge the "status Crow." But she had found herself at Highlander at a pivotal time; she had been affected earlier that spring by the solitary act of a fifteen-year-old girl, Claudette Colvin, who had been arrested for refusing to move from her seat on a bus in Montgomery. The young girl was arrested for disorderly conduct, not a violation of the segregation laws. Still, the news of Colvin's arrest forced Parks to reconsider her longtime efforts to draw up petitions and hold meetings. She later recounted that when she had arrived at Highlander, "I felt that it was time to demonstrate and act in whatever way we could to make it known that we would no longer accept the way that we had been treated as a people."

Clark escorted Parks back to the Atlanta bus terminal after the workshop at Highlander. Parks had been afraid to travel alone. Moved by her description of the Montgomery repression, a UN official who had also attended the workshop told Parks to contact him "if anything happens," and promised support. Virginia Durr later recounted in an embellished but sincere testimony that Parks, "so happy and so liberated" after the Highlander experience, could no longer bear the discrimination in Montgomery.

On December 1, 1955, four months after the workshop, Rosa Parks set off the civil rights movement when she refused to give up her seat on a bus in Montgomery, Alabama, to a white passenger. Another woman, Mary Louise Smith, had also been arrested for the same offense in October. Supported by the Durrs and local activist and unionist E. D. Nixon, Parks's famous case became a rallying call for civil rights in Montgomery and the rest of the South. Her arrest spiraled into a bus boycott that lasted 381 days and focused the nation's attention on the South. The boycott not only altered the segregation laws on transportation, but also produced a prophet of the times. As the spokesman of the new movement, a twenty-six-year-old newcomer to the Montgomery religious circles, Martin Luther King, Jr., stepped into world history.

AS THE KEYNOTE speaker at the twenty-fifth-anniversary celebrations at Highlander in 1957, Martin Luther King praised the school's "dauntless courage and fearless determination" in the emerging civil rights movement. He also heard for the first time, as he recounted on the drive home with Southern activist Anne Braden, a song that "really sticks with you." It was called "We Will Overcome." The song had been the theme of the celebrations, recorded in a film documentary that showed black and white participants singing it together at Highlander.

Singing, of course, in the tradition of the Southern Appalachians, had always been a part of the Highlander experience. When Zilphia Johnson, a young woman from the Arkansas Ozarks, married Horton in 1936, she brought with her an accordion and a musical background, along with a commitment to social justice, all of which fit in well at the mountain school. Within a few years, Zilphia Horton had toured extensively in the region, collecting ballads and encouraging others at strikes and labor meetings to write topical songs that one newspaper hailed as "the genuine article in Southern Highland music." More importantly, Zilphia oversaw the crucial role of music at Highlander's own workshops and classes.

In the summer of 1946, a group of black students from the Food, Tobacco and Agricultural Workers Union in South Carolina attended a workshop at Highlander. As part of the session, Zilphia had called on the union members, who had just won a bitterly contested strike and national boycott, to share any songs. Though none in the group possessed a musical background that could transcribe the song, the tobacco workers sang their version of an old African American spiritual, which they had transformed into "We Will Overcome." Enthused by their singing and newly written verses, altering religious phrasing for union slogans, Zilphia recorded a rough version of the song and then recast her own version with the rhythmic and harmonic structures of an Appalachian mountain ballad.

According to singer and musicologist Bernice Reagon, the song was a variation of a popular nineteenth-century Baptist and Methodist hymn found among African American churches in the low country of the Carolinas; it was generally sung with the refrain "I'll Be All Right." A similar interpretation was transcribed and published by an African American Methodist minister in 1901 under the title "I'll Overcome Someday."

The song quickly became a school institution, passed on to thousands of students, including Rosa Parks. Folksinger Pete Seeger learned it at Highlander later that same year and immediately began spreading his version around the country. Changing the rhythm slightly, Seeger's musical ears preferred "We shall" instead of "We will" in the chorus. Labor unions took up the song immediately. When a young California folksinger, Guy Carawan, learned it from another folksinger in the early 1950s, he had no idea of his eventual role as a modern-day pied piper in spreading the song to civil rights workers at Highlander.

Zilphia died in a tragic accident at Highlander in 1956. Taking her position as the music coordinator at Highlander in 1959, Carawan reintroduced the song to a new generation of college students who had participated in some of the first sit-ins in the South. (The song itself was copyrighted in Zilphia's name, along with Seeger, Frank Hamilton, and Carawan.) At a huge sit-in in Nashville in the spring of 1960, the song received its first national media spotlight, when Carawan and the students were filmed singing on evening television news. "We Shall Overcome" resounded into the living rooms of America for the first, but not last, time.

Later that same spring, at a workshop that included many of the Nashville students who would play a leading role in the establishment of the Student Nonviolent Coordinating Committee (SNCC), Carawan noted the unique success of the song among urbane young people who had often rejected the more folksy rural and traditional ballads. (Recognizing that young people had views and expectations different from their parents, Highlander had been running college leadership workshops on myriad issues for nearly a decade.) Striking a chord among these Nashville students at Highlander, who included future Washington, D.C., mayor Marion Barry and future U.S. Representative John Lewis, the song was passed on at the SNCC founding conference two weeks later in Raleigh.

The historic momentum for integration had been ignited. Joined by black student leaders from around the region, SNCC emerged as a leading civil rights organization in the country, churning out the "young shock troops" alongside King and legions of unknown activists in the civil rights movement.

"We Shall Overcome" became their anthem.

FROM LABOR BATTLES to the civil rights movement, Highlander was more than a remote pioneering school on a mountain. When necessary, it brought the mountain spirit and training programs, like the veterans of Kings Mountain, to the lowland communities in the South. And Horton, as its figurehead and visionary, generally led the charge and transcended his self-deprecating label of "radical hillbilly" in more than one way. As a quiet and not-so-quiet adviser to King's Southern Christian Leadership Conference (SCLC) and virtually every major current in the civil rights movement, hosting the planning meetings for historic events such as the Mississippi Summer Project voting drive in 1964, Horton had a deceptive but undeniably pervasive role in shaping the movement's strategies.

Beyond the more celebrated and news-making events that have received well-deserved attention, some of Highlander's greatest educational successes, such as the Citizenship Schools, remained largely unknown to the public at large. Their impact was nevertheless critical in the transformation of the South.

A story closer to the Highlander home irrevocably changed the nature of segregation in the nation. As early as 1950, residents in the Appalachian community of Clinton, Tennessee, had filed a suit against segregation laws in the schools. Black students had been forced to either travel to Knoxville or attend a segregated school in nearby Rockwood. When the U.S. Supreme Court unanimously struck down the separate-but-equal policy in 1954, the presiding judge in Knoxville declared that the Clinton High School had to open its doors to African American students by the fall of 1956.

Highlander and its Southern associates had long recognized the importance of eastern Tennessee mountain communities in setting a pattern to implement or refuse the new law. Horton had actually been present in Washington, D.C., in support of NAACP attorney Thurgood Marshall, when the historic decision was handed down. Like many others, Horton knew that the Supreme Court case would not simply usher in a new era without a tremendous amount of resistance, terrorism, and massive violence from segregationists, a threat to children throughout the region, and the ultimate use of the National Guard to protect the schools. Clinton High School stood on the front lines.

Along with the early school-desegregation workshops in 1953, Highlander had reached out to educators and community leaders in Clinton and the neighboring communities in Oak Ridge, Norris, and Knoxville.

The school had sponsored interracial summer camps as a first step for children to come together. Principals, counselors, and teachers had attended Highlander workshops in 1954 and 1955 and, joined by community leaders and professors from around the region, assisted in developing a transitional curriculum. In the spring of 1956, for example, schoolchildren had been assigned papers on integration topics. Highlander also published booklets such as "Basic Policies Presentation to Local School Boards" and guides to desegregation for "an orderly transition." One of Highlander's closest associates, local Grundy County author May Justus, whose children's books had gone far in providing a positive view of Appalachian cultures, was so inspired by the meetings and historic regional events that she authored *New Boy in School,* one of the nation's first children's books that dealt with the subject of school desegregation.

The Clinton High School experience started out reasonably calm. Twelve African American students attended the first day without any problems. The white population of the mountain community had accepted the new law as the final word, despite some misgivings. After an outside segregationist leader of the White Citizens Council, whose rallying call had been "segregation or death," arrived in town, a few locals began to protest in front of the school, earning the attention of the news media. The tension heightened over the next month, leading to attacks on some of the students and blacks in the community. When gunfire erupted after a football game, the National Guard was called in to police the town for the rest of the year.

The psychological pressure on the school was immense. The principal, a slight man at 130 pounds, apparently lost 15 pounds over the year; like the majority of the teachers, he resigned the next spring after a year of intense harassment. Shadowy groups phoned in threats on a constant basis. Violence continued to occur in the area. Many of the black students begged their parents to leave; one girl's parents whisked her off to California relatives.

Realizing that the children and their families desperately needed a support network, Highlander convened a number of meetings with agencies and organizations in the South to come to the aid of the "potential martyrs." In an effort to support and boost the morale of the students and teachers, Highlander threw parties for the youngsters and developed a special tutoring program. Students eventually came to Highlander for a secret retreat to relax. As part of this process, longtime educator Clark played a critical role as an African American mentor for the young students, encouraging them to stay the course of their convictions. With the nation watching this pioneering school and its integration drama unfolding, Highlander realized that the bravery of the students had to be matched by a sustained campaign from their advocates.

By the start of the spring semester, only six black students remained enrolled. More attacks occurred. Still, the mountain town's tenacity held. When Bobby Cain walked through the graduation ceremonies in the spring of 1957, he became the first black student to graduate from a desegregated high school in the South.

ACCESS TO EDUCATION was also on the mind of an adult student who had attended one of Highlander's desegregation workshops in 1954. Arriving at the mountain school at Clark's urging, South Carolina businessman Esau Jenkins recounted the experiences of African Americans in the Sea Islands. Being from Charleston, Clark was no stranger to the area; she had taught at a small school on Johns Island in 1916. Cut off from the mainland by any means of transportation outside of boats until the first bridges were built in the 1930s, the string of islands that draped down the Carolinas and Georgia had evolved into a unique Gullah outpost, with a distinct African-influenced language and culture.

The Gullahs' ancestors had been enslaved across West Africa and impressed as the planters and engineers in developing the region's cotton, rice, and indigo plantations. The amazing toil of their enslaved work, its complexity often overlooked, gave rise to the rice kings and their eighteenth- and nineteenth-century aristocracy in Southern cities like Charleston. In Jenkins's report on the Gullah communities in the 1950s, he concluded that voting rights remained one of the most pressing problems facing the disenfranchised people. South Carolina maintained strict literacy laws, which had been upheld by the Supreme Court. In the process, the majority of the Gullah had been prevented from voting. Only 210 blacks on Johns Island, for example, had registered in the last century.

Horton traveled to the Sea Islands the next spring, remaining for several months. Aware of the suspicion of outside white visitors like himself, he sought to observe local affairs by living and working with Gullah farmers and fishing folks. Acting on the initiative of Jenkins, whose bus service to Charleston had been a critical gathering spot for the islanders, Horton, Clark, and others began to formulate a plan to establish evening Citizenship Schools, where black adults could learn to read and write and, ultimately, "seize political power."

Staving off any institutional or outside missionary element, Highlander hired a local hairdresser, Bernice Robinson, to be the first teacher for a model program that opened its doors on January 7, 1957, on Johns Island. Highlander had loaned Jenkins and his associates the funds to purchase an old schoolhouse. In a policy that continued over the years, Horton insisted that only African Americans from the area be hired; the plan was to cultivate local leaders through local initiatives. Beyond the basics of literacy, the schools emphasized discussions and educational activities dealing with immediate problems and needs, voting rights, and what Robinson would later term "big ideas." Before long, she was teaching courses on the South Carolina constitution and the Declaration of Human Rights of the United Nations.

Eight students successfully registered to vote after the first course. As the word traveled in the area, attendance soon soared, and schools opened around the Sea Islands in beauty shops, churches, co-op stores, and community centers. Clark noted in one report that demand for classes far exceeded the facilities. Teachers were suddenly leading their classes in kitchens and under the draping Spanish moss of trees. As the voting ranks increased and local black populations made their voice heard in the 1960 elections, capturing some of the town seats on the island councils, the role of the schools became clear to Jenkins and his white detractors. "Everyone is jubilant for the Highlander Folk School," Jenkins declared. "It has helped them see the light."

Of course, not everyone was thrilled with the integrationist visions of the Citizenship Schools. Editorials appeared in Charleston and other local Carolinian newspapers about the potential horror of registering black voters. The success of the Citizenship Schools brought tremendous pressure and resistance from the white power structure in the low country of the South, as the experience of the workshops spread to other black communities in Georgia, Alabama, and Tennessee. It also overwhelmed the limited resources and staff of Highlander.

Adding to the tension, the radical reputation of the mountain school in Tennessee made it the target again for segregationist forces from around the region. Cleverly mixing anti-integrationist views with anti-communist propaganda, segregationists depicted Horton and his civil rights colleagues as Reds. Anyone who supported integration in the South suddenly found his or her patriotism under suspicion. Billboards arose throughout the South with a photo of King, Horton, and other participants at Highlander's twenty-fifth-anniversary celebration. The caption in huge letters on the billboard accused King of attending "a Communist Training Center."

With a life of their own, the Citizenship Schools began to proliferate informally throughout the South. In 1959, Ella Baker, executive director of King's SCLC and the future mentor for SNCC, journeyed to the Sea Islands to investigate the possibility of replicating the program on a wider level. Baker found the schools inspiring and powerful; she encouraged King and others to implement them as part of their ailing voter registration efforts. By 1961, despite Highlander's being hamstrung by legal battles and violent reprisals, King sent scores of SCLC teachers to the mountain school to train in the Citizenship School program. Recruited by Horton out of New York City, Andrew Young, a young minister who would go on to become the mayor of Atlanta and the U.S. ambassador to the United Nations, was hired to assist in transferring the program to SCLC and set the Citizenship Schools on a fast track in the South.

As the most effective organizing tool of the civil rights movement, according to some historians, the Citizenship Schools reached tens of thousands of African Americans over the next years. Black voting ranks swelled in the South. In the process, the schools produced a generation of black political leaders, such as Fannie Lou Hamer of the Mississippi Freedom Democratic Party, by providing them with their first involvement in civil rights through the training programs.

Young, of course, as one of those leaders, looked back at the schools with a profound appreciation of their ripple effect. In educating and mobilizing the front ranks of the civil rights movement in the South, the schools were "the base," he declared, from which the movement was built.

ON THAT FATEFUL summer night in 1959, when the Tennessee state troopers and local police stormed the ramparts of the Highlander Folk School and found a handful of liquor bottles in Horton's personal cabinet, it was clear that Highlander's role in the burgeoning civil rights movement had simply become too hot for the Southern segregationists. The prosecuting attorney assigned by the Tennessee legislature had declared his intention to make "something stick," in order to shut down the school. He wasn't alone. Hounded by racist elements and segregationist leaders across the region, Highlander was branded by a Chattanooga newspaper as a "sordid story of this festering sore atop the mountains in the heart of Tennessee." Other Southern newspapers, such as the Nashville *Tennessean,* recognized the witch hunt as a front to attack Highlander for "its candid advocacy of integration."

The raid was eventually declared illegal; the whiskey bottles were thrown out. Undaunted, the district attorney scrounged about desperately in petitioning for a hearing against Highlander. He also called for an injunction to padlock the school. "The place has a reputation of being one where people drink and engage in immoral, lewd and unchaste practices," he declared. A judge agreed to hear the case, and Highlander's doors were locked.

The series of trials and hearings over the next year, as the *Chattanooga*

Times noted, did indeed resemble a Scopes-like monkey trial. The more progressive Southern newspaper editors cringed at reviving McCarthyism. Locals, who had axes to grind for whatever reasons with Horton and his staff, recounted all sorts of horrific tales of folly and intrigue. The communist charges were repeatedly dredged up, as were accusations that Horton was running a racket. Highlander pleaded its case, calling in the support of civil rights and public figures from around the country, including luminaries like Eleanor Roosevelt, Jackie Robinson, Martin Luther King, and Reinhold Niebuhr. Roosevelt, in fact, a longtime supporter of Highlander, wrote that the prosecuting attorney would someday "be deeply ashamed" by his actions. Whether or not that ever occurred, the costly trial placed an additional burden on the otherwise depleted school resources. Horton and his associates found themselves scrambling to cover their debts.

In the end, throwing out the barrage of accusations, and sidestepping the 1901 segregation laws in Tennessee, the judge managed to revoke the school's charter on two main offenses: Beer had been "sold" on the premises—following a common tradition in the area, students had made donations to a rotating fund for beer—and he found that Horton had used the nonprofit school for "personal gain." This last offense was erroneous; Highlander had legally transferred a tract of land to Horton in 1957 as back pay for his services as director.

Nonetheless, the Highlander Folk School buildings were shuttered. On a cold winter day in December 1961, after various appeals had been denied or lost, the school's property, the five-thousand-volume library, furniture, bed sheets, farm equipment—everything on the 174-acre grounds—were auctioned to a gaggle of local segregationists anxious to buy goods on the cheap.

Horton and his associates did not attend the auction. They were too busy. They had already drawn up a charter for a new school, the Highlander Research and Education Center, to be temporarily based in Knoxville, Tennessee. A new Highlander-sponsored voting education project had just been launched in Mississippi.

After nearly three decades of social crusades in the South and

Appalachia, an amused but weary Horton dismissed the trial and school closing as a circus. "A school is an idea," he declared. "And you can't padlock an idea."

Horton may have lost his first school and his personal belongings and property, but he had not lost his sense of humor or spirit. He continued to travel the country and the world as a legendary activist and educator until his death in 1991. Highlander continues today on a farm outside Knoxville, still in the forefront of social justice movements.

Epilogue

WE ARE ALL APPALACHIANS

᠊ᢆᢇᢆ᠊

Something like a shadow has fallen between the present and past,
an abyss wide as war that cannot be bridged by any tangible connection, so
that memory is undermined and the image of our beginnings betrayed,
dissolved, rendered not mythical but illusory. We have connived
in the murder of our own origins.

—Edward Abbey,
"Shadows from the Big Woods," *The Journey Home*

In 1839, Washington Irving, the globe-trotting author who gave the world the Rip Van Winkle legend—a tale that would be saddled onto Southern Appalachian backs for the next several generations—wrote a letter opining his belief that the United States of America needed to change its name. That it needed a more pointed geographical reference. Irving had one in mind: He suggested the country's new name should be either the United States of Alleghenia or the United States of Appalachia. In the writer's mind, our nation's southeastern mountain range was the great American landmark. Irving wasn't taken seriously, the United States of America remained intact, and Appalachians would have to wait for another day to claim the country for their own.

Or would they? In truth, Southern Appalachians have roamed to all ends of the United States and the rest of the world, spreading their traditions and changing the way we live. Beyond their contributions to indigenous struggles—the American Revolution; the abolitionist, labor, and civil rights movements; and literary and musical innovations—they have literally peopled the nation. I dare say that if older American families took the time to do a little genealogy, they'd find an Appalachian or two in the woodpile. One of their ancestors would have at least tarried while passing through the Cumberland Gap or ferrying down the Ohio River.

I know mine did, though I didn't realize this when I first stumbled into Southern Appalachia in 1983. A college dropout, I was hitching and hiking along the Appalachian Trail in North Carolina, Tennessee, and southern Virginia, taking day-laborer jobs on various farms. I brought with me a vague sense of my heritage. I had been uprooted as a child and transplanted in the Sonoran Desert of southern Arizona, though I had not been completely purged of a Southern hill culture. For one thing, my grandparents and cousins remained in southern Illinois (and then moved back into Kentucky), in the little-known eastern boot of the state that hides itself in the hilly range of the Shawnee National Forest, also known as the Illinois Ozarks.

Referred to locally as the Garden of the Gods, this range possesses one of the most diverse forest biomes outside Appalachia. The area has also been soaked in Shawnee blood and indigenous ruin. My mother, raised for a spell in an Eagle Mountain hollow in a log cabin with no running water or electricity, came from a family that had tended its homestead for nearly two centuries. The family had farmed its hills, dug its ginseng and other herbs in the forests, worked the coal mines, and eventually parceled out its family members to the steel mills and canning factories in Chicago and Indiana. My grandfather had been a coal miner, among many things; black lung disease haunted his later years. He was buried with pieces of coal embedded in his head, having barely survived a mine explosion. My ancestors maintained a Primitive Baptist subculture, spoke a regional dialect drawn from Cumberland English and Lowland Scots, considered themselves Scotch-Irish, and lived on a molasses, cornbread, and mast-fed pork farm cuisine that could have easily floated down from Appalachia on the Ohio River. The region, also known as

Egypt, defended itself from the same stereotypes of feuds, lawlessness, moonshine, laziness, racism, poverty, superstition, and general backwardness that have plagued Southern Appalachia.

The disparaging connections, in fact, were not as distant as I had imagined. On further digging among the family roots, I found that my ancestors, like most of the pioneers and early waves of immigrants into southern Illinois, had come from the Mountain South. My mother's family branches had come from North Carolina, southwestern Virginia, and northern Alabama; they were not simply Scotch-Irish, as so many Southerners are commonly grouped, but a mixture of Swedish, Scottish, English, Dutch, and Chickasaw. My father's Scottish family had come from eastern Kentucky after the Civil War; they had split over of the issue of slavery. They left behind their hemp farms and slave-owning brothers.

One of the landmark articles in the 1870s that had sullied the Appalachians as "a strange land and peculiar people" included the Egyptians in southern Illinois on that select roster of cultural misfits. Before Grace MacGowan Cooke wrote her groundbreaking novel about cotton mill workers in Appalachia in 1910, she had already published a novel about coal miners in southern Illinois. One of Egypt's bloodiest characters, Billy Potts, was even taken across the river and replanted into Appalachian tales and a celebrated Robert Penn Warren poem. Long before "Bloody Harlan County," there was "Bloody Williamson County" in the coalfields of southern Illinois; Mother Jones, in fact, the labor figure identified with the West Virginia mining wars, was buried in a miner's union cemetery in Egypt at her request.

I discovered these genealogical wonders after two important events in my life. First, picked up by a random driver in the Virginia Blue Ridge, I was taken to the Appalachian South Folklife Center in Pipestem, West Virginia, after I had made a quip about "hillbillies." My driver, a Connecticut transplant named Warren Doyle, who has since become the dean of the Appalachian Trail for his record-breaking expeditions, offered to show me more about mountaineers, or to drop me at the next exit.

Thrust into the farm life and cultural activities of the folk school, which had been founded by the legendary labor activist and poet Don West (who had cofounded the Highlander Folk School with Myles Horton), for the summer, I learned firsthand not only about the need to champion progressive cultural traditions and values, but also how to sort fact from fiction in defending them from the nefarious versions of outsiders. Few people had done more than West over the past half century to nurture an Appalachian identity. He had churned out stacks of articles, poems, stories, and pamphlets on the history of "the other Appalachia." He was certainly controversial, often cantankerous, but committed to getting the story right.

West piled me down with books, starting with his own. In a life-changing summer for me, the Appalachian stalwart forced me to consider the role of writing in reclaiming the hidden histories and stories of the maligned and misunderstood regions in our society. "If you do not know your history," he lectured me, "others will provide it for you, often in a version that is wrong, belittling, and misleading. This is what has happened to Appalachia."

Opening the door to the region's literary treasury—West's own personal library had been burned down by the Ku Klux Klan in Georgia—he was the first person to remind me that some of our nation's most important writers had come from the back hills and mountains of Appalachia. West, though, was not interested in merely making an inventory of literary accomplishments or awards. Nor was he a provincial regionalist who had closed the door to the outside world. He believed the scribes of the Mountain South had played a distinct role in transforming the literature of the United States, especially in reminding our transient and urbanized populations that much of our historical and contemporary identity and stories were still connected to the land.

"You cannot understand America," he told me, "until you understand Appalachia."

TODAY's large stable of nationally acclaimed Appalachian writers has emerged from a long and hard-won literary struggle in the Southern mountains. Notable and best-selling authors abound now, including Robert Morgan, Homer Hickam, Barbara Kingsolver, Rick Bragg,

Dorothy Allison, John Ehle, Jan Karon, Adriana Trigiani, Tony Earley, Lee Smith, Sharyn Crumb, Fred Chappell, Romulus Linney, Wilma Dykeman, Denise Giardina, Silas House, Ron Rash, Jayne Anne Phillips, P. J. Laska, Frank X. Walker, Gretchen Laskas, Chris Offutt—among many, many others—and *Cold Mountain* novelist Charles Frazier, whose National Book Award–winning novel has been translated into dozens of languages.

The first book to be published in the Southern Appalachians dates back to the 1790s. Mountain muckraker Anne Royall knocked off a romance, *The Tennesseans,* in the late 1820s. By the time Martin Delany's serialized novel of insurrection dazzled the *Anglo-African Magazine* readership in the late 1850s, and Rebecca Harding Davis astonished the literary readers of the *Atlantic Monthly* in 1861 with her portrait of the iron mills, another Appalachian literary character had already claimed a national readership: Sut Lovingood, a "nat'ral born durn'd fool." Created by Knoxville writer George Washington Harris in the 1850s for the New York–based *Spirit of the Times* periodical and later published in book form, the Sut stories provided a comic portrayal of the gullible yet conniving backwoodsman whose brains are usually "unhook'd."

Often hailed as a great literary influence on Mark Twain (who was biologically conceived in an Appalachian cabin in the eastern Tennessee mountains, as some historians enjoy footnoting), Harris died in 1869, unaware that his exaggerated tall tales would flower into a century of local-color stories, romance novels, and boorish portraits. In fact, over two hundred books and stories about Appalachia and its mostly bedraggled, shotgun-brandishing, moonshine-swigging denizens and their "olde" English were published by 1920.

One remarkable exception was the return of Pulitzer Prize–winning novelist Willa Cather to her homeland of western Virginia. Her last novel, *Sapphira and the Slave Girl,* published in 1940, took place in Cather's Back Creek valley. A few years earlier, the arrival of another Appalachian writer, Thomas Wolfe, triggered a literary upheaval as dramatic as the stock market crash. His coming-of-age novel, *Look Homeward, Angel,* revealed the scandalous backroom scenes in the fictional mountain town of Altamount. It was published only days before Black Tuesday in 1929. Based in his native

Asheville, North Carolina, the novel devastated any dull facade that had masked small-town America and essentially launched a new vogue for the autobiographical exposé. Compared variably to Walt Whitman, Herman Melville, and Fyodor Dostoyevsky, the towering Wolfe became an overnight sensation in New York and abroad. It took seven years before he managed to return to his outraged hometown in Appalachia.

The true big bang of Southern Appalachian literature occurred in the 1930s, when a trio of students out of Lincoln Memorial University in the Cumberland Gap (they also attended Vanderbilt together) began to publish their stories and poems in national magazines and then widely praised books. The three writers were James Still, from northern Alabama, Jesse Stuart, from eastern Kentucky, and West himself, from northern Georgia. This trio is notable for many things, but a singular Appalachian trait stands out: They were as adept at writing poetry as they were at writing fiction or nonfiction. Stuart's first poetry collection, in 1934, thrust him into the national arena as an "American Robert Burns." West sold over 100,000 copies of a collection of quatrain ballads and labor poems in 1946.

Emerging over the decades as the dean of Appalachian literature, Still wrote several acclaimed volumes of poetry, fiction, and essays. Released in 1940 to great praise, his *River of Earth* novel stunned the nation with its account of rural displacement. Chronicling the pivotal years in the life of mountain farmers in eastern Kentucky before the Great Depression, the novel is a paean to the mountaineers' understanding of the natural world around them and the industrial forces beyond their control. The farmers eventually make the agonizing decision to leave their yeoman independence behind for uncertain work in the coal mines. Steeped in the geography and language of the mountaineers, the novel captures the tremendous changes taking place in Appalachia. *Time* magazine hailed it as "a work of art." Many critics preferred its lyrical prose and dialectal phrasings over John Steinbeck's *Grapes of Wrath,* released the previous year.

River of Earth shared the Southern Authors Award with fellow Appalachian Thomas Wolfe, who had died suddenly at the age of thirty-eight, in 1938. Published posthumously as *You Can't Go Home Again,* Wolfe's novel continues the journey of his alter ego George, who has written a novel, *Home to Our Mountain.* Returning to Appalachia for the first time in years, George finds that "a spirit of drunken waste and wild destructiveness was everywhere apparent." He is soon on the road again, traversing the seas for other countries. The words of a local woman haunt him: "There's no better or more beautiful place on earth than in these mountains—and someday you'll come home again to stay." Wolfe, in fact, was buried in Asheville.

THE LEGACY OF Appalachia's literary community, as Still's and Wolfe's contrasting works show, is as varied and complex as the region. Authors in the Southern mountains have cultivated an extraordinarily rich, diverse, and enduring literary terrain in twentieth-century American literature. Unafraid of tackling the great moral issues of their day, their work has taken on the quintessential American paradox: exploring our nation's sense of place and identity in a time of tremendous change and displacement.

Far from being narrow in scope or regional in tone, contemporary Appalachian writing has mined its mountains and hills as a critical chapter within the broader American experience. Appalachian authors have reminded American readers that you cannot separate a land from its inhabitants; you cannot write about mountains without mountaineers, or hills without hill folk. With a profound understanding of geography and nature, in one of the last regions of the country where *roots* refer to both family deeds that date back to the American Revolution *and* the wilderness that surrounds them, writers have captured the diversity of the region's biomes, rural and urban communities, languages, ethnicities, ways of life and labor, music, and religious visitations. At the brink of some of the most violent clashes in agrarian societies and the rise of industrialization, Appalachian themes have dealt with our nation's most unflinching labor and land wars.

In this respect, Mary Lee Settle's series of largely unknown novels,

The Beulah Quintet, which spans over three hundred years in a breathtaking historical saga of western Virginia families, is one of the most ambitious undertakings by any modern American writer. Begun in 1956, Settle's five volumes were published over twenty-five years. Her story takes us from the debtor prisons of England to a modern-day barroom brawl in Charleston, West Virginia. Written with painstaking attention to historical detail, Settle sought to provide a human story behind the often glossed-over role of America's forced founders, be they serfs, slaves, indigenous, or working class. In one interview, she offered this trigger for her series of novels: "I had a picture of one man hitting another in a West Virginia drunk tank one Saturday night, and the idea was to go all the way back to see what lay behind that blow." She had to "go back" to Cromwell's prisons in the British Isles.

Settle's landmark work on Appalachia has been overlooked in most literary circles. Strangely enough, she won a National Book Award for *Blood Tie,* her novel about expatriates in Turkey.

SUPRISINGLY, a number of twentieth-century Appalachian writers lost their mountaineer and hill folk status altogether, either by joining national literary movements or by moving away. Overlooking the roots and influences at play in their work, many critics have simply deemed them Southern writers. James Agee, a much-celebrated twentieth-century "Southern" writer, is—like Wolfe—rarely associated with Appalachia, even though Agee won the Pulitzer Prize posthumously for his novel *A Death in the Family,* which was based on his childhood in Knoxville.

West Virginia–raised William Demby, one of the celebrated writers in the Harlem Renaissance, wrote a groundbreaking coming-of-age novel in 1950, *Beetlecreek,* which has left a great legacy in African American literature. He took its title from a Thomas Wolfe story. Turning the regional stereotypes on their heads, *Beetlecreek* recounts how it is not the woods or hollows that trap people, but the lair of the provincial town, "the deadly mud backwater in the weeds; this was Beetlecreek." Once

Demby moved to Italy and churned out several experimental works compared to writings by Gertrude Stein (who was actually born in the Appalachian region of Allegheny, Pennsylvania), he was never seen again in Appalachian reviews.

In more recent times, West Virginia–raised Henry Louis Gates, one of our nation's most important cultural critics and African American writers, Pulitzer Prize–winning poet Charles Wright, raised in eastern Tennessee, and Knoxville-born Nikki Giovanni, a leader in the black arts movement and a treasured poet, have been associated more with various academic arenas than their Appalachian roots and work. Tom Robbins, a self-proclaimed "hillbilly from Blowing Rock, North Carolina," became a counterculture genre all to himself with his literary high-jinks novels. (Serialized in the legendary *Whole Earth Catalogue,* Gurney Norman's Appalachian road novel, *Divine Rights Trip: A Folk Tale,* was a countercultural classic in the early 1970s.) Annie Dillard's 1974 Pulitzer Prize–winning *Pilgrim on Tinker's Creek,* based in southwestern Virginia, has become an "American" existential classic in the minds of many, uprooted from its Appalachian base.

On an international level, two famous and widely translated American authors, Pearl Buck and Frances Hodgson Burnett, quietly transformed their Appalachian experiences into foreign scenes.

Buck's novel *The Good Earth,* one of the most widely sold in American literary history, made her a spokeswoman for Far Eastern concerns. Chronicling the travails of farmer Wang Lung and his family in the Anhwei province of China, the novel was an instant best seller in 1931; it remained at the top of the lists for nearly two years and was translated into scores of foreign languages. The MGM studios bought the rights for an enormous sum and made the story into a successful Hollywood film. By the late 1960s, Buck was the most translated American author of her times, with sixty-nine translations of her work appearing in a single year.

Few would know that Appalachia, as well as China, shared the spotlight at the Stockholm ceremony for her Nobel Prize for Literature in 1938, the first ever for an American woman writer. The Nobel committee recognized Buck's biographies about her West Virginia parents, not her best-selling novels on China, as her greatest "literary works of art." In these family biographies, in fact, Buck made the link between her writing and her Appalachian past. In *The Exile,* the first book she ever wrote (though she would publish it years later), Buck recalled how she took solace as a child in hearing her mother's stories about their West Virginian ways. The book chronicled her mother's suffering as the wife of a zealous missionary. Yearning to maintain her connection to their family, Buck saw "America through her [mother's] eyes, enthralled with her stories of my own country, the country I had never seen."

Born in Hillsboro, West Virginia, a background detail that many obituaries, including one distributed by the Associated Press, somehow overlooked, Buck spoke often about her cultural "bifocals." One side came in Chinese; she wrote that she actually formulated her numerous novels and books first in Chinese, and then translated them to English. The other part of her bicultural world originated in the Appalachian hills, where she always maintained "a strong sense that there are my beginnings."

Buck's mother, Carie, whose family had come from Holland, spun stories about the Southern Mountain divisions over the Civil War, and her own brother having to hide out for two years in a hollow near Droop Mountain. She recounted their cultural and racial conflicts; their songs, dresses, and games as children; and the rising fervor of religion in the mountains.

When Buck actually arrived back in the States in her late teens, to attend Randolph-Macon Woman's College in southwestern Virginia, the expatriate refound her roots: "I found myself walking through a wood in Virginia. How can I put the excitement of it into words!" Far from the bustle of the Chinese cities, the southwestern Virginian forests were an "intoxicating revelation of beauty" for the young woman, who had "spiritually" seen the Blue Ridge Mountains before her actual arrival. Her mother "had shown them to me ten years before and ten thousand miles away, so that I knew them."

Despite her world travels, Buck never lost contact with her Appalachian origins. In a blurb for *Best of Hillbilly,* a book collection of newspaper essays by Appalachian writer Jim Comstock, she declared, "for years I have followed *The West Virginia Hillbilly* newspaper."

In a visit to her Hillsboro farm birthplace late in her life, Buck declared, "In spite of our living in China, our Mother always taught us to call America home." That home, in a generous aside, had always made her feel like a West Virginian, and the mountains her "good earth."

Along with her family treasury of tales, Buck's mother surrounded herself with American periodicals, such as the venerable *Godoy's Lady's Book and Magazine.* That very magazine had given birth to the writing career of another bicultural Appalachian émigré who had lived a generation or so before Buck and whose success nearly matched the Nobel Laureate's household fame in her own time.

Few writers today would be so identified with England as Frances Hodgson Burnett. Several of her children's books, such as *Little Lord Fauntleroy* and *The Secret Garden,* will forever ensure her legacy in British literature. She authored fifty-two books and over a dozen plays. Her best-selling and widely translated works were so prodigious that some historians have called Burnett the J. K. Rowling (author of the Harry Potter series phenomenon) of her time.

After her father died and the family's thriving English textile business collapsed in the face of the American Civil War, the sixteen-year-old Burnett and her family crossed the Atlantic and settled in a cabin in the eastern Tennessee mountain hamlet of New Market. Instead of being displaced from her English mores, the young adolescent, as she later wrote, "strange as it may seem . . . was not a stranger here." In fact, Burnett pinpointed a more mystic element to her relocation, as if some mysterious past in her life had been reincarnated with her sojourn in the Southern mountains.

The move was providential. As one reviewer of her era put it, for the young Frances set adrift into the backwoods and storytelling traditions of the Appalachian region, "the spirit of the grand mountain scenery and the subtle influence of the historic and romantic environment" shaped the teenager's "imaginative writing." She began to spin tales for her younger siblings and, for inspiration, looked not to the English gardens or factory towns of her past, but to the forests of the Cherokee and mountaineers.

This influence was not merely a detailed nuance about the joys of nature. Stylistically, Burnett recalled in her memoirs that she "ceased to pretend" once she arrived in Tennessee. Her stories moved beyond yarns and fairy tales into "emotions" and the details of the landscape and cultures. She became rooted in nature. In her memoir, she referred to this time as her "Dryad Days," when "she lived in the woods, and she wrote stories on slates and pieces of papers." In the end, the mountains and hills "became part of one's life."

They also became part of her livelihood. In a desperate bid to earn money for her family, the young woman started writing stories and sending them off to publishers on the East Coast, just as the first travel and local color writers were beginning to "discover" Appalachia. By 1868, she had sold her first story to *Godoy's* magazine; she was only eighteen years old. Within a few years, she had published in numerous magazines, alternating stories based in England or the Appalachians or both, as in the case of the short story "Seth," in which she chronicled the life of a Lancaster immigrant in the Tennessee mountains.

Like Buck, Burnett's tenure in the Southern Appalachians was brief but powerful. After marrying a Tennessee doctor, she moved back to Europe and then New York. The mountain experience, however, was not forgotten, nor was it hidden in Burnett's future works. Years later, Burnett would write: "Not until after I was twenty did I find out that during those years spent among the woods and mountains of East Tennessee, I had been accumulating material out of which I could build and from which I could draw as long as I lived."

As WEST reminded me, no region has been so influenced by the land-driven tales of Southern Appalachian writers as my own transplanted childhood home in the American Southwest. Willa Cather, of course, is quite possibly the American author most identified with nineteenth-century Western frontier life; in her footsteps, New Mexico transplant

Conrad Richter, from a coal-mining Appalachian town in southwest Pennsylvania, won a Pulitzer Prize in 1951 for his frontier novel *The Town*. New York theater critic-turned-naturalist Joseph Krutch, from Knoxville, and novelist Barbara Kingsolver, from eastern Kentucky, who has since returned to southwestern Virginia, have written definitive books on the Sonoran Desert in southern Arizona. Her brilliant debut novel, *The Bean Trees*, depicts the trials of an Appalachian woman reinventing herself in the volatile New West; her most recent novel, *Prodigal Summer*, entangles the conflicting aspirations of preservationists and predators in an Appalachian forest community brought together by nature's desires. Two famous transplants to the Southwest are Cormac McCarthy, author of the National Book Award–winning Border Trilogy novels, and environmental hell-raiser and novelist Edward Abbey.

While McCarthy is mostly known for his Southwestern novels and their bloody meridians, notably the multiple-prize-winning *All the Pretty Horses*, his first four novels took place in Knoxville or the eastern Tennessee mountains, where he was raised, and provided the mythos that would haunt his later work. Far beyond any Southern gothic tradition, McCarthy's work is steeped in the imagery of the Appalachian landscape and the "absolutely overpowering use of language," as Saul Bellow once noted.

The Orchard Keeper, McCarthy's first novel, which was published in 1965, deals with the sordid crimes unearthed by a mountain man who tends a ruined orchard. His subsequent novels, *Outer Dark* and *Child of God*, are parables of incest, necrophilia, and murder, situated in the darker corners of the mountains and their caves. As hideous as their plots may suggest, the novels conjure the otherworldly powers of nature over humans, all of whom are "children of God." Recalling Greek mythology, the Appalachian wilderness plays a role, like the wildness of humankind, in any redemption or salvation. Hiding out in a cave in *Child of God*, the main character literally becomes part of the bowels of the mountains, "where dead people lay like saints."

McCarthy's influence on contemporary Appalachian literature continues to rattle through the bones of stylistic innovators in the mountain region. For poet and novelist Robert Morgan, author of the best-selling

Gap Creek novel, McCarthy's mountain dialogues and prodigious stories in Appalachia "planted a seed" for his own spellbinding fiction work.

A famous recluse, McCarthy followed the trail of Texas hero Sam Houston, who spent his youth in the mountains of Tennessee, and moved to El Paso to pursue his Southwestern novels in the 1970s. One of the few literary friends that McCarthy acknowledged was fellow Appalachian and borderland transplant Abbey, with whom McCarthy had apparently conspired to reintroduce wolves into the region.

Born in southwestern Pennsylvania in 1927, Abbey understood a few things about wolves and wilderness. In his essay "Shadows from the Big Woods," he recalled his youth in the Appalachian forests, which ultimately led to his famous call for environmental defense: "The idea of wilderness needs no defense. It only needs more defenders." Author of the best-selling environmental manifesto *Desert Solitaire* and a novel that inspired a genera-tion of environmental activists, *The Monkey Wrench Gang,* Abbey drew from his Appalachian experience after moving to the Southwest in his twenties. The land, in his work, from Appalachia to Southwestern deserts, still determined the cultural ways of its inhabitants. The mountains pro-vided the backbone of his first sense of place, its loss to industrial change, and his resolve to challenge environmental destruction. His landmark essay, "Shadows from the Big Woods," reveals this sense of place and loss:

> *Now I would not care to revisit those faraway scenes. That forest which seemed so vast to us was only a small thing after all, as the bulldozers, earth movers, and dragline shovels have proved. The woods we thought eternal have been logged by methods formerly considered too destructive, and the very mountainside on which the forest grew has been butchered by strip miners into a shape of crude symmetry, with spoiled banks and head walls and right-angled escarpments where even the running black-berry has a hard time finding a roothold. Stagnant water fills the raw gulches, and the creek below runs sulfur-yellow all year long.*

Abbey did return to Appalachia. He wrote an acclaimed portrait of the Smoky Mountains, "the vegetation cradle of America." In one of his last autobiographical novels, *The Fool's Progress,* his alter ego Henry Lightcap takes a road trip back to his "myth-infested hills of Appalachia," to visit his family and birthplace.

BEING APPALACHIAN, for Abbey, was forever a matter of coming home "to the green hills." Those green hills, though, as he predicted, were rapidly being destroyed, and with them the Appalachian ways of life. I learned this lesson the hard way. When I was taking a walk on the back roads one evening with West at the Appalachian South Folklife Center in the 1980s, the elder Appalachian writer challenged me to "go home" to my green hills of southern Illinois, a coal-infested land I had essentially written off as an impoverished backwash of our family experience, in order to understand my own place in the world. I never did, and I never will get the chance.

Abbey's childhood forest was not the only area to be "butchered by the strip miners." This was my second important lesson about Appalachia: Not quite twenty years after my first visit to the Southern mountains, a region that I would continue to explore for years, my mother's two-hundred-year-old home place and family hollow in the Eagle Mountains was strip-mined through a process now referred to as "mountaintop removal." Despite the land's being on the edge of the Shawnee National Forest, a coal company had managed to squeeze inside some loophole and plunder the area for an untold fortune. My last remaining cousin in the area had sold out under duress, the explosions from the nearby operations destroying his well, shaking his dishes from the shelves, and taking the property and peace from his life.

The land is gone now; it is a black amphitheater of industrial glory. And with it went the farm, the cabin, the cow pond, the four plum trees, and two hundred years of stories, legends, history, and the unknown contributions of a backwoods lifestyle that I will never understand in person.

WILL WE still be able to write about mountaineers and hill folk if we destroy the mountains and hills of Appalachia?

Strip mining, Harry Caudill wrote in his landmark book on Appalachia, *Night Comes to the Cumberlands,* got its "practice" in our southern Illinois and western Kentucky coalfields. By the 1950s, the "rape of Appalachia," in his words, was in full throttle.

A half century later, Appalachia remains on the front lines of the most drastic strip-mining and mountaintop-removal policies in American history. Far from being an employment factor, mountaintop removal is simply the quickest and cheapest way for multinational companies to procure the coal from Appalachia. Unleashed in the last decade, operating on poorly enforced, misconstrued, or relaxed environmental laws, massive machines the size of buildings are literally roaring into the backwoods and knocking the mountains into the valleys and natural drainage routes. Over the last decade, an estimated one million acres of hardwood forests have been leveled in the region; more than 720 miles of streams have been destroyed; more than 1,000 miles of waterways are being wiped out.

The result has been devastating. Filling in natural drainage gullies and wreaking erosive havoc in its deforesting wake, mountaintop removal has completely altered the landscape in some of the most breathtaking parts of the Mountain South and the United States. Entire communities have been lost. Even monumental Blair Mountain in West Virginia, the sacred ground of organized labor in its pivotal insurrection against coal companies in 1921, has been placed on the chopping block. In the process, many mountain homes, hamlets, and towns are now at risk of being flooded out or are following the death pattern of the Buffalo Creek disaster in the 1970s, when over one hundred lives were lost when a coal dam broke in West Virginia.

A mountain the size of Rhode Island is being dismantled.

In truth, *our* mountains, as in our American mountains—the United States of Appalachia that Irving had once envisioned as the natural symbol of our nation's greatness—are being dismantled. And, in the process, *our* heritage, our American heritage that has been profoundly transformed by the Cherokee; the first Washingtonians; the revolutionaries at Kings

Mountain; the courageous abolitionists throughout the Southern mountains; the laborers at Blair Mountain and the other mines, mills, and factories; the civil rights activists at Highlander Folk School; and the generations of innovative artists, musicians, journalists, and writers who have shaped the story of our American experience—all of this rich Appalachian and American heritage is at risk of being erased from our maps.

In looking back at the destruction of his own Appalachian wilderness, Abbey imagined the shadow between our past and present as a growing abyss, inevitably leaving our "beginnings betrayed, dissolved, rendered not mythical but illusory."

Illusory Appalachia? Betrayed, dissolved? The issue of mountaintop removal has emerged in this new century as a defining challenge for our United States of Appalachia. It will determine whether our country's destiny will continue to be entangled in our natural and historical roots; it will ultimately be a part of our national decision to accept whether the Southern hills and mountains are vital to the larger American experience.

From the earliest days of our nation, to its leaps in artistic and creative endeavors, and to its most significant struggles of labor and civil rights and fairness in the nineteenth and twentieth centuries, the Southern Appalachians have been in the vanguard in determining that American destiny. There is no question they will continue to do so. The greater question is whether the rest of the country will "come up to these hills and mountains" and join them.

Acknowledgments

Thank you so much, my dear compañeros, for your time, advice, ideas, and editorial comments these past years: John Morton and Helen Osterman, Ted Olson, Bill Maakestad, Janice Welsch, Peter Cole, Jeri Scott, Ron Rash, P. J. Laska, Yvonne Farley, Gretchen Laskas, Gordon Simmons, Helen Lewis, Warren Doyle, Jim Lorence, Kevin O'Donnell, George Brosi, Edwina Pendarvis, Emily Satterwhite, Judy McCulloh, Sally Maggard, Joyce Brown, Katie Bacon, Robert Gipe, Gary DeNeal, Ed Pavlic, Charlotte Sheedy, Quincy and Margaret Troupe, Luis Rodriguez, Dorothy Allison, Alfredo Vea, Susan Straight, Russell Banks, Demetria Martinez, Bryce Milligan, Fred Craddock, Tony Sears, the indefatigable folks at the Appalachian Studies Association, the Highlander Center, the Appalachian South Folklife Center, Marilyn Auer and the staff at *The Bloomsbury Review,* and William Clark Associates.

Special thanks to Jack Shoemaker for making a risky turn into the mountains, Trish Hoard, Roxy Font, Patty Boyd, and the Avalon Publishing Group.

Eternal gratitude to my family, Mam and Pap, bro and sis and their clans, Uncle Richard and Aunt Jerretta Followell and my Kentucky family, and *la famiglia Paciotto-Piernera e nonna Gigia,* for walking the long road with me. Thanks, Doug, for the hardware. This book would not have been possible without your support.

Grazie a te, Carla, my jo, per avermi messo in cuore le parole e il coraggio per scalare queste montagne e per avermi mostrato i sentieri nascosti che mi hanno riportato a casa.

Bibliographic Notes

＋〜＋

My work owes a great deal of gratitude and debt to the legions of Appalachian writers, scholars, and activists who have been at the grindstone for decades.

The writing of this book took shape over years of reading, researching, traveling, and late-night bouts of listening to and exchanging ideas with Appalachian enthusiasts. The germ dates back to my first visit with Don West at the Appalachian South Folklife Center in 1983, when he shared with me his own vision of Appalachia. The years I spent collecting his papers, manuscripts, and correspondence; roaming the mountains; and serving as coeditor of a collection of his writings, *No Lonesome Road: Selected Prose and Poems of Don West*, broadened my understanding of the region.

Appalachia's rich treasury of literature and its bevy of critics form a long line. A few classics are required reading, of course, if only to remind ourselves of the high bar of excellence: John C. Campbell's *Southern Highlander and His Homeland;* Horace Kephart's *Our Southern Highlanders;* Harriette Simpson Arnow's *Seedtime on the Cumberland;* Cratis Williams's dissertation, *The Southern Mountaineer in Fact and Fiction;* and Harry

Caudill's *Night Comes to the Cumberlands*. A few contemporary polemics have added a lot grist for the mill: Allen Batteau's *Invention of Appalachia;* Henry Shapiro's *Appalachia on Our Mind;* David Whisnant's *Modernizing the Mountaineer;* all of Wilma Dunaway's stunning work on frontier history, economics, and slavery; and Anthony Harkin's *Hillbilly: A Cultural History of an American Icon.* Ronald Eller's *Miners, Millhands and Mountaineers: Industrialization of the Mountain South* remains indispensable. Recent overviews, including John Alexander Williams's *Appalachia: A History;* Richard Drake's *History of Appalachia;* and Michael Frome's *Strangers in High Places: The Story of the Smoky Mountains,* have added a lot to the basics.

I also found these anthologies, among many, great resources: *Voices from the Hills; Appalachia Inside Out; Confronting Appalachian Stereotypes: Back Talk from an American Region; Colonialism in Modern America: The Appalachian Case; Fighting Back in Appalachia: Traditions of Resistance and Change; Appalachians and Race; Bloodroot: Reflections on Place by Appalachian Women; Blacks in Appalachia;* and *Appalachia in the Making: The Mountain South in the Nineteenth Century.*

For general background, my understanding of the region has been deepened by reading its lesser-known local voices. To this purpose, I trolled back issues of *Mountain Life and Work; Appalachian Heritage; Appalachian Journal; Journal of Appalachian Studies;* and *Now and Then,* among the scores of tiny newsletters, small-town newspapers, and fugitive presses hiding in libraries. There are also hundreds of informative Web sites, notably those sponsored by the Appalachian Studies Association; the West Virginia University Libraries Appalachian Collection; West Virginia Archives and History; the Berea College Appalachian Center; and the Eastern Tennessee State University Archives of Appalachia.

Appalshop, a multimedia arts and education center, is a mountain of knowledge all to itself. Check out its Web site, www.appalshop.org, and donate as much as you can.

Many creative works—novels, poems, tales, and songs—by Appalachia's vast pool of novelists, poets, storytellers, and singers might provide the best view into the region's secrets. We all have our favorites; many of mine appear throughout this book.

PROLOGUE: RANK STRANGERS

My work draws from interviews, album liner notes, memoirs, and biographies of the musicians noted, including Nina Simone's *I Put a Spell on You*; W. C. Handy's *Father of the Blues: An Autobiography*; Sidney Bechet's *Treat It Gentle: An Autobiography*; Chris Albertson's *Bessie*; Richard Smith's *Can't You Hear Me Callin': The Life of Bill Monroe, Father of Bluegrass*; Mark Zwonitzer's *Will You Miss Me When I'm Gone? The Carter Family and Their Legacy in American Music*; Jean Ritchie's *Folk Songs of the Southern Appalachians*; John Wright's *Traveling the High Way Home: Ralph Stanley and the World of Traditional Bluegrass Music*; and Loyal Jones's *Minstrel of the Appalachians: The Story of Bascom Lamar Lunsford*. For more information on Nina Simone, Mauro Boscarol's "The Nina Simone Web," a Web page available at www.boscarol .com/nina; and Roger Nupie's "Dr. Nina Simone," the Web site of the International Dr. Nina Simone Fan Club, available at www.ninasimone .com/fans.html, are noteworthy.

A number of other excellent music histories and critiques, too numerous to list here, provided a broad picture of minstrelsy, blues, folk and country music, but I especially appreciated the following sources: Michelle Scott's dissertation, *The Realm of a Blue Empress: Blues Culture and Bessie Smith in Black Chattanooga, TN 1880–1923*; William Mahar's *Behind the Burnt Cork Mask: Early Blackface Minstrelsy and Antebellum American Popular Culture*; Bill Malone's *Don't Get Above Your Raisin': Country Music and the Southern Working Class*; Robert Cantwell's *When We Were Good: The Folk Revival*; Karen Linn's *That Half-Barbaric Twang: The Banjo in American Popular Culture*; Charles Wolfe and Ted Olson's *Bristol Sessions: Writings About the Big Bang of Country Music*; Wolfe's *Kentucky Country: Folk and Country Music of Kentucky*; Maud Karpeles and A. H. Fox-Strangways's *Cecil Sharp: His Life and Work*; Stephen Whitfield's "Is It

True What They Sing About Dixie?" in *Southern Cultures;* and Colin Escott's *Roadkill on the Three-Chord Highway.*

CHAPTER ONE: THE TRAIL OF WORDS

There is a massive amount of literature on the Cherokee. Sequoyah's life story has been recounted variably in Jack Kirkpatrick's *Shadow of Sequoyah;* his *Sequoyah, Earth and Intellect;* Grant Foreman's *Sequoyah;* George Foster's *Sequoyah;* Traveller Bird's opposing *Tell Them They Lie: The Sequoyah Myth;* John Ehle's *Trail of Tears;* and James Mooney's *Myths of the Cherokees.*

Landmark works and collections of Cherokee voices in the late nineteenth century, including those by James Mooney, Charles Royce, a bit in Draper's papers at the Wisconsin Historical Society, and Henry Timberlake's *Memoirs,* are still vital. William McLoughlin's more recent *Cherokee Renascence in the New Republic* is a masterpiece. I also appreciated the various volumes of *The Lost Archives of the Cherokee Nation,* put out by the Eastern Tennessee Historical Society. Wilma Dunaway's growing body of work on the Cherokee is critical, as are Theda Purdue's several volumes, including *Slavery and the Evolution of Cherokee Society,* and *Cherokee Editor: The Writings of Elias Boudinot;* and John Finger's *Eastern Band of Cherokees, 1819–1900.* For language issues, I also consulted Jack Kirkpatrick's *New Echota Letters;* and Margaret Bender's *Signs of Cherokee Culture: Sequoyah's Syllabary in Eastern Cherokee Life.* The back issues of the *Journal of Cherokee Studies* provided invaluable resources for a broader perspective.

For those who are interested, copies of the *Cherokee Phoenix* are available at the American Antiquarian Society in Worcester, Massachusetts; Western Carolina University also features notable Cherokee studies resources. The museum commemorating Sequoyah's birthplace in the Little Tennessee Valley, operated by the Eastern Cherokee tribe, is a good visual starting point. The *Cherokee Phoenix* office is now a tourist site in New Echota, Georgia.

The Gists appear in a wide range of works on the frontier. Christopher Gist's journals are informative documents on early expeditions on the frontier. For my purposes, I also found these most helpful: Duane King's "Long Island of the Holston: Sacred Cherokee Ground," in *Journal of Cherokee Studies;* Samuel C. Williams's "Nathaniel Gist: Father of Sequoyah," in *Chronicle of Oklahoma;* Kenneth Bailey's *Christopher Gist: Colonial Frontiersman, Explorer and Indian Agent;* and Jean Dorsey's *Christopher Gist of Maryland: And Some of His Descendants, 1679–1957.*

CHAPTER TWO: THE FIRST WASHINGTON, D.C.

Works by the nineteenth-century Tennessee historians Moses Fisk, John Haywood, and J. M. G. Ramsey, with a little help from Lyman C. Draper's papers, provided the colorful characters and dramatic stories, while early-twentieth-century stalwarts Samuel C. Williams, A. V. Goodpasture, and Archibald Henderson attempted to clarify a lot of details. Theodore Roosevelt, like many historians of his period, such as George Bancroft, was quite smitten with the Wataugans, whose romance fell out of favor with the revisionists. Later, in the 1960s, Max Dixon and a number of other regional historians, such as Paul Fink, took up the cause again; an interesting debate took place in the 1970s over the community's relevance. Max Dixon's *Wataugans* is the most passionate defense. Dixon's publisher, Overmountain Press, is without a doubt the great promoter of the Wataugans.

A bigger picture emerges today, juxtaposing the works of some modern historians, including Michael Frome's *Strangers in High Places;* Robert Ramsey's *Carolina Cradle: Settlement of the Northwest Carolina Frontier, 1747–1762;* Woody Holton's *Forced Founders;* Edmund S. Morgan's rack of books on early-American history; David Hackett Fischer's books on frontier Virginia; and the mountains of texts on the Scotch-Irish experience on the frontier. I also appreciated the anthology *Appalachian Frontiers: Settlement, Society, and Development in the Preindustrial Era;* T. H. Breen's *Marketplace of Revolution: How Consumer Politics Shaped American Independence;* Max Edling's *Revolution in Favor of Government: Origins of the US Constitution and the Making of the American State;* Barbara Rasmussen's *Absentee Landowning and Exploitation in West Virginia, 1760–1920;* Richard Hooker and Marjoleine Kars' work on the Regulators in North Carolina: *Carolina*

Backcountry on the Eve of Revolution and *Breaking Loose Together;* Reuben Thwaite's collection of Draper's papers in *Dunmore's War;* John Finger's *Tennessee Frontiers;* and Ora Blackmun's *Western North Carolina: Its Mountains and Its People to 1800.* Among the number of Boone biographies, I most appreciated John M. Faragher's *Daniel Boone.*

Primary Wataugan documents are few. William Tatham, an English pioneer and Washington participant, left behind the most extensive memoirs. We need more modern biographies and dissertations on key players, such as John Sevier, James Robertson, and John Carter. Rhys Isaac's *Landon Carter's Uneasy Kingdom* is a sidestep in that direction. I did find many valuable primary sources culling the family genealogical records in the region and especially gained a better sense of the issue of slavery, a detail largely kept out of most versions.

In this regard, any stories about the Appalachian frontier must pass through the filter of Wilma Dunaway's *First American Frontier: Transition to Capitalism in Southern Appalachia, 1700–1860,* and her subsequent work on slavery and Cherokee history.

CHAPTER THREE: DOWN FROM THE MOUNTAIN

Lyman Draper's massive *King's Mountain and Its Heroes* is the nineteenth-century classic on the battle; John Buchanan's *Road to Guilford Courthouse;* Walter Edgar's *Partisans and Redcoats: The Southern Conflict That Turned the Tide of the American Revolution;* and John Alden's *The South in the Revolution, 1763–1789* are modern views about the broader Revolutionary campaigns in the south. Local and regional historical texts on the Battle of Kings Mountain abound; I found Hank Messicks' *King's Mountain: The Epic of the Blue Ridge Mountain Men* among the best.

Samuel Doak's papers and published lectures rest in the Tennessee State Library; a few works on Doak, notably *Washington College: A Study of an Attempt to Provide Higher Education in Eastern Tennessee;* Earle Crawford's *Samuel Doak;* William Calhoun's *Samuel Doak, 1749–1830;* and Ester Pritchett Prigden's master's thesis, "The Influence of Doctor Samuel Doak Upon Education in Early East Tennessee," are useful.

Historians are lacking a modern biography of Isaac Shelby, among other participants. J. G. Hamilton's edited article, "King's Mountain Letters of Colonel Isaac Shelby," was useful, along with other narratives by soldiers, such as "The Narrative of the Battle of King's Mountain by Captain David Vance."

CHAPTER FOUR: THE EMANCIPATORS

Copies of Elihu Embree's *Emancipator* have been bound and published; the *Philanthropist* and Lundy's *Genius of Universal Emancipation* can be found in various libraries. Lundy did leave behind a memoir, *Life of Benjamin Lundy*, as did Underground Railroader Levi Coffin, in *Reminiscences*. John Rankin's letters and a larger body of work are readily available. Elihu Embree's personal papers sit in the Historical Society of Pennsylvania, with some materials at Eastern Tennessee State University's Archives of Appalachia, which also house related research by Samuel C. Williams, among other local historians. For notes on Doak, please refer to notes for Chapter 3.

Important new works on slavery and the abolitionist movements have reshaped our thinking about the antislavery South. I found these most helpful: the excellent anthology *Appalachians and Race: The Mountain South from Slavery to Segregation;* Wilma Dunaway's *Slavery in the Mountain South;* Amy Reynolds's article from her dissertation, "Charles Osborn, Elihu Embree and the Tennessee Manumission Society: How Pioneers of the Abolitionist Movement Conceptualized Free Speech"; Asa Martin's "Pioneer Anti-Slave Press"; Stephen Week's *Southern Quakers and Slavery;* various pieces by Carter Woodson; Ann Hagedorn's biography on John Rankin, *Beyond the River;* Durwood Dunn's *Abolitionist in the Appalachian South: Ezekiel Birdseye on Slavery, Capitalism and Separate Statehood in East Tennessee, 1841–46;* John Thomas's *Liberator: William Lloyd Garrison;* Henry Mayer's *All on Fire: William Lloyd Garrison and the Abolition of Slavery;* Alice D. Adam's *Neglected Period of Antislavery in America, 1808–1831;* Lawrence Goodheart's "Tennessee's Antislavery Movement Reconsidered: The Example of Elihu Embree," in *Tennessee Historical Quarterly;* and some early religious accounts, such as Andrew Murray's *Presbyterians and the Negro;* Walter Posey's *Presbyterian Church in the Old Southwest;* and Ernest Thrice's *Presbyterians in the South.*

CHAPTER FIVE: ALL THE NEWS THAT'S FIT TO PRINT

Most of Anne Royall's *Black Books* can be tracked down, as well as her groundbreaking *Sketches of History, Life, and Manners in the United States;* issues of *Paul Pry* and the *Huntress* are sparse, though the latter is available on microfilm. Bessie James's *Anne Royall's USA* shed some light, as did Sarah Porter's *Life and Times of Anne Royall.*

Robert Levine's *Martin R. Delany: A Documentary Reader* is a fine resource. Thanks to Floyd Miller, Martin Delany's *Blake; or, The Huts of America* is now in print. I also learned a considerable amount on Delany and his era from Robert Levine's *Martin Delany, Frederick Douglass and the Politics of Identity;* Dorothy Sterling's *Making of an Afro-American: Martin Robinson Delany, 1812–1885;* Victor Ullman's *Martin Delany: The Beginnings of Black Nationalism;* Frank Rollin's nineteenth-century account, *Life and Service of Martin R. Delany;* and the anthology *Race, Citizenship and Law in American Literature.* There is also a great pool of resources on Delany and the *Mystery* on the West Virginia University Libraries' Web site.

I found a tremendous number of primary sources, including correspondence, clippings, and testimonies, on Adolph Ochs in Chattanooga's historical archives. Additional resources provided a broader view, including Gerald Johnson's *Titan;* Susan Twifft's *Trust: The Private and Powerful Family Behind the New York Times;* Joseph W. Campbell's *Yellow Journalism;* Wendy Besmann's *Separate Circle: Jewish Life in Knoxville, Tennessee;* Kevin O'Donnell's work on tourism, travel writing, and the Reconstruction; Deborah R. Weiner's articles on Jewish traditions in Appalachia, including "Middlemen of the Coalfields: The Role of Jews in the Economy of Southern West Virginia Coal Towns, 1890–1950"; and the historical review *The Chattanooga County, 1540–1951.*

I also drew on background from the anthology *Appalachia in the Making: The Mountain South in the 19th Century;* and Eller's *Miners, Millhands and Mountaineers.*

CHAPTER SIX: THE GREAT AMERICAN INDUSTRIAL SAGA

Thanks to Tillie Olsen and others, Rebecca Harding Davis's "Life in the Iron Mills" is now in print, and a veritable field of study has emerged around her life and times. Other works are also worth the time to track down, including Harding Davis's memoirs, *Bits of Gossip.* Among the various biographies and social criticism, I found these to be the most useful: Tillie Olsen's postscript to "Life in the Iron Mills"; Jean Pfaelzer's *Parlor Radical: Rebecca Harding Davis and the Origins of American Social Realism;* and Anne Knowles's "Iron and the Welsh: A Geographical Reading of 'Life in the Iron Mills.'"

Thanks to Elizabeth Englehardt, Grace MacGowan Cooke's *Power and the Glory* is back in print. Elizabeth Englehardt's *Tangled Roots of Feminism, Environmentalism and Appalachian Literature;* and her edited *Beyond Hill and Hollow* are tremendous new works.

In terms of the cotton mills, I relied heavily on Jacquelyn Dowd Hall's inimitable and prodigious research in the field, especially the classic *Like a Family: The Making of the Southern Cotton Mill World;* and the auxiliary article, "Disorderly Women: Gender and Labor Militancy in the Appalachian South." I also found several other resources of value, namely, Tom Tippett's classic *When Southern Labor Stirs;* John Salmond's *Gastonia 1929;* and Liston Pope's *Millhands and Preachers: A Study of Gastonia.* Two of the best proletarian novels about the Gastonia strike are Olive Dargan's *Call Home the Heart;* and Grace Lumpkin's *To Make My Bread.*

The literature on the coal wars of Appalachia is vast, controversial, and still full of emotion. Some of the enduring classic texts on the conflicts around the region include David Corbin's *West Virginia Mine Wars* and *Life, Work and Rebellion in the Coal Fields;* John Hevener's *Which Side Are You On? The Autobiography of Mother Jones;* Howard Lee's *Bloodletting in Appalachia;* Eller's *Miners, Millhands and Mountaineers: Industrialization of the Mountain South;* and John Gaventa's *Power and Powerlessness.* Good background material was gained from more recent works: Robert Shogan's *Battle of Blair Mountain: The Story of America's Largest Labor Uprising;* Lon Savage's *Thunder in the Mountains;* and Barbara Freese's *Coal.*

Goldenseal Magazine published an interesting collection of essays over twenty years. The collection is titled *The Goldenseal Book of the West Virginia Mine Wars.* David C. Duke's *Writers and Miners* is a fascinating perspective of coal mining's creative endeavors.

Works on the radical women balladeers abound, especially on Florence Reece, who published her own collection of stories and songs, *Against the Current.* I found these helpful: Shelly Romalis's *Pistol Packin' Mama: Aunt Molly Jackson and the Politics of Folksong;* Lynn Haessly's thesis on Ella May Wiggins, "Mill Mother's Lament"; John Greenway's *American Folksongs of Protest;* and Archie Green's classic *Only a Miner.*

Carter Woodson's numerous works can be found in most libraries. His *Mis-Education of the Negro* is now in print. Booker T. Washington's autobiography, *Up from Slavery,* is also required reading. Two works on African American miners in Appalachia, Joe Trotter's "Introduction to Black Migration" and Thomas Wagner and Phillip Obermiller's *African American Miners and Migrants,* are important resources. Walter Reuther's story is well known. I found these good guides: Nelson Lichtenstein's *Walter Reuther: The Most Dangerous Man in Detroit;* and Bill Goode's *Infighting in the United Auto Workers: The 1946 Election and the Ascendancy of Walter Reuther.*

Harriette Arnow's masterpiece, *The Dollmaker,* should be required reading for all Americans.

CHAPTER SEVEN: WE SHALL OVERCOME

I drew from Highlander's primary documents, including their reports, newsletters, correspondence, and interviews and Myles Horton papers, housed at the Highlander Research and Education Center in Knoxville and at the Wisconsin State Archives. Several portraits of Highlander are useful: Frank Adam's *Unearthing the Seeds of Fire;* John Glen's *Highlander: No Ordinary School;* Aimee Horton's *The Highlander Folk School: A History of Its Major Programs;* Septima Clark's *Septima's Story* and *Ready from Within;* Rosa Parks's numerous interviews and memoirs; Guy and Candie Carawan's *Voices from the Mountains;* Bernice Johnson Reagon's dissertation, "Songs of the Civil Rights Movement 1955–1965: A Study in Cultural History"; and Myles Horton's own memoir, *The Long Haul.* Two classics on the pre-civil-rights-movement era are also critical: John Egerton's *Speak Now Against the Day;* and Eliot Wigginton's collection of interviews, *Refuse to Stand Silently By.* Several books on the student role in the civil rights movement were helpful: Clayborne Carson's *In Struggle: SNCC and the Black Awakening in the 1960s;* and Howard Zinn's *SNCC: The New Abolitionists.*

EPILOGUE: WE ARE ALL APPALACHIANS

The works of the authors reviewed in this chapter speak for themselves. My apologies to the many great Appalachian scribes for any novels, stories, or collections of poetry that I have failed to mention. There are many, many others.

My work is indebted to Cratis Williams's dissertation, "The Southern Mountaineer in Fact and Fiction"; and several literary anthologies, including *Listen Here: Women Writing in Appalachia; Voices from the Hills; Appalachia Inside Out;* and *Confronting Appalachian Stereotypes: Back Talk from an American Region.* For material on Cormac McCarthy, I also drew from the anthology *Sacred Violence: Cormac McCarthy's Appalachian Works.* For material on Frances Burnett, I appreciated Gretchen Gerzina's *Frances Hodgson Burnett: The Unexpected Life of the Author of 'The Secret Garden.'*

In a perfect world, the president, the head of the Environmental Protection Agency, the entire U.S. Congress, leaders of the United Mine Workers, state officials, judges, and all other important leaders would board helicopters and fly over the areas of Appalachia ravaged by mountaintop removal, visit a few hollows and their communities, and then shuttle back to their respective corridors and change the way we mine coal, and develop an energy policy of independence based on sustainable resources in the process.

In the meantime, the scores of Appalachian groups and their alliances need support. Two film documentaries should be required viewing before any American goes to his or her comfortable bed: *Mucked* and *Razing Appalachia*. Chad Montrie's *To Save the Land and People: A History of Opposition to Surface Coal Mining in Appalachia* also deserves a wide readership.

Speak now against the day, as William Faulkner admonished his generation.

Index

Abbey, Edward, 195, 207, 208–209, 211
Abercrombie & Fitch, xiii
abolitionism/abolitionists
    black, 116–125
    early movement, 83–98
    gradual vs. immediate, 115–116, 122
    publications, 92, 92–96, 97–98, 99, 100–101
    societies, 84, 86, 87–89, 91, 94, 97, 101
    Southern Appalachian influence on, xi–xii,
      98–102
    Southern backlash against, 95, 99
Acuff, Roy, 3
Adams, John Quincy, 106, 109
African Americans
    as abolitionist journalists, 116–125
    in American Revolution, 78
    Appalachian settlement and, 50–51
    authors, 199, 202–203
    as coal miners, 162–164
    colonization to Africa, 85, 90, 91, 94, 96, 97, 124
    lynchings of, 125
    musical influence of, 3–4, 6–24
    political leaders, 191–192
    prohibited from education, 114
    voting rights for, 189–192, 193
    See also civil rights movement;
      desegregation; slavery; *specific person*

African Methodist Episcopal Church, 120
Agee, James, 202
agriculture, 175
Akron (Ohio), 164
Alabama, 40, 82, 90, 138, 180, 197
Alamance (N.C.), Battle of the (1771), 52
Alcott, Louisa May, 143–144, 145
Allegheny (Pa.), 203
Allison, Dorothy, 199
Alloway, Harry, 131
All Southern Conference for Civil Rights (1935),
    179
American Anti-Slavery Society, 101, 116
American Colonization Society, 91
American Convention for Promoting the
    Abolition of Slavery, 91
American Revolution (1775–1783), 34
    battles, 67, 69, 70, 73, 77–80, 87
    beginning of, 52, 62, 70
    British southern campaign, 68–70, 72, 75–80
    as civil war, 77–78
    Cornwallis's surrender (1781), 80
    Dunmore's War (1774), 58–59, 70, 72
    land rights and, 48
    in Washington District, 64–66
    Washingtonian annexation petition, xii,
      45–46, 64–66